I. M. DESTLER   HIDEO SATO
PRISCILLA CLAPP   HARUHIRO FUKUI

MANAGING AN ALLIANCE

The Politics of U.S.–Japanese Relations

D1112376

THE BROOKINGS INSTITUTION
Washington, D.C.

Copyright © 1976 by

THE BROOKINGS INSTITUTION

1775 Massachusetts Avenue, N.W., Washington, D.C. 20036

Library of Congress Cataloging in Publication Data:

Main entry under title:
Managing an alliance.
    Bibliography: p.
    Includes index.
        1. United States—Foreign relations—Japan.
    2. Japan—Foreign relations—United States.
    I. Destler, I.M.
    E183.8.J3M3   327.73'052   75-44501
    ISBN 0-8157-1820-9
    ISBN 0-8157-1819-5 pbk.

1 2 3 4 5 6 7 8 9

MANAGING AN ALLIANCE

THE BROOKINGS INSTITUTION is an independent organization devoted to nonpartisan research, education, and publication in economics, government, foreign policy, and the social sciences generally. Its principal purposes are to aid in the development of sound public policies and to promote public understanding of issues of national importance.

The Institution was founded on December 8, 1927, to merge the activities of the Institute for Government Research, founded in 1916, the Institute of Economics, founded in 1922, and the Robert Brookings Graduate School of Economics and Government, founded in 1924.

The Board of Trustees is responsible for the general administration of the Institution, while the immediate direction of the policies, program, and staff is vested in the President, assisted by an advisory committee of the officers and staff. The bylaws of the Institution state: "It is the function of the Trustees to make possible the conduct of scientific research, and publication, under the most favorable conditions, and to safeguard the independence of the research staff in the pursuit of their studies and in the publication of the results of such studies. It is not a part of their function to determine, control, or influence the conduct of particular investigations or the conclusions reached."

The President bears final responsibility for the decision to publish a manuscript as a Brookings book. In reaching his judgment on the competence, accuracy, and objectivity of each study, the President is advised by the director of the appropriate research program and weighs the views of a panel of expert outside readers who report to him in confidence on the quality of the work. Publication of a work signifies that it is deemed a competent treatment worthy of public consideration but does not imply endorsement of conclusions or recommendations.

The Institution maintains its position of neutrality on issues of public policy in order to safeguard the intellectual freedom of the staff. Hence interpretations or conclusions in Brookings publications should be understood to be solely those of the authors and should not be attributed to the Institution, to its trustees, officers, or other staff members, or to the organizations that support its research.

Foreword

NEGOTIATIONS between governments are sometimes regarded as encounters in which diplomats on each side press clearly defined national objectives, adjusting them only as the positions and tactics of those across the table make compromise essential. But the conduct of diplomacy is often much more complicated. Negotiators have to bargain not only with their foreign counterparts, but also with officials of their own government—to establish basic policy and to ensure that agreements reached abroad have support at home.

The authors of this book find such a pattern in relations between the United States and its most important single ally—Japan. They trace the manner in which misunderstanding of the constraints binding leaders and officials can disrupt particular negotiations and provoke domestic political crises that damage bilateral relations on a broader range of issues. To shed light on how such setbacks can be avoided, the authors analyze the politics of Japanese-American relations since 1945, examining the causes of failure and the lessons to be drawn from success. They focus on the security treaty revision of 1957–60 and later negotiations, but also touch on events before the Second World War to illustrate specific points.

The book stems from a project conceived and organized by Morton H. Halperin in 1971, when he was a Brookings senior fellow. To reflect attitudes and viewpoints on both sides of the Pacific, the project brought together two Japanese and two American scholars to pursue parallel, collaborative research and analysis. They concentrated first on specific negotiations, interviewing many participants in Tokyo and Washington. Particular attention was given to the Okinawa reversion question and the textile dispute of 1969–71. They then applied their findings to a general study of U.S. and Japanese domestic decision-making and its influence on bilateral issues, of which this book is the result.

All four authors were Brookings research associates while working on the project. Their individual contributions cannot be defined precisely, because the ideas and analysis that emerged result from several years of teamwork. Priscilla Clapp focused on the historical and case background in chapter 2, with important contributions from Haruhiro Fukui. I. M. Destler was responsible for the comparative analysis of Japanese and American policymaking in chapter 3, also with important contributions from Fukui. Hideo Sato developed most of the analysis of misperceptions in chapter 4 and a large part of the analysis of Japanese-American interaction in chapter 5. In addition, Destler assumed the major coordinating and final writing responsibility. In the course of revision, however, all four authors influenced each chapter, and all participated in the case studies—Destler, Fukui, and Sato in that on the textile dispute, and Clapp and Fukui in that on Okinawa reversion.

The study was financed by the National Endowment for the Humanities, the Ford Foundation, and the Rockefeller Foundation. The authors thank Morton H. Halperin, Henry Owen, William P. Bundy, Joseph S. Nye, Leon V. Sigal, and Philip H. Trezise for their comments on drafts. They are also grateful to Laurel Rabin, who reviewed the manuscript for clarity and accuracy; to Donna Daniels Verdier for her administrative support as the study took shape; to her and Delores Burton for deciphering and typing successive drafts; to Alice M. Carroll for editing the book; and to Florence Robinson for preparing the index.

The views expressed here are solely those of the authors and should not be ascribed to the trustees, officers, or other staff members of the Brookings Institution, or to the National Endowment for the Humanities, the Ford Foundation, or the Rockefeller Foundation.

GILBERT Y. STEINER
Acting President

June 1976
Washington, D.C.

Contents

CHAPTER ONE

Introduction

JAPAN'S ECONOMIC expansion since 1945 is one of the remarkable and least expected success stories of the past thirty years. A related success story, the U.S.-Japanese alliance, has likewise exceeded the hopes of most participants and observers. Just as Japan's shattered industries and demoralized population seemed unlikely sources of an economic miracle, the prospects for a close, mutually beneficial relationship between two bitter wartime enemies were not exactly encouraging. Yet such a relationship emerged and has persisted. Japanese leaders found the United States to be a dependable and generally beneficent patron as they built new policies founded on cooperative relations with the nations of the West. For American leaders, Japan proved to be a vital geographical link in the Pacific network of defenses, as well as a loyal ally willing to follow the American lead in international policy.

Achieving and maintaining such a partnership has required sustained effort by leaders and officials on both sides of the Pacific, because of the ever-present potential for serious misunderstanding and disagreement. Deep divisions within Japan about the virtue of the American connection fueled a severe crisis in 1960 when the bilateral security treaty was revised. A decade later, just as a similar crisis was being avoided by agreement on returning Okinawa to Japanese control, the two countries became engaged in a bitter three-year dispute over textiles. And before this was resolved, the alliance was further shaken when the United States made its surprise opening to China in July 1971 and when President Nixon suspended the dollar's convertibility into gold a month later and imposed a temporary surcharge on imports. As the imbalance in trade—a major target of Nixon's economic measures—grew to $4 billion in Japan's favor in 1972, Japanese-American tension continued. But after Japan established diplomatic relations with Peking late that year, and a sharp upsurge in U.S. exports closed the trade gap, the tension subsided. By the mid-seventies it was clear that the alliance had survived these crises and entered a new if somewhat uncertain era. Gerald Ford, in the fourth month of his presidency, undertook as his first overseas venture the visit to Tokyo that protest demonstrations had forced President Dwight Eisenhower to cancel in 1960. And Emperor Hirohito's return visit in 1975 was even more symbolic of the ability of both countries to look beyond past conflicts.

Yet problems—actual and potential—continue. Americans inevitably worry about whether Japan will one day choose to acquire nuclear arms and about the impact of such a choice on world power relationships. And although Japan's particular vulnerability to the recent economic ills of the industrialized world has tempered visions of an economic superstate, Americans worry about the possibility of future Japanese trade offensives. Underlying these genuine substantive concerns is a widespread anxiety about what "the Japanese" really want, who "the Japanese" really are. For many Americans, the cultural gap raises questions about the foundations of the relationship and the extent of mutual understanding, about what officials on the other side of the negotiating table are really thinking. And in Japan, where the psychology of the junior partner still prevails, concern about "the Americans" is far more pervasive. Opposition Communists and Socialists have long challenged American policies; now conservative politicians and bureaucrats worry about the dependability of U.S. policies. The "Nixon shocks" of 1971 suggested to them either a purposive U.S. administration determined to shake up and loosen the alliance, or else a willful, capricious giant paying little heed to U.S.-Japanese relations as it pursued matters of current preoccupation. The communist victory in Indochina in April 1975 raised further concerns about the American security commitment.

All of these uncertainties seem related to a deeper change in the international economic and political structure, for the U.S.-Japanese alliance of the fifties and sixties flourished under circumstances that clearly no longer exist. The American policy of isolating and containing China then made the Japanese connection, and Japanese bases, critically important; they seem less crucial in a multipolar world. Until the 1960s the Japanese economy had limited impact internationally, so that remarkably effective growth and export policies could be pursued—and encouraged by the United States—without threatening the domestic markets of too many American industries; now the sheer size of Japan's economy demands attention to how its domestic policies affect the international order. Furthermore, the oil embargo of 1973 and the ensuing fourfold oil price increase illustrated dramatically the limitations of American ability and determination to protect Japan from her economic vulnerabilities, and resulted inevitably in differing national policy responses. Obviously, the U.S.-Japanese relationship must be reshaped to fit the new realities, to manage and mediate economic rivalry, to maintain basic trust and mutual confidence while independent overtures to third powers are being undertaken by both sides. By 1975, leaders in both countries were showing sensitivity to this requirement, recognizing both the value and the vulnerability of the relationship. But there remains the ever-present need to translate such general predispositions into concrete, mutually beneficial cooperation within an altered world environment.

An important determinant of the future of the relationship will be how the American and Japanese governments deal with one another on the major policy issues that arise between them. Ideally, the actions of each should be based on careful, rational calculations of the impact of such actions on the other and the other's likely response. But powerful political facts of life work against this—the inevitable existence of other policy goals that compete with good U.S.-Japanese relations; the dispersion of power within the two governments and societies that makes coherent central policies difficult for leaders to achieve whatever their priorities may be. Thus the major foreign policy actions that emerge from both governments have their roots in politics at home, both bureaucratic politics within each government and the broader national interplay labeled domestic politics.[1] The politics of U.S.-Japanese relations involves far more than the direct dealings of Japanese and American officials with one another. Constructive U.S.-Japanese relations require far more than mutual understanding and effective

1. While this book is not an explicit effort to determine either the utility or the limitations of the bureaucratic politics approach to the study of foreign policy, our basic orientation owes much to works such as Graham Allison, *Essence of Decision: Explaining the Cuban Missile Crisis* (Little, Brown, 1971); and Morton H. Halperin with the assistance of Priscilla Clapp and Arnold Kanter, *Bureaucratic Politics and Foreign Policy* (Brookings Institution, 1974). Like those writers, we consider politics and decisionmaking inside each government as part of a broader national political process, and in our study we give considerable attention to such broader domestic politics. On this general point, see Halperin, *Bureaucratic Politics*, pp. 4–5.

communication between the officials who specialize in maintaining them. For these officials must also work within their own governments and societies to reach solutions to particular problems that will have sufficient domestic support. Otherwise, officials with quite different perspectives and priorities are likely to gain the upper hand.

In the dispute over textiles in 1969–71, for example, the objectives of industrialists and their government supporters came to dominate the bilateral negotiating process. Those in Washington who argued for compromise in order to avoid a disruption of bilateral relations could not win the support of the President, who was determined to honor his pledge to protect the U.S. textile industry against the influx of Japanese synthetic and wool textiles. Those whom the President assigned to negotiate textile quotas with the Japanese had little stake in the objective of maintaining good relations with Japan and even less sensitivity to the fact that a demanding American approach was likely to stiffen Japanese resistance. Thus in 1969, instead of using quiet diplomacy with Japan to pursue his objective of textile quotas, the American official in charge of the issue, Secretary of Commerce Maurice Stans, led a highly visible mission to Europe seeking to line up support for a multilateral agreement aimed at Asian textile products. Inevitably Japanese national pride was aroused, and when Stans arrived in Tokyo a month later to deal directly with Japanese negotiators he was greeted with a unanimous Diet resolution opposing an agreement on textile quotas, as well as by a foreign minister whose opening statement expressed official unwillingness to discuss the problem.

Why were American official actions of the sort that would trigger the very kinds of Japanese policy responses that U.S. officials wished to avoid? U.S. tactics did not, of course, create the substantive difference between the two governments. The fact that Nixon wanted thoroughgoing quotas and Japanese leaders no more than a very loose restrictive arrangement was bound to make resolution difficult. But why transform textiles from a tough negotiating problem into a confrontation before negotiations had even begun, and a confrontation, moreover, with an atypically unified and unusually adamant coalition of Japanese actors and interests? How might American officials have done better? Could they have understood enough about Japanese politics and decisionmaking to facilitate U.S. policy choices aimed at resolving or preventing crisis rather than precipitating it? Or were Japanese politics and decisionmaking too alien, too "Oriental" for Westerners to comprehend?

Do Japanese decisionmakers do any better in understanding the U.S. system, or in shaping their actions consciously to affect it? Or are officials in each country so preoccupied with the politics of their own system that they have no time to comprehend the other? If so, then how does one explain the successes like Okinawa reversion?

For even as the secretary of commerce was bringing the textile issue to a point of confrontation with Japan, U.S. and Japanese officials were reaching an amicable agreement in principle to return Okinawa to full Japanese sovereignty. Indeed the Okinawa question in itself was more complex and held greater potential for creating bilateral animosity than textiles. The Okinawa question reached far more deeply into Japanese politics and national consciousness than textiles and held crucial implications to Japanese for the sincerity of American professions of partnership and alliance. Until 1967, the American government had consistently held a more rigid and less compromising position on the Okinawa issue than it had on earlier negotiations for textile quotas. How was a satisfactory settlement reached? Why would the two governments allow an interest as narrow as textiles (a modest and declining portion of the total trade relationship and the two domestic economies) to diminish the gains for the alliance which reversion was bringing?

These are the types of problems this book seeks to address. Although it does not assume that adequate official American understanding of Japanese politics and policymaking—or vice versa—would in itself resolve difficult policy issues, it does assume that misunderstanding is likely to compound the real problems that already exist. Although it does not claim that improving the process of U.S.-Japanese relations would in itself eliminate the significant substantive differences that are bound to arise, it does rest on the belief that how communications and negotiations between the two countries are handled will affect the prospects for relatively expeditious and amicable resolutions of substantive differences that arise in the future, just as it has in the past.

Chapter 2 introduces the three main cases that are used illustratively throughout the book. These three cases—the revision of the security treaty, the reversion of Okinawa, and the textile dispute—span a twenty-year period and required the attention of both governments at all levels. Chapter 3 opens our more general discussion by focusing on the national political and bureaucratic institutions through which policy decisions and actions are taken. Here the emphasis falls overwhelmingly on Japan, since we are writing mainly for Americans who are already familiar with their own system. One important purpose of the chapter is to demonstrate that many of the institutional differences can be explained by political concepts and variables with which Americans are very familiar. The general discussion moves next, in chapter 4, to a consideration of how officials in each government tend to perceive actions taken by the other—and particularly to recurrent patterns of misperceptions. Some of these seem common to any bilateral relationship between large, complex democracies. Others, however, stem from cultural differences and, in treating them, we give attention to elements of Japanese culture that seem particularly prone to American misunderstanding.

Chapter 5 takes a more comprehensive look at the interplay between the two governments. Here our focus is on the origin and communication of initiatives, the types of negotiating channels brought into play, and some of the ways that actions by actors in one system have an impact on decisionmaking in the other—whether or not the effect is intended. For example, we examine how the specific steps that officials in one country take can strengthen or weaken potential allies in the other.

And finally, in chapter 6, we develop and summarize our conclusions and our policy recommendations. Here we continue to focus particularly on U.S. relations with Japan. But we organize our analysis so as to indicate which of our findings might also be applicable to other U.S. relationships with large allies.

In basing our study on a set of specific cases, we inevitably oversimplify some of the negotiating problems involved. Managing the relationship requires more than resolving individual, bilateral negotiating issues; actors on both sides are always involved in a range of U.S.-Japan issues at the same time, bilateral and multilateral, with each affecting the others. Indeed, the U.S.-Japan relationship itself cannot be fully understood outside its broader international context; the recent oil crisis, and the Japanese government's tilt toward the Arab countries, diverging sharply from the U.S. stance, is a case in point. But focusing on bilateral issues helped make our research manageable, and simplifies the presentation of the analysis. Furthermore, a look at the postwar record will show such specific cases have been very important in shaping broader U.S.-Japan dealings in the past. Chapter 6 includes our argument for the relevance of our findings to current multilateral issues as well.

Another kind of problem arises from the potential evolution of Japanese policymaking. Postwar policies have been shaped by conservative, Liberal Democratic party (LDP) cabinets working with senior bureaucrats who shared their general assumptions about international issues. The cases we have studied all reflect this pattern. If the LDP were to lose its diminished Diet majority, and especially if a Socialist-Communist coalition were to take power, this pattern would undergo major change, much more fundamental than shifts between parties in the United States. It would affect many of the specific institutional relationships analyzed in this study. Nevertheless, even in the case of sharp leadership shifts, an understanding of the institutions currently dominant would be important for predicting and interpreting the institutional changes most likely to occur under basic political change. In the more probable case of either a continuing LDP majority government or a trend toward LDP-led coalitions, the future would bear much greater resemblance to the present.

Finally, for the reader close to policymaking in either government, our single-minded focus on the U.S.-Japan relationship may seem a bit artificial, since actors in both countries necessarily have to take account of other values as well. We recognize, of course, that no U.S. president and no Japanese prime minister could adopt this focus in its absolute form—there is no reason, after all, why the claims of "good U.S.-Japanese relations" should take priority in every case over other policy interests and goals of groups and governments. Indeed, the very existence of substantive differences that need to be resolved attests to the importance of these other goals and interests. Yet constructive overall U.S.-Japanese relations are an important goal, fully worthy of an analysis of how they can be politically and procedurally advanced. Thus for purposes of this book, we are only secondarily concerned with the specific substance of particular U.S.-Japan questions—what types of export or import quotas there should be, if any; what changes should take place, if any, in security obligations and arrangements. Instead, we seek to emphasize how the way these issues are perceived and managed by influential policy actors in both countries can affect the prospects for mutually acceptable resolutions.

CHAPTER TWO

Three Postwar Cases

THREE MAJOR postwar negotiations illustrate the interplay between domestic politics and U.S.-Japanese relations: revision of the bilateral security treaty (completed in 1960); the reversion of Okinawan administrative rights to Japan (agreed to in 1969); and the dispute over quotas for Japanese textile exports to the United States (resolved in 1971). Each became a major political issue between the two countries. Each involved not only dealings between foreign offices, but struggles over national politics and policy in Tokyo and Washington.

Security treaty revision and Okinawa reversion were both deeply significant bilateral issues involving Japan's basic alignment in world politics and her territorial integrity. The public demonstrations and political turmoil surrounding ratification of the revised security treaty in 1960 were unprecedented in postwar Japan. The policy community in Washington was surprised at the depth of controversy in Japan over an alliance that Americans saw as so generous and beneficial.

The lessons of the treaty revision remained in the minds of policymakers in Washington and Tokyo as they began to grapple with the highly complex problem of Okinawa several years later. To Japanese, Okinawa represented the unresolved status of Japanese sovereignty, a reminder of the war and defeat, an anachronism in times of surging Japanese economic power and renewed national pride. To Americans, Okinawa was a thorny security problem. As a sprawling collection of bases had developed on the island, so had the attitude that American administrative control was essential to maintaining the bases. There was significant resistance in Washington to the idea of compromising larger U.S.

8

security interests simply for the sake of returning to Japan the administrative rights over a few outlying islands. It took a long, complex process
of domestic bargaining—on both sides—to recast the issue and reach
an equitable solution that averted repetition of the 1960 crisis.[1]

The textile dispute, by contrast, was significant not because of what
was directly at stake, but because of the political crisis it provoked. In
substance it was a market struggle between two declining national textile industries carried out through their governments. But its resolution
became equated with the commitment and effectiveness of the two countries' top leaders. Because this dispute coincided with a series of dazzling
Japanese economic successes, it tended to reinforce American perceptions that Japanese economic advances were rapidly becoming a threat
to American interests. And frustrations arising from this particular negotiation were an important cause of the shock treatment applied to Japan
by the Nixon administration in 1971.[2]

Together these three cases provide a convenient means of exploring
nearly a twenty-year span in the postwar U.S.-Japanese relationship.
The histories of all three overlap, most significantly those of Okinawa
reversion and textiles. A description of how each arose and was resolved
affords a view of the politics of U.S.-Japanese relations and the general
perspectives of each country during the postwar period. But our purpose in describing them here is less to offer history for its own sake than
to build a foundation for the chapters that follow. In our subsequent
efforts to generalize about the politics of U.S.-Japanese relations, we
shall draw mainly—though not exclusively—on these three cases for
illustrative examples and supporting evidence. And introducing the
cases at this point has one further purpose. While they are interesting as
self-contained stories, many of their specific episodes are difficult to
understand without the broader analysis of policymaking patterns and
interaction that follows. Thus we hope that their presentation will both
establish the need for such analysis and develop the reader's interest in
the questions that analysis will treat.

1. The discussion of Okinawa in this study is drawn from Priscilla Clapp and
Haruhiro Fukui, "Decisionmaking in U.S.-Japanese Relations: Okinawa Reversion"
(1976; processed).

2. The discussion of the textile dispute in this study is drawn from I. M. Destler,
Hideo Sato, and Haruhiro Fukui, "The Textile Wrangle: Conflict in Japanese-American Relations 1969–71" (1976; processed).

The Postwar Setting

On September 8, 1951, Japan and forty-eight other nations affixed signatures to a treaty of peace ending the state of war that had existed officially for nearly ten years. The set of understandings and agreements that evolved between the United States and Japan as a prelude to the peace settlement did much to define the relationship between the two countries for the next twenty years. The peace settlement was nonpunitive (and economically supportive) by design, and these generous terms helped foster bonds of alliance and friendship between the former enemies. But Japan was compelled to sacrifice certain areas of sovereignty to accommodate American security interests, and the unusual arrangements devised for the purpose became sources of domestic resentment and friction in Japan.

For American leaders—as President Truman instructed his special negotiator John Foster Dulles in January 1951—the principal purpose of the peace settlement was to "secure the adherence of the Japanese nation to the free nations of the world, and to assure that it will play its full part in resisting the further expansion of Communist imperialism."[3] To this end, Dulles won the acquiescence of other World War II allies to Japan's reentry into the international community, despite their preference for strong reparations requirements and other sanctions. And the United States worked in the ensuing years to open access to world markets for the Japanese, whose products had been discriminated against before the war. The United States sponsored and pressed the case for Japan's membership in the postwar General Agreement on Tariffs and Trade (GATT) structure aimed at nondiscriminatory international commerce.

The United States also negotiated a mutual security treaty with the Japanese, which came into effect simultaneously with the peace treaty. Dulles's goal here was an alliance modeled on the principles of the North Atlantic Treaty Organization, with each member contributing to the common defense according to its abilities. During the initial stages, Japanese security would be guaranteed by the continued presence of American forces in Japan, but Japan would rebuild its own forces as

3. Quoted in Townsend Hoopes, *The Devil and John Foster Dulles* (Little, Brown, 1973), p. 105.

rapidly as possible to replace and augment American strength. Japan's eventual contribution would be toward insuring the security of neighboring Asian countries. But for a Japan still reeling from the devastation of war and the psychological agony of national self-recrimination, that was an unwelcome prospect. Dulles soon modified his demand for immediate large-scale rearmament not only in response to the pleas of the Japanese premier, but under pressure from nervous Asian allies and dissenters within the American government. He settled for assurance from Prime Minister Shigeru Yoshida that Japan would undertake a gradual program of rearmament within the limits of economic capability and constitutional law.[4] In turn, the United States withheld an explicit commitment to Japan's security and pressed other provisions on Japan limiting its sovereignty.

Japanese territorial jurisdiction also fell victim to the pressing American concern for security. With the outbreak of the Korean War and the subsequent American commitment to that war, the American bases on Okinawa, like those in Japan, became active staging centers. There was a general feeling in Washington that continued U.S. administrative control over Okinawa and other outlying Japanese islands would prove a valuable strategic asset in the long run. Japanese officials were understandably concerned that these territories not be permanently separated from Japan, although they may have recognized the strategic significance of the Okinawa bases. To satisfy the long-run interests of harmony with Japan and, at the same time, retain the flexibility of the Okinawa bases afforded by direct American administrative control, Dulles devised a unique formula whereby Japan would retain "residual sovereignty" over the outlying islands. When and if the islands would return to full Japanese sovereignty were questions to be answered by future generations.

Finally, with the division of China under a communist Peking government and a nationalist Taipei government there arose the question of which to include in the San Francisco peace conference as signatory to

4. Article Nine of Japan's constitution stipulates: "Aspiring sincerely to an international peace based on justice and order, the Japanese people forever renounce war as a sovereign right of the nation and the threat or use of force as a means of settling international disputes. In order to accomplish the aim of the preceding paragraph, land, sea, and air forces, as well as other war potential, will never be maintained. The right of belligerency of the state will not be recognized." However, this language has been construed by postwar governments as permitting the creation of limited military forces for self-defense.

the treaty with Japan. The United States was, by 1951, heavily committed against Peking. Great Britain, however, had recognized the communist regime and favored her participation in the settlement. It was decided that neither China would be invited and Japan would be left to settle the question of peace with China later. However, the powerful pro-Nationalist China lobby in the U.S. Congress was not satisfied with this disposition of the issue and demanded assurances from Japan that it would indeed conclude a peace treaty with the Taipei government. Against his preference that Japan take a less committed position on the China question, Prime Minister Yoshida acceded to Dulles's request for assurances that would satisfy Congress. To have refused would have jeopardized Senate ratification of the peace treaty. On April 28, 1952, the day such ratification took place, Japanese officials signed a separate peace treaty with Nationalist China. This episode came to symbolize American unreadiness to accept the normalization of Japanese relations with mainland China. It symbolized also Japan's dependence on the United States, the asymmetry of the relationship which colored all three of the postwar cases treated here.

Revision of the Security Treaty

The revised security treaty signed in January 1960 was the product of the first major postwar negotiation between Japan and the United States, and American officials tended to view it as a demonstration to Japan of American faith in the alliance. The negotiation had been primarily aimed at meeting conditions of mutuality that Japanese leaders had argued were essential for their country's security and sovereignty. These conditions had apparently been satisfied, and the new treaty had the approval of a political majority in Tokyo. Why, in the months after its signing, was the opposition so successful in using the treaty to create an extreme political crisis in Japan? As surprising to many Americans as the furor of the storm was the rapidity with which it faded after mid-year. Conservatives consolidated their rule and gained in subsequent elections; the U.S. alliance survived intact, if not strengthened.

The origins of the 1960 crisis lie, at least partially, in the terms of the security treaty included in the peace package of 1951. Because of American disappointment over Japan's contributions to free world defense, there were no explicit provisions for mutual security: the United States was "presently *willing* to maintain certain of its armed forces in and about Japan," forces which "*may* be utilized to contribute to the maintenance of the international peace and security . . . in the Far East . . . and to the security of Japan against armed attack from without."[5] Indeed, the treaty even authorized the use of these U.S. forces, "at the express request of the Japanese government," to control externally instigated insurrection within Japan. There were no other provisions for mutual consultation on the deployment or use of U.S. forces in Japan, except whatever "conditions" might be "determined by administrative agreements." The treaty also called upon Japan "increasingly [to] assume responsibility for its own defense against direct and indirect aggression," and it prohibited Japan from granting any base rights to a third power without the consent of the United States. In sum, the treaty was—for the Japanese—only a modest step from occupation. And it was very different from other security treaties concluded by the United States in the forties and fifties.

The small circle of Japanese politicians and officials who negotiated the security treaty nonetheless favored a security arrangement with the United States because they shared, to some extent, American concern about the communist threat in Asia, particularly the possibility of a communist victory in South Korea. They accepted the continued presence of American forces in or around Japan as a means of guaranteeing Japanese security against such an external threat. In return for this guarantee, they were willing to allow American bases to be used to guarantee the larger security of Asia. For them, this contribution to the free world cause was a reasonable quid pro quo for an explicit American commitment to ensure Japanese security, which would provide the basis for a *mutual* security pact.

American leaders, on the other hand, particularly John Foster Dulles, viewed mutual security fundamentally as a parallel commitment by two or more governments to the defense of each other. This implied parallel contributions by each country, according to ability, in material resources and explicit concern for collective defense. What the Japanese viewed as their contribution to mutuality—commitment to the free world and the provision of Japanese bases—Americans did not consider equal or parallel to their own contribution. Under the Japanese equation, the

5. For the text of the treaty, see Martin E. Weinstein, *Japan's Postwar Defense Policy, 1947–1968* (Columbia University Press, 1971), pp. 137–38. Emphasis added.

United States would be providing most of the resources for Japanese security. As long as Japan was unwilling to contribute materially to collective security or to make an explicit commitment to the security of its neighbors, Americans could see no justification for offering a comprehensive guarantee for Japan's security. Even if American officials could grasp the significance and intrinsic value of the Japanese quid pro quo, they felt they could never convince Congress, which was always looking for the direct return on dollars spent. Thus the same Dulles who had negotiated the security treaty continued to press for major Japanese rearmament after he became President Eisenhower's secretary of state. On at least one occasion he even disparaged Japanese defense efforts by comparing the size of her forces with those in neighboring South Korea, which had been fighting a war for three years.[6] For Dulles and most Americans, however, that war underscored the fundamental struggle between the free world and its communist adversaries; and they saw the strengthening of anticommunist military forces in Europe and Asia as essential because of that struggle.

Japanese leaders were fearful of undertaking rearmament so soon after the war, not only because of the memories of Japan's prewar expansionism it would evoke among its Asian neighbors, but because of the intolerable domestic division it would create. Premier Yoshida and his advisers knew that to commit Japan to the level of rearmament that Dulles had requested in 1951 would cause enough of a drain on reconstruction to cause widespread social unrest. Furthermore, rearmament might lead to a revival of Japanese militarism, if it were undertaken so quickly that the prewar generation of military officers had to be brought back to power. There might be international economic repercussions as well. If other countries, particularly Asian neighbors, saw Japan rebuilding its military machine to become the strong partner in an Asian collective security arrangement, they would be reluctant to provide the markets and raw materials on which Japan's economic reconstruction depended. For this would awaken memories of the prewar Japanese scheme for a Greater East Asian Co-Prosperity Sphere.

Even the quid pro quo defined by Japanese governmental leaders met considerable domestic opposition. There was broad support for Japanese neutrality in international relations, extending beyond the So-

6. See John M. Allison, *Ambassador from the Prairie: or Allison Wonderland* (Houghton Mifflin, 1973), p. 242.

cialist and Communist party opposition to include many articulate intellectuals. Advocates of neutrality saw a commitment to the free world as increasing the risk that Japan would be needlessly drawn into conflict—either directly or by implication. At the very least, such a commitment would seriously inhibit Japanese relations with communist countries. And it was hard for conservatives to counter the argument that American bases in Japan were simply a revised form of American occupation, for in substance the security treaty seemed little more than an arrangement for continued stationing of U.S. troops. Thus any Japanese government, no matter how it defined the international situation and Japan's security needs, would pay a domestic political price for a security treaty with the United States.

The gap in approaches to the security relationship was dramatically illustrated when three senior Japanese leaders met with John Foster Dulles in August 1955, carrying with them Prime Minister Ichiro Hatoyama's request for revision of the security treaty. They cited domestic discontent with Japan's "unequal" status under the 1951 arrangement, and argued that without changes Japan's conservatives would be hard pressed to stay in power. Dulles sternly rejected their request and apparently lectured them on Japan's refusal to make a significant contribution to regional defense.[7] At the conclusion of the discussion Foreign Minister Shigemitsu signed a joint communiqué committing Japan "to contribute to the preservation of international peace and security in the Western Pacific." In Japan the Hatoyama government was quickly accused by both conservative and opposition politicians of violating Japanese law and the constitution by agreeing to such a commitment. And the government found it necessary to deny that this was the intention of the communiqué, forcing Shigemitsu to retreat from the position he had taken in Washington.

Nevertheless, substantial policy adjustments by both governments were already under way. The United States had begun reducing the number of troops stationed in Japan; they dropped from almost 200,000 in late 1954 to about 90,000 in December 1956. Successive Japanese governments had been taking significant strides toward rearmament. In

---

7. Interview, Ichirō Kōno, a member of the delegation, Sept. 30, 1964 (Dulles Oral History Library, Princeton University). See also Asahi Shimbun Staff, *The Pacific Rivals: A Japanese View of Japanese-American Relations* (Weatherhill/Asahi, 1972), pp. 231–32; Allison, *Ambassador from the Prairie*, pp. 266–67; and Dan Kurzman, *Kishi and Japan: The Search for the Sun* (Obolensky, 1960), p. 288.

1952 the National Police Reserve, which had been formed by the American occupation to assume responsibility for internal security, was reorganized (with the Maritime Safety Force) into a National Security Force and designated for gradual expansion. In 1954, legislation was passed to establish national Self-Defense Forces, composed of separate ground, air, and naval arms. Their authorized strength reached 214,182 men by late 1956,[8] well under the 350,000 that Dulles continued to seek, but a substantial rise nonetheless. By 1957, moreover, the Japanese and U.S. governments had reached a series of understandings on limitations to the security treaty that were not contained in the document itself. Generally, these understandings evolved from consultations between the two governments on details about the deployment and use of U.S. forces in Japan which had not been made explicit in the security treaty or administrative agreement.

Even more important for the security relationship, however, was the adjustment in Japan to postoccupation self-government. With the release of those prewar leaders who had been purged from political activity during the occupation, the number of competing forces within the Japanese conservative leadership increased dramatically. Prime Minister Yoshida was forced to resign in late 1954 with the advent of renewed factional rivalry. Almost overnight the task of rising to and maintaining the position of prime minister became an incredibly complex problem of balancing factional coalitions and outmaneuvering numerous actual and would-be rivals. Conservative politicians aspiring to party leadership would seize upon salient foreign policy issues, safely removed from immediate domestic impact or informed public scrutiny, to gain valuable publicity and an advantage over their competitors.

Such maneuvering was evident in the August 1955 delegation to Washington. It was apparently a device for Prime Minister Hatoyama to demonstrate concern about the security arrangements to his domestic audience; if he could initiate revision of the treaty it would be an additional political plum. Because the senior Japanese representative in the delegation, Foreign Minister Shigemitsu, was not considered forceful enough to impress American leaders with Japan's position, Hatoyama had asked Nobusuke Kishi, chairman of the ruling Democratic party, to accompany Shigemitsu. Kishi was reluctant to appear in Washington

8. This and U.S. troop figures are from Weinstein, *Japan's Postwar Defense Policy,* p. 77.

as Shigemitsu's aide, because he already saw himself as a contender for top leadership. But he agreed to go in return for Hatoyama's endorsement of his campaign for merger of the two conservative parties, the Democrats and the Liberals, which Kishi saw as enhancing his premiership prospects.[9]

And indeed, Kishi did rise in early 1957 to the presidency of the newly consolidated Liberal Democratic party.[10] He was now clearly the strongest of the conservative leaders. He was certainly not the most popular, however, either within the party or with the public more generally. He was openly contemptuous of the press, and the dislike was reciprocated. His maneuvering within the party to advance and solidify his own position did not win him the affection of his conservative colleagues. And his identification with the prewar Japanese government (he had been minister of commerce in the Tōjō cabinet and was subsequently jailed as a war criminal) made him an easy target for an opposition seeking to arouse public anxiety about his "undemocratic" behavior. Kishi seems to have felt that only through personal forcefulness could he lead the nation in the direction he calculated to be best. But among other Japanese political actors there was an undercurrent of suspicion that whatever Kishi was pushing was more directly relevant to his own personal advancement than to the national interest.

Kishi addressed the security treaty question directly at his first press conference as prime minister: "From the point of view of national sentiment, the Japanese people desire that the present security treaty and administrative agreement between Japan and the United States should be abolished."[11] Those arrangements had become the more irritating as Japan recovered her economic strength and national self-confidence. The large number of American troops in Japan was causing multiple frictions with the local population and providing a constant

9. Kurzman, *Kishi and Japan,* p. 288. Kishi further used the Washington trip to push his cause when he returned to Tokyo, by arguing that only conservative unification would make it possible for Japan to improve its relations with the United States.

10. The Liberal and Democratic parties managed to effect a merger in November 1955. In December 1956, Tanzan Ishibashi narrowly defeated Kishi for the LDP presidency, and thus succeeded Hatoyama as prime minister. Kishi, who had been appointed deputy prime minister and foreign minister, took over two months later when Ishibashi was forced by illness to resign. Kishi was formally elected party president in March 1957.

11. As cited in George Packard III, *Protest in Tokyo* (Princeton University Press, 1966), p. 44.

reminder of defeat and occupation. Yet as far as the public could see, Yoshida's security treaty gave Japan no choice in the matter. Although there was no single mind on how best to achieve security, there appears to have been a consensus that the treaty was a temporary device, which must eventually be revised or eliminated, and that it was highly undesirable to become involved in an alliance that would bring Japan into conflict where its own interests were not at stake.[12]

In moving to take the matter up with the American government, Kishi had reason to presume that he might make headway. The substantial increase in size of the Japanese Self-Defense Forces under the Hatoyama government was practical evidence of Japan's awareness of and contribution to its own defense needs. Furthermore, Kishi had spent considerable effort before his ascendancy to convince American officials of his own commitment to a strong U.S.-Japanese alliance (as well as to educate them to the realities of what was and was not politically acceptable in Japan). Moreover, there had emerged within the U.S. government a strong, increasingly influential opposition to the Dulles-Pentagon stress on maximum Japanese military effort. Officials concerned with Japan at the U.S. embassy in Tokyo and the State Department in Washington argued for modification of the stern Dulles conditions. They developed a more political approach to the Japanese alliance, identifying U.S.-Japanese relations with the future of Kishi and the new Liberal Democratic party, favoring steps that might strengthen them domestically. Under their influence, Dulles personally seems to have softened his stance by the spring of 1957. Thus when Kishi traveled to Washington to meet President Eisenhower in June 1957, the situation was far more propitious than it had proved two years earlier.

For Japan the most important result of the 1957 summit meeting was mutual recognition of the "understanding that the Security Treaty of 1951 was designed to be transitional in character and not in that form to remain in perpetuity." Furthermore, a joint committee was established "to study problems arising in relation to the Security Treaty," which, as Kishi pointed out after his return to Japan, did not exclude matters relating to revision.[13] In return, Premier Kishi recognized the "major threat"

12. Ibid., pp. 31–32.

13. For his own purposes, Secretary of State Dulles indicated that revision was not in fact under way and that the joint committee had not been established expressly for revision of the treaty. Needless to say, Kishi was confronted with Dulles's comments at home.

of international communism and acknowledged the "deterrent power of the free world" in preventing aggression in Asia. Although the prime minister may actually have hoped to achieve an American commitment to revision at the summit meeting, from the American perspective an agreement in principle would not be possible until there was clear mutual understanding of the specific issues involved. Kishi himself has acknowledged a conversation with Secretary of State Dulles—probably during this visit—in which they discussed the pros and cons of merely amending the current treaty to avoid the legislative process or going ahead with full revision and accepting the political consequences. The latter course was taken.[14]

A year later Foreign Minister Aiichiro Fujiyama began discussions with American Ambassador Douglas MacArthur II that were clearly preliminary to an explicit plan for negotiation. In September 1958, Fujiyama and Dulles officially agreed to undertake negotiations, and talks began in Tokyo. At this point, however, factionalism within the Liberal Democratic party forced Kishi to suspend official negotiations until he reestablished his position and developed some base of agreement among party leaders. Although none of his LDP colleagues and rivals were taking a stand against revision of the treaty, several publicly criticized details in the government's approach. This apparently was more a reflection of anti-Kishi feeling and factional rivalry than of deep conviction, but the effect was to delay progress in the negotiations and force Kishi to spend considerable time building consensus and buttressing his strength within the party. Clear party unity was never achieved on the terms of revision and the continuing intraparty struggle sapped Kishi's power over time and left him at a psychological disadvantage in the matter of treaty revision. "The treaty was clearly to be his 'last act' as far as all the other LDP leaders were concerned."[15]

Debate within the LDP seems also to have increased the broader public anxiety about the American alliance, an anxiety that the opposi-

14. Interview, Nobusuke Kishi, Oct. 2, 1964 (Dulles Oral History Library, Princeton University). When the revision question was formally raised the first American response was to suggest three possibilities: (1) a simple base-lease agreement; (2) amendment of the current treaty; and (3) a new treaty. Kishi apparently chose the third over the advice of the Foreign Ministry that amendment was preferable because there would be strong popular resistance to a new treaty. (See Packard, *Protest in Tokyo*, p. 70.) Similar differences arose between Sato and the Foreign Ministry on Okinawa reversion several years later.

15. Packard, *Protest in Tokyo*, p. 81.

tion parties both reflected and fanned. Premier Hatoyama had struck a responsive public chord by negotiating a peace agreement with the Soviet Union in 1956; many Japanese favored a similar opening toward China and saw the American alliance as the major roadblock. The late fifties, moreover, was a period of recurrent cold war tension—over Berlin and across the Taiwan straits. The latter were patrolled by the U.S. Seventh Fleet, and a Japan tied to the United States could in no way assume a neutral position. Not only did it look more likely that military alliance with the United States might draw Japan into useless conflict, but the strength of the Soviet Union seemed clearly on the rise and the United States no longer looked like an unassailable protector. Thus, even as Japanese negotiators were winning major concessions from the Americans, a deeper Japanese uneasiness with the U.S. relationship persisted and grew.

In January 1960, Kishi flew to Washington to sign the revised treaty negotiated by Foreign Minister Fujiyama and Ambassador MacArthur over the previous fifteen months. In substance, the premier could claim considerable achievement. The new treaty was fully mutual in form, with each party committed to join in resisting "armed attack against either Party in the territories under the administration of Japan." Japan did not have to assume any broader collective security responsibilities in the region. The condescending tone of the earlier agreement was not duplicated, nor were its specific infringements on Japanese sovereignty. And in an exchange of diplomatic notes accompanying the treaty, agreement was reached on a "prior consultation" formula: "Major changes in the deployment into Japan of United States armed forces, major changes in the equipment, and the use of facilities and areas in Japan as bases for military combat operations to be undertaken from Japan other than those conducted under Article V [in response to an attack against Japan], of the said Treaty, shall be the subjects of prior consultation with the Government of Japan."[16] To symbolize the new relationship, it was announced that President Eisenhower and Crown Prince Akihito would exchange state visits, with the President to arrive in Tokyo the following June.

The treaty was submitted to the Diet for ratification in April and it became the subject of renewed debate. The responses of Prime Minister

16. Weinstein, *Japan's Postwar Defense Policy*, p. 96. For the text of the treaty, see ibid., pp. 139–41.

Kishi and his cabinet to opposition questions only exacerbated the tension. When the Socialist party disrupted the Diet session in order to stall ratification, Kishi counterattacked on May 19 with a series of maneuvers that resulted in ratification of the treaty by the LDP members of the lower house, in the absence of the opposition members.[17] Under the Japanese constitution, this meant that the treaty would automatically take effect thirty days thereafter—the precise day of Eisenhower's planned arrival in Japan. The whole sequence looked a little too clever to be publicly acceptable. Widespread anger focused on Kishi, "whose insolence," in the words of a Japanese observer, "typified the worst aspects of prewar bureaucracy."[18] Not a few critics saw Kishi's arbitrary exploitation of his Diet majority and failure to take heed of opposition concerns as threats to Japanese democracy. Demonstrators, urged on by Communist and Socialist opposition, descended in ever-increasing numbers on Kishi and the Diet building. Their objective quickly became the cancellation of Eisenhower's visit.

In part, this was due to unhappiness with the treaty, but even more, it was anti-Kishi. The Eisenhower visit became the test-crucible of the premier's tenure in office. Not only did Kishi himself so identify it, but the opposition and the demonstrators also did and began planning for disruption of the visit as the ultimate means to discredit Kishi. When Eisenhower's press secretary, James Hagerty, led an advance party on June 10 to make final preparations, the limousine taking him from the airport was surrounded by a crowd that trapped Hagerty for about an hour before he could be rescued by helicopter. Nonetheless, Kishi remained determined to welcome Eisenhower, and neither the U.S. embassy nor the White House seemed to wish a postponement.

For the embassy, the problem was partly protocol—it was the Japanese government's responsibility to protect a state visitor, or to request a postponement if it could not do so. A cable from Ambassador Mac-Arthur shortly after the lower house action argued that "it would be great mistake for President to take initiative in postponing his visit to Japan," though a change in timing might be acceptable if "initiative be

17. Opposition members of the Diet had tried physically to keep the speaker of the lower house in his office so that he could not initiate a vote on the treaty ratification before the time ran out on that Diet session. They were removed from the building bodily by the police and when the vote was initiated, they did not know the Diet had reconvened. The majority LDP members, however, were present and voted for ratification.

18. Quoted in Packard, *Protest in Tokyo*, p. 246.

that of GOJ [Government of Japan]."[19] But the embassy's support of
the Kishi government encouraged sticking with the trip on policy
grounds as well, especially since cancellation would damage both national leaders. And MacArthur feared that if the Kishi government were
to collapse, final ratification of the new security treaty would be "very
seriously jeopardized"[20] (though all that was now legally required was
that the Diet remain in session for thirty days after May 19). And if
treaty ratification were thus blocked, it would be "the greatest victory
communists could gain in Asia" and a devastating blow to Japanese
democracy.[21] Thus for the embassy, persevering with the Eisenhower
visit was essential to hold the line against communist encroachment in
Asia.

President Eisenhower also remained ready to proceed. He wanted
to end his career as president on a note of international peace and a
reconfirmation of the strength of the free world alliance. Thus in 1959
he had embarked on a series of state visits that would take him to Asian
and European allies and also, he had hoped, to the Soviet Union. The
visit to Tokyo would be the most important stop on his Asian itinerary.
Then, in May 1960, the Russian invitation was dramatically withdrawn
after an American U-2 plane was shot down over Russia. Eisenhower
did not wish a second such public humiliation, and when he left on
June 12 for the Philippines—his first Far Eastern stop—he hoped that
the Tokyo visit would still be possible. But on June 15 the Tokyo
demonstrations provoked a major battle between police and demonstrators, during which a young woman student was crushed to death. Despite
the fact that Japanese public opinion was now moving against the left,
Kishi concluded that the President's safety could not be guaranteed;
indeed, Kishi himself could not move about freely. So on June 16 in
Manila, Eisenhower learned that the invitation had been withdrawn.

A week after the cancellation, Premier Kishi resigned. The wave of
public emotion and demonstrations in Tokyo quickly subsided, and the
conservatives actually made gains in the Diet elections the following
November. Controversy over the security treaty also receded into the

19. Cable no. 3825, U.S. Embassy, Tokyo, to Secretary of State (eyes only),
May 25, 1960. This is one of a number of State Department documents on the
period declassified in 1975 under the Freedom of Information Act.

20. Cable no. 3798, U.S. Embassy, Tokyo, to Secretary of State, May 23, 1960.

21. Ibid.; and cable no. 4017, U.S. Embassy, Tokyo, to Secretary of State, June
4, 1960.

background and Japanese politicians, both conservative and opposition, expressed regret that the crisis in Tokyo had taken on such a strong tone of anti-Americanism.

The initial White House comment on the cancellation of Eisenhower's trip was "that a small organized minority, led by professional Communist agitators acting under external direction and control, have been able by resort to force and violence to prevent his good-will visit."[22] Later, a more subtle interpretation began to emerge at higher levels in Washington. Senator Sparkman concluded, for example, that one cause of the crisis was Kishi's failure to engage in public discussion and develop public support for his policies, and he warned that "it served notice on our country that Japan cannot be taken for granted."[23] A respected expert on Japan, Harvard professor Edwin O. Reischauer, wrote that this current of discontent in Japan "cannot be disregarded, for it is made up, not just of the formally organized Socialist opposition, centering around the trade-union movement, but also the bulk of Japan's intellectuals and college students—that is, the would-be ideological pathfinders and the generation to which the future of Japan belongs."[24] Within a year, Reischauer was named U.S. ambassador to Japan by the new Democratic President John F. Kennedy, specifically "to establish ties that might reach deeper into Japanese society than the Foreign Office."[25] And for years to come the lessons of 1960 remained vivid in the minds of policymakers, conditioning the approach of both American and Japanese officials to matters concerning the security treaty.

Okinawa Reversion

On May 15, 1972, the U.S. military administration of Okinawa ended and full sovereignty was returned to Japan. On the Japanese side, the issue of reversion not only reopened public debate about the security

22. A. Merriman Smith, *A President's Odyssey* (Harper, 1961), p. 222.

23. Senator John Sparkman, *The Far East and the Middle East,* Report to the Senate Committee on Foreign Relations, 86:2 (Government Printing Office, 1960), pp. 1–9. Eisenhower himself later expressed the view, according to Smith, that Kishi "generated trouble for himself the way he rammed the defense treaty with the United States through the lower house of the Diet." (*A President's Odyssey,* p. 258.)

24. Edwin O. Reischauer, "The Broken Dialogue with Japan," *Foreign Affairs,* vol. 39 (October 1960), p. 13.

25. W. W. Rostow, *The Diffusion of Power, 1957–1972* (Macmillan, 1972), p. 237.

alliance with the United States but raised sensitive questions of national sovereignty. On the American side, and within official Japanese circles, the Okinawa decision required a strategic reassessment, which inevitably produced severe resistance from those whose operations and missions were likely to be affected by change. The question had all the potential for a repetition of the crisis of 1960. Moreover, Okinawa became directly linked to the tenth anniversary of the mutual security treaty, for after 1970 either side could cancel the treaty on a year's notice. If Okinawa's status was not renegotiated before 1970, it was widely feared that Japanese resentment would lead to major demonstrations against maintaining the treaty.

Thus the issue to be resolved through bilateral negotiation was highly complex. In Japan and Okinawa there was strong public reaction against U.S. military ventures in Southeast Asia and the possible implication of Japan. In Washington there was severe military resistance to giving up Okinawa. How was it possible to reach an amicable decision in time to avert a crisis? What was required on the U.S. side to avoid resistance from military leaders and to gain their acquiescence to a decision that also acceded to Japanese antinuclear sentiment? How did the Sato government in Japan manage to withstand the political consequences of engaging in public debate about the security alliance, the issue that had brought Kishi's downfall in 1960?

Although he was the first Japanese premier to pledge himself to the resolution of the Okinawa question, Sato was not the first to discuss the issue with American officials. When Premier Hayato Ikeda visited Washington in 1961, he expressed concern to President John F. Kennedy that his most difficult domestic political problem arising from Japan's relations with the United States was the continued American military administration of the Ryūkyū[26] and Bonin islands. For during

26. The terms *Okinawa* and *Ryūkyū Islands* are used interchangeably in this study; they refer to those islands under postwar U.S. administration that reverted to Japan under the agreement effective in May 1972. Geographically, *Okinawa* can also mean just the main island and *Okinawa Islands* can mean that plus the small group of islands immediately around it. *Ryūkyū Islands* can include other islands not included in the U.S. administration (*Ryūkyū Rettō*), or be limited (as in this study) to the area of that administration (*Ryūkyū Shotō*). More important, the alternative designations have a political significance. When the territory was separated administratively from Japan in 1945, Americans (inclined to deemphasize the islands' ties to Japan) reverted to the old Chinese designation, Ryūkyū Islands, and called only the largest island Okinawa. Japanese continued to call them the Okinawa Islands after the former prefecture of Okinawa.

the 1950s the United States had clung steadfastly to the position that reversion of these administrative rights to Japan could not be considered as long as tension and aggression in Asia persisted. Discussions with the Japanese had never been allowed to go beyond this position. The U.S. Department of the Army, invested with the responsibility of governing Okinawa and the Bonins, had followed blueprints developed for the occupation of Europe after World War II. Under Dulles, the Department of State strongly supported military estimates of the importance of maintaining total control over Okinawa and the notion that Japan's "residual sovereignty" would continue into the indefinite future. (The State Department did not participate in the U.S. administration.)

Nevertheless, Ikeda's suggestion to President Kennedy fell on fertile ground. On Okinawa, pressures against the U.S. bases had been rising and it was generally believed in both the White House and State Department that at least part of the solution to this problem might be sought in negotiation with Japan (the rest would be in increased U.S. aid to Okinawa). In 1961, probably in response to Ikeda's concern, a special U.S. government commission was formed to study the matter. Its objectives were to find means of relieving pressures against the Okinawa bases and demonstrating good faith to the Japanese of American intentions to return the islands one day; consideration of reversion was not included. The few officials who saw a base rights agreement for Okinawa similar to that in Japan as a workable alternative were not willing to challenge unified military claims that such an arrangement would seriously impair American military operations. Furthermore, without the support of the military for whatever measures were to be taken, it was thought that Congress would not approve increased aid to Okinawa, which was the Kennedy administration's most important objective.[27] Acting on the commission's recommendations, President Kennedy announced the intentions of the U.S. government "to discharge more effectively our responsibilities towards the people of the Ryūkyūs, and to minimize the stresses that will accompany the anticipated eventual restoration of the Ryūkyū Islands to Japanese administration." He proposed that Congress increase aid to Okinawa, that arrangements be made for Japanese cooperation in economic assistance to Okinawa, and

27. Previous appropriations from Congress for civil aid to Okinawa had not been adequate to meet the needs, and there was hope that increased aid and economic growth would make the local population less inclined to disrupt base operations.

that a civilian be appointed to fill the position of civil administrator in the U.S. administrative structure on Okinawa.[28]

This unilateral gesture by the American President was received with renewed hope in Japan, although very little substantive change in the administration of Okinawa resulted. Within the American government it lent credence to the concept of Japanese residual sovereignty and emphasized the impermanence of American control. Furthermore, the commission's work created awareness of the Okinawa problem among middle-level officials in both the Pentagon and the State Department; they now saw a need to pay close attention to developments on the islands. However, it also drew out the opposition—the belief that Okinawa was no longer Japanese and should never return to Japan was represented eloquently by the high commissioner, General Paul W. Caraway. Although he could agree wholeheartedly with the need for increased U.S. aid to Okinawa, he was firmly set against any Japanese aid contributions. And until Caraway was replaced in 1964, there were none.[29] For the time being, Washington hesitated to enforce the intent of the President's recommendations. From this point, opinion appears to have polarized within the U.S. government between those who advocated concessions to local sentiment in order to preserve harmony with Japan and those who insisted that even a single concession would lead to a series of concessions, resulting eventually in total degradation of the strategic value of the Okinawa bases.

In the LDP presidential elections of 1964, one of the candidates, Eisaku Sato, chose to speak out boldly on the issue of Okinawa reversion as a means of distinguishing his platform from those of his opponents, but, as characteristic of political gambits, with no particular strategy for fulfilling his promise. Although Sato lost the election to Ikeda, he did come to office four months later when illness forced Ikeda's resignation. He renewed his pledge to pursue the matter of Okinawa reversion with American leaders. Sato had picked up the issue almost casually, but as premier he became increasingly attached to it emotionally as well as politically, and the final Japanese position on the terms of reversion bore the stamp of his personality.

Sato had risen through the ranks of the Liberal Democratic party

28. Statement by the President Upon Signing Order Relating to the Administration of the Ryūkyū Islands, March 19, 1962, in *Public Papers of the President, 1962*, p. 247.

29. The 1964 appointee, General Albert Watson, was far more conciliatory.

as a protégé of Shigeru Yoshida, and his political style was one of extreme patience and caution. Once Sato had defined the issue of Okinawa reversion as an important foreign policy objective, he almost immediately stepped back and began a waiting game that was to last for more than three years. As a former bureaucrat, he was inclined to lean heavily on the counsel of the Foreign Ministry professionals, but he consistently weighed this against the views and recommendations of individuals and groups outside the government, whom he considered more in tune with domestic politics.

Career officials in the Japanese Foreign Ministry (the Gaimushō) in the postwar period have probably been most concerned with maintaining and strengthening the basic framework of cooperation with the United States that was defined at the time of the peace treaty. Although they recognized in 1951 the inherent difficulties of the peace package, they worked more consistently and methodically than any other group in Japan over the next twenty years to remove those aspects of the arrangement that might turn the Japanese public against the United States, and to avoid weakening the security and economic relationship with the United States, which they considered essential to Japan's well-being.[30] One of their greatest concerns was balancing the vagaries of LDP factional politics, which tended to raise contentious issues prematurely, with what they calculated to be feasible in negotiations with the United States.

In 1957, when Premier Kishi chose to pursue treaty revision with American leaders, the Foreign Ministry had already succeeded in establishing with American officials a series of understandings that made revision almost the next logical step. When Premier Sato brought up the subject of Okinawa reversion in 1965, none of the incremental steps had yet been taken and, as far as the Foreign Ministry was concerned, Japan was far from prepared to assume the responsibility for administering Okinawa or to work out the complex arrangements that would have to be made to accommodate the operations of the American bases on Okinawa. Above all, it was important to avoid creating a domestic political situation that would lead to a rupture in the existing security structure between Japan and the United States. Until 1967, when public

30. For example, Gaimushō officials tended to view the prior consultation formula arrived at in the revised security treaty of 1960 as insurance against an abrupt American withdrawal from Japan, as much as it was cast publicly as insurance against American introduction of unwanted troops or weapons.

pressure for an early solution of the problem was steadily growing and Sato began to search for a concrete diplomatic strategy to bring it about, senior Foreign Ministry officials deliberately avoided personal involvement. But the initial steps toward moving Okinawa into a position for reunion with Japan had begun in 1966, and after 1967 the momentum was consciously sustained through a series of negotiated adjustments that in effect Japanized Okinawa.

There had been considerable discussion within the American government before 1966 about the need to begin planning for reversion. Diplomats anticipated initiatives by the Japanese government to negotiate a settlement of the problem and military officials could see merit in the argument that 1970 might be the crucial decision point. The expiration of the security treaty would offer a clear opportunity for the opposition parties in Japan to mount a major offensive against the entire security relationship and renew the horrors of 1960. If the United States did not take steps to return full Japanese sovereignty over Okinawa by 1970, the opposition could rouse public sentiment against the security treaty, jeopardizing the entire alliance with Japan.

Recognition of this threat did not affect the formal position of the Joint Chiefs of Staff on reversion, however. Apparently, they would not endorse Ambassador Reischauer's recommendations that the U.S. government begin discussion of the problem with the Japanese government, nor would they consider reversion as a real option for discussion within the American government. Their reluctance to accept the State Department's sense of urgency stalled attempts in late 1965 and early 1966 to focus on the problem within a small interdepartmental forum. Finally it was agreed that a special study group, chaired by the State Department's country director for Japan, should analyze the local pressures in both Japan and Okinawa before any consideration was given to the possible effects of reversion on base operations.

The formation of this group marked the beginning of American consensus building. Concerned with the potential of local discontent for disrupting the operations of American bases on Okinawa, representatives of the State Department, the Joint Chiefs of Staff, the Department of the Army, and the Office of International Security Affairs (part of the secretary of defense's staff) were able to agree that 1970 was indeed a crucial year. Whatever problems existed would demand a solution within five years. The objective for the American government, they decided, should be to retain maximum flexibility for using the Okinawa

bases and yet accommodate Japanese public demands in order to preserve the larger security arrangement with Japan proper. The bases on
Okinawa were highly valued, but the alliance with Japan was much
more important.

From their agreement that there was an urgent local problem requiring immediate consideration of reversion, the interdepartmental
group went on to define a need for better coordination between the
American administrative organ on Okinawa and the embassy in Tokyo,
as well as between these two entities and Washington. All of the parties
to this highly complex problem would have to communicate effectively,
if the issue were to be resolved systematically by the crucial deadline.
They recommended that both the high commissioner and the ambassador report regularly to Washington on the mounting local pressures
and their recommendations for dealing with them. This would serve
the dual purpose of educating Washington and monitoring the field
operations.

In late 1966 a new ambassador to Japan and a new high commissioner for Okinawa were named with conscious recognition that the
reversion to Japan of administrative rights over Okinawa would be the
next major agreement between Japan and the United States. Ambassador U. Alexis Johnson and High Commissioner General Ferdinand
Unger met in Washington before they left for their posts and agreed to
work together to prepare the way. The effect of this conscious planning
by two high U.S. government officials was felt most strongly on Okinawa. Shortly after his arrival, Unger announced to the Okinawan legislature that it was time for them to begin preparing for return to Japanese administration. It was the first time an American military leader
had broached the subject publicly in anything but a negative sense.

During 1967 the Washington study group produced a second report
aimed at establishing an American position preparatory to the summit
meeting between the Japanese prime minister and the American president scheduled for the autumn. This report compared the conventional
operational capabilities of the American bases on Okinawa with the
capabilities they would have if their status were the same as that of
the bases in Japan. The conclusion was that very little would be lost if
Okinawa reverted to Japanese administration.[31] Thus with the full par-

---

31. The strategic role of the bases, in particular as a depot for storing nuclear
weapons, was not considered in this evaluation.

ticipation of the Joint Chiefs of Staff the widely entertained idea that
reversion would render the bases virtually useless began to dissipate.
The foundation had now been laid for direct discussions with Japanese
officials.

In the months before the 1967 summit meeting Japanese Foreign
Ministry officials began to perceive that Washington's wall of resistance
to the return of Okinawa had begun to crack. Possibilities suddenly
appeared for negotiating the incremental steps that would lead to full
reversion. It soon became evident that the summit would at least produce agreement on the return of the Bonin Islands. When Premier Sato
learned this, he decided that he would seek to go a step further and
achieve agreement in principle on the early reversion of Okinawa.
Shortly before the summit he signaled his wishes to the White House
through a private emissary. The answering signal from Washington
was that the U.S. government was not prepared for an agreement in
principle until the exact status of the Okinawan bases after reversion
had been discussed and agreed upon bilaterally.[32] Neither Sato, nor
his unofficial advisers, nor the Foreign Ministry were prepared to make
such a detailed commitment. There had been no serious public discussion and there was no way of defining the specific terms that would
settle well in Japan, particularly if the Americans were seeking special
status for these bases, as their position seemed to suggest. The compromise finally reached in hectic last-minute negotiations was a recognition by President Johnson of the Japanese desire for the return of
administrative rights over Okinawa within a few years.[33] Meanwhile,
negotiations for the return of administrative rights over the smaller
and less strategic Bonin Islands would begin as soon as possible.

In Tokyo, the reaction to Sato's negotiating achievements was equiv-
ocal, but not ultimately damaging to his position. There was satisfaction with the explicit arrangements in the communiqué for bringing

32. When Sato's proposal for agreement in principle on early reversion arrived,
President Johnson asked that it be discussed with key senators and congressmen. The
chairman of the Senate Armed Services Committee objected adamantly and Sato's
proposal was rejected. Apparently, senior State Department officials—and perhaps
President Johnson himself—saw a subtle connection between congressional reactions
and the attitudes of military leaders. In other words, they suspected that the interdepartmental bargaining process had not produced a full expression of military sentiments and that Congress would provide the public sounding board.

33. In the Japanese version of the joint communiqué the word *few* was interpreted
as *two to three*, so that Sato could point to a positive move toward reversion of
Okinawa as a result of his trip to Washington.

Okinawa into line with Japan economically and socially in preparation for reversion, because this was recognized as a means of maintaining momentum through concrete measures. However, the ambiguity of the American position on reversion itself was suspect and argument continued on whether the American government had actually committed itself to early reversion.

But for American officials who had been working toward reversion the 1967 summit represented a breakthrough. The absence in the communiqué of the standard rhetoric on retaining control of Okinawa until tensions in the Far East subsided—especially considering that tensions were actually at a peak in 1967—indicated to the careful observer that substantial movement had been made in the U.S. bureaucracy toward the reversion of Okinawa. Furthermore, the language devised for the agreement on the return of the Bonins set the precedent for negotiations on the reversion of Okinawa with the Joint Chiefs of Staff and it avoided the sticky issue of nuclear weapons storage, which was best left to the president himself. To the Japanese public and media, the reversion of the Bonins was related only indirectly to the reversion of Okinawa. Moreover, the opposition claimed that it was a substitute for, rather than a prelude to, the return of Okinawa. Only the specialists in the Foreign Ministry shared the American view of its significance.

On his return from Washington Sato initiated a year of debate on "defense-mindedness" in Japan. In a speech before both houses of the Diet on December 5, 1967, he declared that, "if the people become determined to defend their own country in unity and to take realistic steps toward that end, not only the international stature of our country will rise and we shall be better able to contribute to the stability of Asia, but, I am convinced, it will bring about the reversion of Okinawa in the near future."[34] Although Sato publicly held to his position that the terms of reversion were as yet a "blank sheet" on the Japanese side, he also indicated that the Japanese people would have to consider the possibility that the reversion of Okinawa could not be achieved without Japanese acceptance of a special status for the Okinawan bases allowing the continued presence of nuclear weapons. Voices outside the government began to rise in favor of nonnuclear status for the bases under the same restrictions that applied to the American bases in Japan proper, the so-called home-level formula. Within the Foreign Ministry

34. *Yomiuri*, Dec. 25, 1967.

the view continued to prevail that the Americans would not agree to open negotiations if Japan ruled out entirely the possibility of basing nuclear weapons on Okinawa.

In late January 1969, Foreign Minister Aichi announced that he had arrived at a two-step formula under which the current status of the bases would be maintained without modification for a certain period after reversion and, when the specific period was over, the bases would be reduced to home-level status. Almost immediately there was a strong reaction from within the LDP, and the movement favoring home-level status for the Okinawan bases grew quickly, threatening to become a partywide revolt against the prime minister. This indication of opinion from within his own party undoubtedly was the final sign to Sato that a public consensus had jelled. In early March 1969 Sato stated in the Diet that he would try to persuade the American government that the continued presence of nuclear weapons on Okinawa would alienate the local population to the point where the usefulness of the American bases would be jeopardized.

In the United States, 1968 was a presidential election year that brought the Republicans back to the White House. Richard Nixon, perceiving a need for strong, centralized presidential control over foreign policymaking, designed, even before his inauguration, a new National Security Council (NSC) system and ordered a series of studies on specific foreign policy problems. Two key members of the interdepartmental study group on Okinawa became members of the new NSC staff, and one of the first studies ordered was of U.S. relations with Japan. Thus at the same time that the Japanese premier was moving into a definitive position on the postreversion status of the bases, the American government was making its final calculations on whether the loss of nuclear storage facilities on Okinawa would seriously affect U.S. strategic operations in Asia. By now, American military leaders had become aware of the momentum in Japan toward a reversion arrangement and the fact that the President would have to come to a decision before the 1969 summit meeting with the Japanese prime minister.[35]

35. The State Department was arguing that to retain the long-term usefulness of the bases in both Japan and Okinawa there was a need for the United States to demonstrate its commitment to a strong alliance with Japan. Specifically, the Sato group within the Liberal Democratic party was the most pro-American and most firmly committed to preserving the U.S.-Japan relationship over the long run. Sato had staked his reputation on Okinawa reversion and, if he did not achieve this within his term as premier, he would not be in a position to determine his successor.

Although they were inclined to believe that some sort of nuclear storage arrangement could be negotiated with the Japanese government, they were also prepared to defer to the President's judgment if he ruled otherwise. Careful analysis had shown that the value of such nuclear storage was marginal. But when the President authorized the State Department to begin negotiations with the Japanese government in the late spring, he reserved his position on the issue.

The Japanese Foreign Ministry, once the premier had declared himself on the side of nuclear-free reversion, could now begin formulating a concrete negotiating position. On the basis of conversations with American officials during the last year, Gaimushō officials knew that the American side was most interested in Japanese concessions on the understanding on prior consultation, and specific commitment to security interests outside Japan. The Japanese government had been taking the position publicly that the prior consultation formula under the 1960 treaty meant a Japanese veto over any American request for major troop or weapons movements into Japan. If the Japanese government were willing to indicate that it would respond favorably to an American request in an emergency and to express Japanese interest in the security of other Asian countries, the strategic flexibility of all the American bases in Japan would be increased. Foreign Ministry negotiators believed these to be reasonable concessions in return for home-level status for the Okinawa bases, which only a few months earlier they had believed to be highly improbable. Thus the two sides went into the communiqué negotiations with similar perceptions of the fair exchange to be achieved; the differences between them were only a matter of degree.

Throughout the five-month negotiation, the Japanese officials were given no indication from the American side about its disposition toward the matter of nuclear weapons.[36] As they proceeded to negotiate their

---

If the United States, having already committed itself in principle to early reversion, were to impede the process at this point, it would appear to be a conscious judgment on the part of the U.S. government to alter the relationship with Japan. This would add fuel to the public hostility that already existed toward the U.S. bases in Japan and Okinawa, and would hasten the day when the United States would have to pull out altogether.

36. According to Armin H. Meyer, U.S. ambassador to Tokyo, "no Okinawa negotiating session would pass without a Japanese appeal for the incorporation of clear assurance in the communiqué that no nuclear weapons would be stationed on post-reversion Okinawa. Just as often, the American negotiators would parry the

own concessions to reversion, they (and the premier) became increasingly anxious that other factors were going to be brought into play by
the American government—from one quarter or another—to force upon
Japan a higher price in return for nuclear-free reversion than would be
publicly acceptable. Above all, they did not want to become involved
in a secret agreement on nuclear storage. Apparently to make doubly
sure that the negotiations would produce nuclear-free reversion, and
realizing that the real authority for decision was not in the State Department, Premier Sato opened up his own private channel to the
president's assistant for national security affairs, Henry Kissinger. This
appears to have produced the desired assurance, although at the price
of a promise to agree to restrict textile exports to the United States.

On November 19, 1969, Premier Sato arrived in Washington. Two
days later the joint communiqué was released to the public, announcing
that he and President Nixon had agreed on the reversion to Japan of
administrative rights over Okinawa, consistent with the policy of the
Japanese government with regard to nuclear weapons. The communiqué included Japanese recognition of some common interest in the
security of Korea, and possibly Taiwan. (No common position on Viet-
man was taken, except for a mutual expression of hope that the war
would have ended by the time reversion occurred.) American officials
were still concerned, however, that the connection between the Japanese commitments and the status of the bases in Japan after reversion
be made clear to the military audience to insure against a reaction from
Congress. Thus both Under Secretary of State U. Alexis Johnson and
the Japanese prime minister explained to the press the significance of
the new Japanese commitments to Asian security and the relaxation
of the meaning of prior consultation. In effect the Japanese commitment was overstated for American consumption.

In Japan reactions were mixed, with the opposition parties taking a
predictably negative stand. Premier Sato and the Foreign Ministry had
to answer publicly in Tokyo for his postcommuniqué assurances to
the American public. There was little prospect, however, for the opposition to arouse widespread public emotion about the issue, because
the basic domestic concerns had been satisfied. Okinawa would return

---

question. Actually a decision had been made within the top levels of the American
government some months earlier, but it was to be left to the President to convey the
good news to Prime Minister Sato in November." (*Assignment: Tokyo* [Bobbs-
Merrill, 1974], pp. 37–38.)

to full Japanese sovereignty, without the continued presence of American nuclear weapons, and with the same restrictions on the bases as applied to those in Japan under the security treaty.

With this basic decision as a framework, the detailed negotiations for the return of Okinawa to Japanese administration took place in 1970–71. Among the myriad thorny questions to be resolved were not only issues between the two governments, but also matters vital to the future interests of the Okinawan population, including the desire of private American businesses to retain a preferential status on Okinawa. Agreement was reached in mid-1971 and the treaty was submitted for legislative ratification. On May 15, 1972, Okinawa returned to Japan.

The Textile Dispute

Even as the United States and Japan were reaching an amicable solution to the territorial question that had clouded Japan's political sovereignty for nearly twenty years, one of the most severe bilateral confrontations of the postwar period was emerging. In his race for the presidency, Richard Nixon had pledged his support to the cause of the American textile manufacturers, as part of his quest for southern votes at the Republican nominating convention and the November election. Once in office, President Nixon proceeded to make good on his promise, pressing for the stringent controls on imports of Japanese synthetic and wool textile products that were being sought by the American manufacturers.

As a domestic political issue useful in an aspiring leader's campaign, the textile question paralleled Okinawa. It was parallel in several other respects as well. Each was a prime U.S.-Japan issue for at least two years and each had a major broader impact on the relationship. Each dominated summit conferences and the attention of those officials most concerned with U.S.-Japanese relations. And the resolution of each required concessions by a specific interest (the U.S. military, the Japanese textile industry) that would not be easily won. Yet a fundamental political difference between the issues facilitated resolution of Okinawa while rendering textiles more intractable. Okinawa reversion represented, for almost all Japanese, a deeply felt "national interest" of the most fundamental sort; its importance in Tokyo politics stemmed from the basic belief that Okinawa was part of the Japanese nation and should, by rights, be under Japanese control. Textiles in U.S. politics was the very opposite, a narrow, particular interest of the industry's management and workers, and of a politician in securing their political and financial support. Many Japanese considered U.S. textile demands in a certain sense illegitimate; this was not the sort of serious, important U.S. national interest that they would feel obligated to accommodate. Okinawa, by contrast, was recognized as a legitimate and important Japanese interest by almost all American actors. Without such recognition, its status would not have been so constructively resolved.

The very contrast between the two issues—the "high politics" of Okinawa versus the "low politics" of textiles—makes even more astounding the political prominence that the textile issue attained and the bitterness it created, not just between the respective textile interests but among officials and even national leaders. Nixon had recognized the need for concessions to Japanese domestic politics and national aspirations in agreeing to return Okinawa to Japanese sovereignty. How could he turn around and make rigid, uncompromising demands on the Japanese premier for textile export quotas that would place him under strong political attack? When the extent of domestic resistance in Japan became fully apparent, why did Washington continue to pursue an uncompromising position? And why, since textile exports had long been declining in importance to Japan, did the government in Tokyo resist so adamantly for so long? How could the same two governments that were skillfully negotiating the return of Okinawa for the sake of a harmonious, long-term relationship be unable to negotiate a seemingly more simple and less consequential problem?

The impact of low-cost Japanese textiles on the U.S. market had been a source of minor friction even before the Pacific war. It arose again in the early fifties when the Japanese textile industry, having recovered from its wartime devastation with the help of American financial and technical aid, began to make substantial sales in the United States. These sales remained a small fraction of the overall U.S. textile market but were concentrated in specific product lines like cotton blouses and velveteen cloth. The textile industry, politically very strong in the southern states and New England, pressed for quota restrictions.

The Eisenhower administration resisted efforts to legislate quotas but supported voluntary Japanese export limitations, which were incorporated into a bilateral agreement in 1957. In 1961 the Kennedy administration sought broader restrictions from a group of exporting countries, leading to negotiation of the Long-Term Arrangement on Cotton Textiles (LTA) in February 1962. This fulfilled a campaign commitment by the new President, and also paved the way for the major trade liberalization initiative he was developing—the Trade Expansion Act of 1962—by eliminating textile industry opposition. The Japanese government went along with the agreement, partly because it seemed to offer Japan greater prospects for gradually increased exports to the United States than the 1956–61 bilateral agreements which had kept Japan's sales stagnant while those from Hong Kong and other Asian competitors shot dramatically upward. But implementation of the long-term arrangement required detailed, virtually continuous bilateral negotiations, and these proved increasingly contentious. The industries in both countries intensified their pressure on the governments, and their influence was enhanced by the increasing influence of their official spokesmen: in Japan, the Textile and General Merchandise Bureau of the Ministry of International Trade and Industry (MITI); and in the United States, the Commerce Department and the inter-agency textile committees which it chaired and staffed.

During the same period, the United States was also pressing Japan to limit exports in a number of other product lines. But the general thrust of U.S. policy was to encourage Japanese economic expansion. The predominant official American view was that a full-employment economy in Japan depended on trade and that Japanese democracy, in turn, depended on a healthy economy. It was also important that Western markets be open to Japanese trade so that Japan would not have to turn toward the communist countries. Furthermore, it was believed, if special barriers were erected against Japan and Japan were treated like an outcast, hostile forces might once again become dominant there. The United States strongly supported Japan's entry into the General Agreement on Tariffs and Trade (GATT) against the strong resistance of countries such as Britain. Also, because Japan was so vulnerable and weak economically, special measures to protect Japan's economy, such as import restrictions, were believed justifiable. Thus during the 1950s and well into the 1960s the attitudes of American and Japanese officials on free trade for Japan were basically parallel, stressing (except on special products) nondiscriminatory treatment of Japanese exports and not expecting Japanese reciprocity on imports. The United States did apply pressure on Japan, however, to minimize its trade with communist countries, particularly China.

Taking full advantage of postwar economic opportunities, Japan expanded her production and trade remarkably in the fifties, and even more rapidly in the sixties. Her economy came to bear little resemblance to the outdated American image of an economy dependent on cheap labor producing mainly handcrafted products and low-quality textiles. And as Japan's share of total U.S. cotton textile imports deteriorated through the 1960s, her overall trade with the United States was rapidly expanding. By 1969, sales of machine tools, appliances, motor vehicles, and so forth, had risen to 45 percent of Japan's total exports, and the trade balance with the United States had shifted from chronic deficit to what would become chronic surplus. Rapidly growing also, however, were sales of textiles from manmade fibers, whose importance was multiplied by a worldwide revolution in textile manufacturing. It was to controls on these products, which remained outside of the painfully negotiated restrictions on cotton products, that candidate Nixon pledged himself. And he promised to seek controls on wool textiles as well. He did so at a time of broad and growing American unhappiness with Japan's foreign economic policies—particularly the maintenance of import and capital restrictions well after Japan's economy had, to American eyes, outgrown the need for them. By this time, also, the capacity for considerable bilateral cooperation in textile relations, which had existed until the early sixties, had given way to intense competition and mutual resentment.

Presumably unaware of the recent antagonisms over textiles, but well aware of Kennedy's success in 1961 and 1962, Nixon sought to deliver quickly on his promise. Like Kennedy, he pursued his goal not by asking Congress to enact textile import quotas—this seemed likely to lead Congress to impose quotas on other products, which Nixon didn't want—but by the proven course of negotiating an agreement with the Japanese under which they would restrict their exports "voluntarily." He separated textiles from broader foreign and trade policy, assigning it as a special negotiating task briefly to a White House aide and then to his politically loyal secretary of commerce, Maurice Stans.

Stans's first major efforts came on a general trade mission to Europe in April 1969, when he urged officials in five countries to join in meeting the common threat of low-priced synthetic textiles from Asia. After meeting a cool reception there, he traveled a month later to Tokyo to confront a major political storm, as industry and political figures had already mobilized to resist what was seen as a new and flagrant effort to line up Western countries against Eastern products. From this and a subsequent discussion with Japan's minister of international trade and industry, Stans gained only an agreement to hold "fact-finding" talks in September 1969, which accomplished nothing. But President Nixon's evident concern about the issue led Premier Sato to fear that continued Japanese resistance on textiles might jeopardize his chances of gaining Nixon's agreement on Okinawa reversion without nuclear weapons at the forthcoming November summit. It had been made clear to Japanese negotiators that the nuclear question was being reserved for a presidential decision, and that the President had a personal stake in achieving a strong textile quota agreement. Thus before the summit meeting, Sato initiated talks through a private emissary that formed the basis for his discussions with President Nixon at the meeting. What resulted was an understanding—later portrayed as a misunderstanding—on how future negotiations for voluntary Japanese quotas would be carried on, and what their outcome would be.

Faced with elections shortly after his return to Tokyo, Sato answered public speculation about a "secret deal" on textiles by denial, and he resisted behaving in any way that would indicate publicly the existence of a private understanding. American officials, particularly those who had been privy to the details of the back-channel exchange, expected that the prime minister would be able to move his government to accommodate the President's request, and they became frustrated when official Japanese resistance failed to dissolve after the LDP triumphed at the polls in late December. Sato himself had met firm opposition from MITI and the Japanese textile industry. Hoping to break this resistance, he used a cabinet reshuffle to replace the MITI minister with a man who he felt would be more responsive to him personally. But the new minister, finding he could not persuade the industry and the MITI bureaucracy to seek accommodation with American demands, rather quickly began to espouse the MITI view. Contributing to his stand was an embarrassing fact that plagued the talks throughout—that the Americans were unable to demonstrate widespread, serious injury to the U.S. industry caused by imports. This was the accepted international criterion for quota restrictions, though it had not been applied in the cotton textile negotiations a decade earlier. Thus very few Japanese thought the U.S. case had much substantive merit.

By March 1970, nearly a year after the initial American requests, the two sides had become locked in irreconcilable opposition. The situation had become a cause for concern in both Washington and Tokyo. American textile leaders and their advocates in government were understandably dissatisfied at the failure to gain Japanese restraint. However, free traders in the United States—though opposed to the Nixon textile initiative on trade grounds—were now disturbed by signs that Congress, pressured by the textile firms and other import-affected industries, might enact highly restrictive general quota legislation. Failure to gain some textile concessions from Japan would make such protectionist legislation much more likely. Although the Japanese textile industry and most MITI officials were quite satisfied with the failure of the negotiations and tended to believe that the U.S. Congress would never actually enact comprehensive quotas, officials in the Ministry of Foreign Affairs and the Japanese embassy in Washington were very concerned about the quota campaign emerging in Congress.

Thus the circumstances were ripe for new initiatives aiming at compromise, and they began to spring up left and right during the spring of 1970. At this point, communications between the two governments became extremely confused, with official, semiofficial, and private spokesmen sending messages and proposing compromises. New American suggestions for solution proliferated, but none of the proposals met with success in Tokyo. Those that were directed into the Japanese system through the premier or the Foreign Ministry would meet with resistance in the MITI, where the formulas were considered too rigid, or where proof of injury was stressed as a precondition for restraint. One plan, put forward by free-trader Donald Kendall, that might have won eventual Tokyo acceptance lost its impetus when its revelation brought forth vehement industry objections in the United States, and considerable industry opposition in Japan as well.

In the midst of this confusion, U.S. Secretary of Commerce Maurice Stans and Japanese Minister of International Trade and Industry Kiichi Miyazawa began dealing through an intermediary of their own to see if they could find some ground for compromise. In late June 1970 Miyazawa visited Washington to meet directly with Stans. Despite the commerce secretary's belief that their back-channel communications made success probable, the talks with his Japanese counterpart failed. Thereupon the Nixon administration "reluctantly" endorsed proposed legislation for textile import controls that it had heretofore resisted, carefully pointing out that textiles was a special case and repeating its opposition to statutory quotas on other products.

Through the summer, the prospects of more general quota legislation in Congress seemed to brighten, creating widespread concern in the international trade community and increasing pressure on Japan for textile concessions that might stem the protectionist drive. In September 1970 President Nixon shifted textile responsibility from Stans to Presidential Assistant Peter Flanigan. During the same month, Tokyo requested a meeting with the American President during Sato's October visit to the United Nations. The Japanese embassy in Washington attempted to reopen communications on the textile issue in advance of the summit, but met with a new formulation of the hard-line position in the White House developed under the guidance of Flanigan and Henry Kissinger. The idea was to remain immovable in order to maximize the pressure on Sato, and it proved successful. Prime Minister Sato arrived at the summit meeting without having agreed to the terms on which the Americans were insisting, hoping perhaps to talk the matter out generally. But under strong pressure from Nixon and Kissinger, he left the meeting having agreed in substance to the American demands.

The negotiations that followed this summit agreement slowly began to show promise. Though the Japanese government was having trouble agreeing on a position at all close to what Sato had endorsed at the summit, progress was made in drafting an agreement with the impact Americans desired but in a form relatively palatable to Japanese. In the third week of December, however, just as the U.S. and Japanese negotiators felt they were on the verge of agreement, the U.S. textile industry reacted negatively to certain provisions, and this led to a presidential determination that the United States had to harden its position. After this, the negotiations once again became stalemated. The trade legislation died in the closing days of Congress, removing this immediate pressure. And the Sato government, subjected to vehement attacks from its textile industry and other critics of the mid-December formula, was hardly ready to make further major concessions.

The failure of the December negotiations led to still another inconclusive episode, this one intended by neither government and damaging to both. In early 1971, U.S. Congressman Wilbur Mills, the chairman of the powerful Ways and Means Committee who had been supporting protectionist legislation against his own free-trade instincts, decided to intervene directly to obviate the need for congressional action. By now leaders of the Japanese textile industry, concerned with the broader threat posed to exports by quota legislation, were seriously considering the possibility of designing and implementing their own voluntary quotas, applying criteria less stringent than the U.S. government had sought but perhaps significant enough to undercut the drive for something stronger. In March 1971 Mills and the Japanese industry leaders succeeded in reaching agreement on such a formula, which was then endorsed by the Japanese prime minister's office as resolving the problem. The U.S. textile industry was up in arms. So, apparently, was President Nixon, who saw himself not only upstaged on the textile issue but also undercut in his constitutional prerogative to negotiate trade agreements with foreign governments. Three days after the Japan Textile Federation announced its program, the President issued a strongly worded statement denouncing both its substance and the manner of its negotiation. There was dismay in Tokyo, because by now all major actors on the Japanese side had joined in support of the plan and there was no respectable way of abandoning it. Japanese decisionmakers found it inconceivable that a powerful member of the legislature could have taken major policy action without the knowledge and at least tacit approval of the chief of government. To President Nixon, on the other hand, it looked as if the Japanese premier had maneuvered to renege on his personal promises, by conspiring with a leading member of the Democratic opposition in a way that discredited and humiliated the Republican President.

This fiasco occurred against the background of mounting concern in the United States, both official and unofficial, about the widening imbalance in U.S. trade with Japan. Already, many Americans had begun to back away from the belief that the Japanese economy needed particularly benevolent U.S. economic policies for its survival, or even that Japanese economic expansion was in America's interest. They were uneasy about the U.S. deficit in the bilateral trade balance, about the shift in Japanese exports toward more technologically sophisticated products, about the growing imbalance in overall U.S. trade and payments, and about Japan's rapid rise to economic power.

By the third year of the Nixon administration, therefore, U.S. officials concerned with economic relations with Japan were divided into two groups with sharply divergent views of Japan. The more dramatic was reflected by the "Japan, Inc." concept espoused in the Commerce Department and by some on the White House staff. The Japanese, in this view, had developed a powerful, rapidly growing, purposively managed, and relentlessly self-interested economic juggernaut which was posing a fundamental challenge to U.S. economic supremacy.[37] Strong defensive action would be required by the United States if the world economy was to cope with this Japanese threat. The rival view, prevalent among Japan specialists both inside and outside the government, saw important limiting factors in Japanese economic growth and management, and warned that severe or insensitive pressure on Japan would destroy the cooperative political alliance which had been so carefully nurtured in the postwar period (and which was basic to preventing the conditions that had led to war in the first place). Adherents of this view, naturally, argued against forcing comprehensive textile quotas on the Japanese, although they did see the need for some Japanese export restraint. But they too found fault with Japanese slowness in dismantling the postwar system of import and investment restrictions. And they believed that the yen had become undervalued and thus gave Japanese products an unfair advantage in world markets.

In Japan, there were many in and out of government who felt policy changes in these areas were necessary. But movement toward liberalizing trade restrictions was slow, and on the yen nonexistent, thus adding to the frustration of American officials and American businessmen as well. Leaders of Japanese industry and government still presumed on American benevolence to maintain a somewhat unbalanced trade relationship in recognition of what they regarded as severe economic vulnerabilities peculiar to Japan. Moreover, economic growth had been accompanied by a resurgence of nationalistic sentiment and consequent resistance to the long-standing practice of yielding to specific American export control pressures, which had been Japan's side of the de facto postwar bilateral economic bargain. Thus on both sides of the Pacific, resolution of the textile dispute was complicated by the unraveling of the assumptions about the economic relationship under which earlier textile deals had been struck. And on each side, the textile issue generated strong resentment of the other. Japanese felt bitter about "unreasonable" U.S. economic demands for which they saw little substantive justification; Americans railed against an island nation that seemed

37. An unidentified member of the Nixon cabinet was quoted in *Time*, May 10, 1971, as saying: "The Japanese are still fighting the war, only now instead of a shooting war it is an economic war. Their immediate intention is to try to dominate the Pacific and then perhaps the world."

relentlessly on the make economically, unwilling to make trade concessions to the nation that had provided for her defense and "generously"
agreed to return Okinawa.

In the spring of 1971, after his denunciation of the Mills plan, President Nixon assigned responsibility for the textile issue to Ambassador-
at-Large David Kennedy, and granted him wide authority to pursue
agreement with Japan. In Tokyo, Premier Sato was arranging a cabinet
reshuffle that would result in a new MITI minister, future Premier
Kakuei Tanaka, who he hoped would take care of the problem once and
for all. For Sato, the textile issue threatened the success of what he saw
as his major historic achievement, the reversion of Okinawa.

Suddenly, on July 15, Tokyo was hit with the shock of Nixon's announcement of his plans to visit China. And in another dramatic decision, on August 15, Nixon announced plans to stimulate the sagging
U.S. economy and right the international imbalance through tax cuts, a
temporary freeze on wages and prices, the imposition of a temporary
10 percent surcharge on imports, and a floating of the dollar aimed at
forcing a readjustment of international exchange rates—especially that
of the yen. Just as the China shock seemed to challenge the foundations
of the international political structure, so the announcement of August
15 hit at the heart of the postwar economic structure. Japan took the
brunt of both blows, and nothing was done by those few U.S. officials
who had prior knowledge of either announcement to soften their impact.

Shortly thereafter the United States indicated that it would impose textile quotas by executive order under the tenuous authority of the
Trading with the Enemy Act if agreement were not reached by October
15.[38] Japanese government leaders, and leaders of industries other than
textiles, were now preoccupied with larger economic concerns, and saw
acceptance of an unpleasant textile agreement as necessary to help
salvage the larger U.S.-Japan relationship. Premier Sato and his advisers

---

38. Though the act was passed originally in 1917 when the "enemy" was
Germany, the authority to be invoked had last been clarified—and expanded—in an
amendment enacted just after Pearl Harbor. It provided that, "during the time of
war or during any other period of national emergency declared by the President, the
President may . . . regulate . . . any . . . importation or exportation of . . . any property
in which any foreign country or a national thereof has any interest." President Nixon
had declared a national emergency in his August 15 announcement. Moreover,
previous "national emergencies" had never been rescinded. But many lawyers thought
this authority insufficient because other, more recent legislation aimed specifically at
trade regulation did not give the president this power.

saw no reasonable alternative except to yield to the American pressure, so Tanaka negotiated the matter personally and forced the terms on a weary industry and bureaucracy. On the evening of October 15, after frenetic eleventh-hour negotiations in Tokyo, Tanaka and Kennedy initialed a memorandum of understanding bringing to a conclusion the bitter three-year controversy.

Ironically, Japanese exports of manmade textiles to the United States declined dramatically after 1971 for reasons largely unrelated to the quotas. Most Japanese textiles had long been losing their competitive advantage vis à vis those of other Asian countries, but revaluation plus Japanese domestic inflation sharply accelerated this trend. By 1973, Japan was importing more textile made-up goods than she was exporting (exports had been five times as great as imports in 1970). Not surprisingly, Japanese textile industry leaders concerned with protecting their home market became interested in the same types of international trade restrictions that they had for decades resisted. As revaluation of the yen began to take effect in 1973, moreover, and as Japan did finally liberalize her import regime, the balance of payments between the United States and Japan moved into relative equilibrium. Bilateral trade issues receded into the background, with multilateral questions centering about the energy crisis arising in their place. Still, the controversy of 1969–71 remained more than an unhappy memory. Its intractability and bitterness spurred larger doubts about the relationship on both sides of the Pacific, doubts that persist to this day. And the very fact that such an issue could escalate out of control was grounds for future concern.

Conclusions

The root problems in negotiating the security treaty were problems of Japanese domestic politics. As an exercise in adjustment between official government positions, the issue was dealt with quite intelligently: the existence of a problem (the old "unequal" treaty) became mutually recognized, and national policy positions were adjusted sufficiently to achieve a negotiated solution. Particularly important was the American willingness to yield on full reciprocity of obligations and to compromise on Japanese rearmament. But on both sides, officials underestimated the depth and potential impact of Japanese domestic opposition, particularly the combustible combination of a controversial treaty identified with an unpopular premier. And after the antitreaty movement had gathered strength, those in power fanned the flames further—Kishi by pressing his parliamentary majority and forcing ratification; both national leaders in holding to plans for the state visit which became, inevitably, the movement's new target.

Thus, most obviously, the treaty revision underscores the fundamental need for an alliance to maintain political support within its member countries. But the specific politics of the issue in Tokyo was quite different from what Americans encounter at home. Leading members of the ruling Liberal Democratic party fought publicly in 1958 and 1959 over the terms the government was negotiating; the greatest popular resentment was triggered when the prime minister insisted that a majority of the elected Diet be able to act on ratification. And behind these particular events were more enduring political institutions—the strength of factions within Japan's ruling party; the polarization between establishment conservatives and the left opposition; the place of consensus in Japanese cultural values and practices.

Okinawa and textiles stand, broadly, as the "success" and "failure" stories of the sixties and early seventies. Yet in some respects they were strikingly similar. Each was publicly controversial in Japan more than the United States. Each engaged a strong interest in the United States whose perceived needs—if pressed too far—could both make resolution difficult and weaken the alliance more generally. On Okinawa, however, the Japanese premier managed to keep on top of the issue, and the perceived needs of the U.S. military were both scaled down and satisfied. On textiles, that same premier faced enormous resistance inside and outside of his party, and the U.S. textile industry managed to control the U.S. position throughout; its demands were never significantly modified, and the issue was resolved only after severe damage was done to U.S.-Japanese trust and dealings on other issues. Why did the politics of the two issues lead to such opposite outcomes? And why was an Okinawa-for-textile-quotas trade, so inescapably logical as a bilateral bargain, so elusive in practice?

Succeeding chapters delve more generally into such questions: problems of politics and policymaking within the two countries; problems of perception and interaction between them. Why would Kishi's conservative rivals let factional strife affect relations with their major ally and protector? A fuller answer requires an analysis of Japan's ruling party and the political system within which it operates. Why did the U.S.

embassy (and the president) not pull back earlier from the aborted Eisenhower visit? An explanation requires a look at the political and cultural barriers affecting perception of events in one country by officials in the other. Why did proponents of a moderate settlement in both capitals succeed in supporting one another on Okinawa, while failing on textiles? What were the differences in how negotiations were conducted, in how steps taken in one capital affected the politics of the issue in the other? Fuller development of the partial, tentative answers offered in this chapter requires a more general effort to analyze these two national policymaking systems and their impact on one another.

CHAPTER THREE

Foreign Policymaking in Japan and the United States

THE OKINAWA and textile issues were brought to prominence by politicians, Sato and Nixon, who aspired to national leadership in 1964 and 1968 and raised these issues as part of their campaigns. Neither man sought first to discover whether reversion or new textile quotas would actually be negotiable with the other government. But once each issue was raised, success in resolving it would turn on whether, in that other government, political leaders and senior bureaucrats were willing and able to mobilize sufficient support for granting what the leader in the initiating country sought.

On Okinawa (a critical issue to Japanese), American officials proved willing and able to manage the process to achieve such an outcome. On textiles (not of comparable general importance to Americans), Japanese officials were not, at least not in time to avert a major crisis. But in both cases, an issue that arose from political interplay within one country could not be put to rest until it was confronted and resolved in the politics of the other.

In both cases, moreover, government officials played key roles in the politics of decisionmaking. On Okinawa, the U.S. decision to grant reversion by 1972 was the product of careful internal bargaining between State Department and Pentagon officials; the White House was favorably inclined toward reversion but unwilling to move if there were strong military or congressional opposition. On textiles, Japanese resistance owed no little to the stubbornness of Ministry of International Trade and Industry (MITI) bureaucrats operating in a domestic political climate of strong opposition to quotas, and to the limited leverage of a premier who sought repeatedly to win acquiescence to Japanese concessions. Security treaty revision was even more dominated in the negotiating stage by inside actors both bureaucratic and political; ministers and foreign office officials in both capitals came together on a new security agreement which was, to them, the culminating achievement of the successful relationship they had constructed after the occupation. The fact that it triggered a major crisis in Japan underscores the importance of the broader domestic political arena. Consensus within governments may be necessary, but it is not sufficient. Major foreign policy agreements by democratic states require broader national support and consensus (or at least acquiescence) if these agreements, and the politicians who sponsor them, are to survive and prosper.

Understanding the politics of U.S.-Japanese relations, then, requires understanding the politics of policymaking within each country as it copes, internally, with issues important to that relationship. It requires particular attention to the governments that generate the decisions and actions, but attention also to the larger national political processes within which these governments operate.[1]

Japan's Political System: The Major Actors

In prewar Japan, under the imperial constitution, power was shared by several competing groups. The strongest of these were the emperor's personal advisers (elder statesmen called *jūshin* or *genrō*) and the military and civil bureaucracies, but the hereditary peerage who dominated the upper chamber of the Imperial Diet and the political parties that held precarious control over the lower chamber also had a role in shaping foreign policy. *Jūshin* spoke directly on current issues through the extraparliamentary privy council, and their substantial influence on the actions of the cabinet was enhanced through the exercise of their customary right to appoint the prime minister. The military, on the other hand, had the important advantage of direct access to the throne under the principle of the "independence of military command." Both by law and by convention they also controlled the cabinet portfolios of war and

---

1. In describing these governments and processes, we have found it necessary to go beyond the case evidence which is the major basis for other chapters in this study. Thus we draw also on other sources as noted, and on our general research into foreign policymaking in both capitals. Since we write primarily for an American audience, and since the U.S. foreign policymaking system has been extensively analyzed elsewhere, we give particular emphasis to the Japanese side. Readers desiring more about the American system may wish to consult the books on foreign policymaking and organization in the bibliography.

the navy and through them manipulated cabinet decisions on foreign policy and security issues. By the late 1930s the military had clearly become the major force in Japan's foreign policy. They did not, however, dominate all major foreign policymaking decisions and actions. The Tōjō cabinet which presided over the decisions directly leading to Pearl Harbor in late 1941 was not a true military dictatorship but represented a form of collaboration and compromise between military and civil bureaucrats, with the elder statesmen ever-active behind the scenes.[2]

The structure of the Japanese government was drastically altered by the 1947 constitution. The emperor ceased to rule even in form; the *jūshin* and the privy council were abolished, as were the hereditary peerage and the House of Peers and the military services. The legal centerpiece of the new system was the reconstituted Diet ("the highest organ of state power"). The Diet was to oversee all actions of the cabinet, control the purse-strings of the state, and ratify international treaties. From its members the Diet designates the prime minister, who appoints his own cabinet, a majority of whom must be Diet members. The cabinet is responsible for administering the democratized civil service.

The Diet is composed of two houses, both popularly elected. The more powerful House of Representatives (lower house) is chosen in its entirety in elections held at least every four years—and more often if the cabinet so decides. The House of Councillors (upper house) has basically a checking and restraining function; its members hold office for fixed six-year terms, with half elected every three years. If the lower house votes a resolution of no confidence, the entire cabinet must resign unless new elections are promptly held. After such elections the new Diet must act either to renew the premier's mandate or to replace him.

In postwar practice, most of the Diet's power has been exercised by the Diet members belonging to the majority Liberal Democratic party (LDP), and particularly by the senior LDP members, who fill most cabinet positions and other leadership posts. And though the constitutionally defined role of the bureaucracy is to implement policies and legislation, bureaucrats have taken an active part in policymaking and legislative activities. Big businessmen (the *zaikai*) have also exerted a great deal of political influence in government policymaking by means

2. For extended discussion of Japan's prewar system, see Seiichi Imai, "Cabinet, Emperor, and Senior Statesmen," in Dorothy Borg and Shumpei Okamoto, eds., *Pearl Harbor as History: Japanese-American Relations, 1931–1941* (Columbia University Press, 1973), pp. 53–79.

of their close personal and financial ties to LDP politicians and working relations with government bureaucrats. Together, the party, bureaucracy, and business communities are frequently characterized as the "tripartite power elite" of postwar Japan.[3]

But other groups are active also—particularly on foreign policy matters. For a pervasive feature of postwar Japanese politics has been the domestic divisiveness of major foreign policy issues in general and U.S.-Japan issues in particular. Opposition Diet members and intellectuals have questioned the very basis of the establishment's foreign policy, and their recurrent criticism—reported and sometimes headlined in the media—has brought a particular pattern to the politics of foreign policy issues in Tokyo, especially those involving U.S. security ties.

The Conservative Establishment

The Liberal Democratic party has held absolute (though diminishing) majorities in both houses of the Diet ever since it was created in 1955, and has been generally able to maintain party discipline in parliamentary voting. Thus the LDP president has always been elected premier, and his government prevails on legislation when it comes to be voted on. The LDP is correctly labeled "conservative": leaders and members support economic growth based on private, capitalist enterprise domestically, and a foreign policy founded on the alliance and security treaty with the United States. However, the party is anything but dogmatic. There is considerable diversity of view within the party, and its leaders have proved flexible and pragmatic on particular issues (like the 1972 establishment of diplomatic relations with mainland China).

The major components of the LDP are its factions—well established, formally organized groups of Diet members, each headed by a senior LDP leader. Factions are sometimes identified with substantive policy orientations: in 1975, that of Deputy Premier Takeo Fukuda was generally considered conservative, whereas the faction under Prime Minister Takeo Miki was identified with its leader's progressive, reformist positions. But the main cement holding factions together is reciprocal personal political interests. A member needs the leader's help in winning party endorsement of his candidacy, in obtaining campaign funding

3. For a discussion of the prevalence of this concept in studies of recent Japanese politics, see Haruhiro Fukui, "Foreign Policy-Making in Japan: Case Studies for Empirical Theory" (paper prepared for delivery at 1974 meeting of the Association for Asian Studies; processed), pp. 4–8.

and other election help, and in seeking particular posts in the Diet, the party, and (eventually) the cabinet. The leader needs a solid group of supporters to enhance his political power and his quest for the premiership or other senior cabinet positions.

Aside from the president, the three major party officials are the secretary-general, the chairman of the executive council, and the chairman of the policy affairs research council (PARC). The PARC organizes the party's participation in debate on current policy issues through a series of standing and special policy committees under its jurisdiction. The standing committees correspond both to the executive ministries and agencies and to the Diet committees. These party committees do not usually initiate foreign policy proposals of their own because they have neither the technical nor the manpower resources to do so. But they often react forcefully to foreign policy initiatives coming from the cabinet and bureaucracy, as on security treaty revision, Okinawa reversion, textiles, and China. And the government pays close attention to "party opinion," which can literally break or make a prime minister and his cabinet.

Because the party has received especially strong electoral support from rural areas, it is particularly responsive to agricultural interests. The drawing of electoral districts favors the LDP by giving disproportionate representation to rural voters. As if to compensate, however, the system of multimember electoral districts gives the opposition parties greater opportunities than winner-take-all, single-member districts like those in the United States, where a party with 40 percent of the vote would generally prevail over several smaller rival parties unless these latter could coalesce behind a single candidate.

The LDP leaders work in close cooperation with the permanent bureaucracy. As in other parliamentary democracies, Japan's cabinet system is supported by a strong and influential civil service. The ministries are dominated by career officers who know the details of policy issues and manage the specific instruments of governmental action. The cabinet ministers who lead them often serve for limited periods, and rather than recruiting their own subordinates, they rely on the career officials for most of the information, analysis, and advice they require. Many ministers enter politics after having served in the bureaucracy and for them relationships with ministry officials are enhanced by a sense of common profession. Also contributing to cooperation between politicians and bureaucrats is a shared consensus about basic policies. For like LDP leaders, senior bureaucrats have overwhelmingly favored strong, business-based growth policies at home and a foreign policy based on the U.S. alliance abroad.

Japan's big business community, a key component of the ruling establishment, also shares these values. Businessmen supply politicians needed funds and support, and the amounts of money spent in election campaigns are very large. In turn, they make use of many opportunities to influence government policies and internal LDP politics, and though they may not always prevail, their views and interests are given very full consideration, especially on issues where they have direct economic stakes. Businessmen also have close, reciprocal working relationships with bureaucrats on the many issues that affect their interests. These relationships are deepened by the frequent practice of bureaucrats retiring from high official posts to senior corporate positions.

The big business community also operates through several national organizations. The four major ones are Keidanren (Federation of Economic Organizations), Nikkeiren (Japan Federation of Employers' Associations), Keizai Dōyūkai (Japan Committee for Economic Development), and Nisshō (Japan Chamber of Commerce and Industry). Leaders of these groups seek to develop and promote a view of business interests—and Japanese national interests—that is broader than that of particular economic interests and firms. They do not always prevail, however; in 1969 and 1970, Keidanren efforts to soften the textile leaders' stance on quotas were repeatedly unavailing. Still, these organizations are considerably more prestigious and influential than American counterparts like the Chamber of Commerce and the National Association of Manufacturers.

Opposition Groups and Other Actors

Standing outside the ruling establishment, sharing neither their involvement nor their consensus about policy, are other political actors who represent many millions of Japanese. They include the opposition political parties and allied labor unions, and large segments of the intellectual community. Their influence on government policymaking is mainly indirect, but their impact has been significant, and may be more so if the LDP's Diet majorities continue to shrink. In the lower house election of 1960 the party gained 58 percent of the vote and 63 percent of the seats; in 1972, it won 47 percent of the vote and 55 percent of the seats. The 1974 upper house election saw the LDP win just 42 percent of the vote, and its majority was reduced to a bare 127 out of 251 seats.

The ruling party has been further beset by the formation of cross-factional groups of relatively junior members dissatisfied with both the policies of the leadership and the continuation of the same old faces in power. Also weakening the establishment coalition—and offering opportunities to the opposition—are policy predicaments rooted in the economic successes of the fifties and sixties. Rapid growth has been accompanied by environmental damage—but efforts to reverse such damage produce strains in the government-business coalition. And the economic crisis brought on by skyrocketing energy costs, double-digit inflation, and minimal real economic growth has halted—at least temporarily—the steady rise in economic well-being which has contributed no little to the LDP's public support. Also damaging to the LDP have been well-documented charges of high-level corruption and "money politics," the most dramatic of which drove Prime Minister Kakuei Tanaka from power in December 1974. These have not only provided ammunition for critics of the regime, but strained LDP-business ties by making businessmen reluctant to supply political funds, and forcing LDP politicians to demonstrate publicly that they are not simply captives of business interests.

OPPOSITION PARTIES. Even when the LDP Diet majority is large, the government leadership cannot totally ignore the opposition parties. Cabinet members, including the prime minister, must respond regularly to interpellations from all Diet members—and those from opposition members are particularly sharp and pointed. Their responses are attacked by opposition Diet members and reported in detail by a lively and frequently critical press. During the textile issue Socialists and Democratic Socialists pressed Premier Sato on whether he had made a secret textile-Okinawa deal with President Nixon. Each denial of such a deal by Sato only served to fuel the public suspicions.

Most Japanese opposition parties espouse leftist ideologies. The Japan Socialist party (JSP), the largest, has frequently appeared more radical than the Japan Communist party (JCP), its principal rival. Both the JSP and the JCP are particularly sensitive to foreign policy issues, favoring nonalignment and demilitarization, reduction or dissolution of the Japan Self-Defense Forces, and an end to the U.S.-Japan Mutual Security Treaty.[4] The more moderate Democratic Socialist party (DSP) does not

4. Over the years the two parties' attitudes toward national defense and the U.S. alliance have become somewhat more pragmatic and flexible. While still calling for the dissolution of the Self-Defense Forces, the JSP favors a gradual replacement of

oppose the security treaty but would allow stationing of U.S. troops in Japan only in case of emergency. The non-Marxist Kōmeitō (the political arm of the Sōka Gakkai Buddhist organization) calls for gradual dissolution of the security treaty. The JSP holds more Diet seats than the other three opposition parties combined. But it has declined sharply in relative terms since 1960, with the Communists and the Kōmeitō making significant gains.

The government has tried to minimize public discussion of security and foreign policy issues in order to avoid confrontation with the opposition. But the opposition parties actively seek public airing of such issues, mounting publicity campaigns against certain government policies both in and out of the Diet. Wide press coverage of heated Diet interpellations and press exposure of any controversial behavior of the government or of individual government leaders are helpful to them. In October 1974, for example, Japanese newspapers headlined the testimony of retired U.S. Admiral Gene LaRocque before a U.S. congressional subcommittee that American ships carrying nuclear weapons "do not offload them when they go into foreign ports such as Japan." The government, which had long sought to convey the impression that no U.S. nuclear weapons entered Japan, was immediately confronted with widespread public demonstrations and attacks from opposition Diet members. The generalized reassurances it hastily obtained from the U.S. government did not absolve the Japanese government of culpability in the eyes of its critics, and the opposition succeeded in rekindling public debate on an issue the LDP government wished to keep out of the spotlight.[5]

Once an issue becomes controversial in the public arena, it is difficult for the government to overrule the opposition for fear of being accused

---

the SDF by what they call a "peaceful land development force," supposedly a much less military-oriented organization. The JCP now recognizes the inherent right of self-defense for Japan and talks in terms of reducing the size of the SDF. See *Asahi nenkan* [Asahi almanac], *1956, 1967,* and *1974.* Further softening of their formal and informal stands has been evident since 1974.

5. The United States assured Japan in a formal note that it had "faithfully honored its commitments to Japan." This was a reference to the "prior consultation" formula of 1960 covering any "major changes" in U.S. force or equipment deployments in Japan. The Japanese government insisted in turn that the United States had not asked for consultations on nuclear weapons transit. But this left unresolved the question of whether there had been a secret arrangement on nuclear transit reached in 1960, as reported in the press. (See *New York Times,* Oct. 8, 15, and 17, 1974; *Japan Times Weekly,* Oct. 19, 1974; *Washington Post,* Oct. 23, 1974; and T. J. Pempel, "Japan's Nuclear Allergy," *Current History,* April 1975, pp. 169–73.)

of "tyranny of the majority," particularly if Diet action is required. Despite their minority status, opposition members can also win concessions on policies developed in the legislative committees they serve on. And on a few upper house committees, non-LDP members have come into the majority owing to the thinning of overall LDP control.

LABOR UNIONS. None of the major labor unions in Japan supports the party in power. The largest and most influential is the Sohyo (General Council of Japanese Trade Unions) with 4.3 million members as of June 1973 from the public and private sectors. The Sohyo is the power base for the JSP (some of the Sohyo's affiliates also cooperate with the JCP). Its largest affiliate is the Jichirō (All Japan Prefectural and Municipal Workers' Union) with a little more than a million government workers, followed by the Nikkyōso (Japan Teachers' Union) with nearly 600,000 members. The second largest union grouping, the Dōmei (Japanese Confederation of Labor) with 2,277,900 members, officially supports the Democratic Socialist party. Its largest affiliate, the Zensen Dōmei (Japan Federation of Textile Workers' Union), has 543,000 members. The Chūritsu Rōren (Liaison Conference of Neutral Labor Unions) with 1,374,300 members is not affiliated with any specific political party but usually works jointly with the Sohyo and the Dōmei for advancing common labor objectives, including an annual wage hike.

Like the business organizations, these labor unions often articulate their demands through regular government channels (relevant divisions and bureaus of the ministries, such as Labor and Finance). And if the business groups work politically through the LDP, the labor groups work through the opposition parties, particularly those with which they have ties. Beyond this, the unions resort to street demonstrations, rallies, and strikes to influence government policies. Their actions range from annual wage demands (often called the "spring offensives") to opposition to the U.S.-Japanese defense alliance. Labor unionists played a key role in the mammoth demonstrations in 1960 against the revised U.S.-Japan mutual security treaty and against President Eisenhower's scheduled Tokyo visit. They sponsored a nationwide railroad strike in opposing President Ford's visit to Japan. The Zensen Dōmei was the focal point of the popular protest against the imposition of export controls during the U.S.-Japan textile negotiations.

ACADEMIA AND INTELLECTUALS. In Japan the government and academia have been for the most part mutually exclusive communities. The government seldom brings in professors for short-term service, and professional bureaucrats who see themselves as their society's elite do practically all policy research and planning for the government. The academic community, for its part, is suspicious of scholars maintaining close relations with the government, especially scholars in the social sciences. One reason is that older scholars have a sense of guilt over their collaboration with the government that eventually brought about the war and suppression of thought. And their natural desire for independent thinking has been reinforced by the polarized Japanese political system. Many intellectuals have identified with the opposition, though this commitment seems to have weakened in recent years.

Intellectuals' reluctance to identify themselves with the government has also been related to the strong influence of Marxism in academia in postwar Japan. Even if most scholars are not Marxist, many have been sympathetic. And others have refrained from "selling themselves" to the capitalist government for fear of being accused of helping the establishment by their colleagues and students, some of whose leaders are aggressive Marxists or Maoists belonging to the radical national student organization, the Zengakuren. As a result, only a very small circle of scholars has been willing to advise the government, and some of them prefer to do so anonymously.

Since academia is generally critical of government policies, and the bureaucracy is in any case a rather closed community, the government principally works with those like-minded scholars it considers "safe." This relationship between the government and the small circle of its "chosen" scholars (who are pejoratively called goyō gakusha, or "government's scholars," by other intellectuals) inevitably limits the range of new ideas or perspectives considered. In many cases, the scholars end up telling the government what it wants to hear. Nevertheless, these scholars can sometimes play a significant role. In January 1969, for instance, several Japanese scholars close to Premier Sato convened a U.S.-Japanese conference on Okinawa at Kyoto to try to make influential Americans more sympathetic toward the home-level reversion formula. They were among the few Japanese intellectuals able to communicate effectively and comfortably with Americans, and their major contribution on the issue was their service as interpreters of Japanese domestic sentiment to these Americans (and vice versa). But they were also useful to Sato because they were more sensitive to Japanese domestic politics than were Gaimushō officials advising the premier on the same issue.

THE PRESS. Japan has a truly national press, which influences policymaking through its sometimes-conflicting roles of purveyor of information (including many leaks), vocal critic of the government, and confidant of politicians and senior officials. The average Japanese reads at least one of the five dailies with national circulation (*Asahi, Mainichi, Yomiuri, Sankei,* and *Nihon keizai*), and the average family owns at least one television set. Most Americans, by contrast; read only local newspapers.

Only a limited number of top-ranking Japanese politicians and bureaucrats have access to confidential information channeled through the Foreign Ministry. Thus for most Japanese—LDP members and *zaikai* included—the press is the main source of information on what is happening outside the country. The Japanese press gives a great deal of play to news on the United States and it boasts the largest foreign press corps in the United States. Japanese views or images of the United States have been, to a large extent, shaped by these correspondents, whose reports are frequently prepared in a hurry and sometimes over-dramatized to appeal to the audience back home.

The press in Japan is also influential as the mirror of public opinion. The general political climate of the nation has an important constraining effect on the government, which is reinforced by the Japanese tendency to emphasize consensus. To some extent public opinion comes to be identified with press reports and editorials. Beyond this, public opinion in Japan is often made by the press. The press was instrumental in setting the anti-Kishi mood in 1959–60, in fueling Okinawa reversion sentiment during the 1965–69 period, and in promoting a sense of national resistance to textile quotas in 1969–71. Philosophically, the press perceives itself as filling a vacuum created by the lack of an effective and practical political opposition—in essence, checking "the government's Pisa-like leanings toward America."[6]

The press exerts further influence on policymaking because of its ability to expose individuals or groups in a position of power, often with cooperation from dissident government officials. Frequent leaks to the Japanese press of official or private proposals helped exacerbate the textile issue. Press exposure of the LaRocque testimony on nuclear weapons in the fall of 1974 was a serious blow to the government of Premier Kakuei Tanaka, which had already been weakened by an electoral setback the previous summer. And the detailed reports of *Bungei shunjū,*

6. Yukio Matsuyama, "Japanese Press and Japan's Foreign Policy," *Journal of International Affairs,* vol. 26, no. 2 (1972), p. 153.

a monthly magazine, on Tanaka's allegedly shady financial dealings precipitated a crisis that led to the end of his rule in December. The extent to which the press criticizes particular government leaders or their factions is sometimes limited, however, by its financial dependence on the banks having close ties with such leaders, and by the unwritten code of conduct and sense of reciprocal obligation between individual politicians or bureaucrats and news reporters on their beats. Indeed, Japanese papers did not give the *Bungei shunjū* revelations prominent play until twelve days after the article was published, when Tanaka was questioned about it at the Foreign Correspondents' Club in Tokyo.[7]

Frequently those journalists who maintain close relations with government leaders serve as informal advisers. Very often, decisionmakers turn to their journalist friends to sound out possible public reactions to different policy alternatives. This is usually done during informal nighttime chats (*yomawari*) that newsmen regularly engage in with important politicians and bureaucrats.

The Effect of Polarization

The overall pattern of Japanese national politics, then, is one of sharp differences over the fundamental lines of foreign policy. There is considerable consensus on basic policy directions among the ruling party leaders and senior foreign office officials. They have consistently favored alignment with the United States as the primary means of protecting Japan's security, accommodation to certain U.S. military interests (for example, bases in Japan) in order to maintain the alliance and fulfill its purposes, and moderate Japanese rearmament. The business community has favored these as well. But the opposition parties have opposed, with varying degrees of militancy, the U.S.-Japan security treaty and the American military presence on Japanese soil. And public reaction against rearmament and nuclear weapons—far from fading as many expected—has endured and emerged as a fundamental factor in Japanese foreign policy and international identity.

Domestic politics has imposed substantial limits on the security policies LDP governments could pursue. Full-scale rearmament was out, as was any military role for Japan's forces outside of Japanese territory. Special public sensitivity on the nuclear issue meant that Premier Sato had to negotiate nuclear-free Okinawa reversion, though personally he

7. On their long-time silence on this issue, see Don Oberdorfer, "The Lockjaw of Tokyo Dailies," *Washington Post*, Jan. 4, 1975.

might have accepted an agreement calling for continued presence of nuclear weapons on Okinawa after reversion.

As important, however, has been the impact of domestic politics on how Japan's leaders have handled security issues with the public. The lack of consensus has reinforced a tendency toward minimal disclosure and maximum secrecy, toward conveying a vague and sometimes misleading picture of the purposes and operations of the bilateral security relationship. Thus in public forums ruling politicians and senior bureaucrats have emphasized aspects of Japan's foreign policy (such as pacifism, economic intercourse, and rejection of nuclear arms) that elicited overwhelming domestic acceptance, and refrained from explaining their own conception of Japanese security interests except when internal or external political pressure made some such articulation unavoidable. In the immediate postwar years, Premier Shigeru Yoshida "shared with his advisers a predisposition against discussing the real elements of high policy in public."[8] This elitist approach, characteristic also of the Gaimushō from which Yoshida had come, was regularly reinforced by short-term political pressures. During the Korean War, Yoshida could not have spoken of important Japanese interests in military and political developments on the Korean peninsula—a constant of Japanese foreign policy—without seeming to echo the discredited imperial past. In the decades that followed, LDP leaders were most successful politically when they could emphasize domestic issues—above all, economic growth—and minimize or defuse U.S.-Japan security questions.

Such a closed leadership style has sometimes kept potentially volatile matters from the opposition and the press. But it has left the leaders vulnerable when evidence surfaces that appears to contradict repeated governmental reassurances, as the LaRocque episode demonstrated.

Institutions of Political Leadership

All of these actors must work within the postwar parliamentary system. How does that system distribute power in practice—over policy issues in general and foreign policy issues in particular? And how does this compare with the presidential system as it operates in the United States?

8. Martin E. Weinstein, *Japan's Postwar Defense Policy, 1947–1968* (Columbia University Press, 1971), p. 56.

Prime Minister and President

To win and keep his office, the prime minister must command the support of a majority of the Diet. In practice this has meant the Liberal Democratic party. A party conference composed mainly of LDP Diet members chooses a party president by a direct ballot; then the LDP unites in the Diet to elect him prime minister.[9] Since the party is divided into factions, the premier must win and maintain the support of a majority (or "mainstream") factional coalition. Thus he chooses his cabinet with the factional balance uppermost in his mind. In both gaining the premiership and keeping it, therefore, he must concentrate primarily on intraparty politics.[10] But the desires and values of the broad national political community have their impact too, since party politicians see the premier's public standing as an important influence on the party's electoral prospects. Before he succeeded Sato as premier in 1972, for example, Kakuei Tanaka developed a reputation as a man of "decision and action" who could capture the public's imagination and lead aggressively to new policies; this was seen as an attractive contrast to Sato's cautious, insider style. And Tanaka's departure from office was preceded by his fall to record lows in public opinion polls, when he came to be seen as an ineffective yet arbitrary leader and a prime practitioner of "money politics."

Once in power, the premier is in a relatively strong personal position vis à vis his cabinet colleagues. Unlike prewar premiers who were hostage to the *jūshin* and the military, he has sole power to designate and remove other ministers and he is clearly the central figure in his cabinet. He seldom directly fires a minister—this would be considered too blatant an exercise of authority (and would alienate the target, who as a senior party member might be needed one day as an ally). But he can—and frequently does—remove a minister as part of a cabinet reshuffle—and such reshuffles are almost annual.

9. The present general rule is to hold such a conference every three years; they were held every two years up to 1972. In special circumstances like the forced resignation of Tanaka in 1974, ad hoc procedures are followed. In that particular case, an LDP elder statesman—Etsusaburō Shiina—negotiated with major faction leaders and gained consensus support for Takeo Miki, who was then chosen without opposition by the party's Diet members. More typically, however, the selection is openly contested and the formal intraparty ballot is crucial.

10. This would change, of course, were the LDP to lose its majority. Then a premier's support coalition would have to include at least some of the Diet opposition. A broader coalition might also arise if the LDP were to split.

Yet the premier's authority over his ministers is far more limited and constrained than that of an American president. The president's cabinet members are clearly his subordinates, usually brought to prominence by him, usually lacking independent bases, and thus dependent on his support and confidence if they are to play leading roles in the administration. The prime minister's cabinet is composed of fellow politicians, long-time colleagues who frequently have their own political bases as leaders of rival factions. Presidents can, and do, act above and around cabinet members, depleting their authority. The Japanese premier is much less free to ignore ministers in their spheres of formally designated responsibility. And if a U.S. president is expected to exercise visible leadership, get out front on issues, the ideal prime minister is more often seen as the overseer of a broad participatory decision process, remaining at the center and somehow moving things forward, but avoiding "arbitrary" actions.

He also needs to keep relations with the opposition within tolerable bounds. As long as the premier stays in power, his numerical majority in the Diet is sufficient to enact any legislation the cabinet submits. However, the opposition parties can—and often do—employ a variety of tactics to delay legislation and to underscore their opposition. It is considered improper for the premier to use his majority bluntly, so the views and interests of opposition politicians are frequently considered and to some degree accommodated. When a premier seeks—as did Kishi in 1960—to force through a controversial matter like renewal of the U.S.-Japan security treaty, he risks a strong public reaction against such "coercive" tactics even if he has beyond question the necessary Diet votes, and even if it was the opposition that resorted to obstructionist tactics in the first place. Such a reaction drove Kishi from office. In fact, it was exploited by rivals within his party who forced his replacement by a competing faction leader, Hayato Ikeda.

As the Kishi example shows, LDP factional politics are never very far below the surface in Japanese foreign policymaking on publicly controversial issues. In some cases, they can bring new policy initiatives and commitments to the surface. Sato was competing for the LDP presidency-cum-premiership when he first asserted that the postwar period would not end for Japan until Okinawa reverted to Japanese administrative control. Tanaka used the China issue to his advantage in 1972 by lining up weaker faction leaders in favor of a thoroughgoing China policy shift against the more cautious stance of the other major contender, Takeo Fukuda. And each leader took action on his issue once he reached power.

Factionalism can also, however, lead LDP leaders to temporize on foreign policy questions. A leader may fear that too dramatic an action will put him in a politically exposed position. Masayoshi Ohira, minister of international trade and industry in 1969, resisted efforts to settle the textile issue at least partly out of fear that identification with unpopular concessions would hurt his prospects of one day becoming premier. In 1974, Ohira as *foreign* minister moved cautiously toward an aviation agreement with Peking—which he favored personally—because of opposition from LDP members oriented toward Taiwan; ultimately, however, he seemed to conclude it was in his interest to act decisively and demonstrate his ability to prevail over his intraparty opponents on a controversial issue. And sometimes, as in early 1959 on security treaty revision, LDP leaders take publicly conflicting positions in their maneuvering for the succession. Similar maneuvering—and similar disarray— was evident in the Japanese response to the Arab oil export cutbacks in the fall of 1973, as several ministers took conflicting stances in their search for initiatives that could enhance their prestige and party standing. By contrast, Sato successfully avoided major factional complications on Okinawa by his cautious handling of the issue after he came to power. He also changed foreign ministers at a crucial stage, replacing rival faction leader Miki with a loyal supporter, Kiichi Aichi.

But though in most respects the Japanese prime minister is more constrained—and certainly less autonomous—than the U.S. president, the power differences are not all in favor of the latter. In relations with his legislature, it is the Japanese chief of government who has the advantage.

The Diet and Congress

Linked with the prime minister's dependence on the Diet is its responsiveness to him—as long as it supports his regime, it can usually be counted on to back his legislation. The American president's autonomy cuts both ways too—many presidential programs die for lack of congressional action. The president's colleagues (whose power and roles he must take account of and accommodate) are the congressional power barons—chairmen of standing committees who remain in their posts year after year and develop close relationships with senior bureaucrats and major interest groups in their substantive bailiwicks. Sometimes also congressional party leaders attain such power as to require considerable presidential deference, as did Senate Majority Leader Lyndon Johnson during the Eisenhower administration and Senate Minority Leader Everett Dirksen in the 1960s.

The influence of Representative Wilbur Mills on the textile issue was based on his position as House Ways and Means Committee chairman and his use of that position to establish himself as the most influential congressman on taxation and trade policy.[11] Mills could not control the U.S. negotiating position on the issue, but he had decisive influence on whether Congress would: (1) credibly threaten to enact statutory import quotas (more damaging to Japanese exports than a negotiated arrangement) and thereby strengthen the leverage of Nixon's negotiators; and (2) actually enact such quotas if negotiations failed.

Mills strongly preferred a negotiated quota arrangement to quotas by legislation, fearing that any bill containing statutory textile import limits would be quickly amended to include quotas for other products as well. But he collaborated with the Nixon administration in 1969 and early 1970 by threatening to push a quota bill through the House of Representatives unless negotiations with Japan were successful. When the White House surprised the Ways and Means chairman in June of 1970 by actually endorsing Mills's bill, he was left with no choice (in his eyes) but to move on legislation he disliked and feared. Quotas for other products were added, and the bill passed the House, only to die on the Senate floor as the congressional session expired in December 1970. Mills was determined to avoid such quota legislation in 1971. So he seized upon and pressed the proposal that the Japanese textile industry adopt its own export quotas, in a form far less stringent than the administration was demanding. This in turn was deeply resented by President Nixon, who saw his negotiating stance and political credibility being undercut. But for Mills it was enough trade restraint to support a claim that he had done something for textiles, and he stood adamantly against quota legislation thereafter.

An earlier exercise of congressional power resulted in the "Yoshida letter" of December 1951; negotiator Dulles extracted from Premier Yoshida a commitment to recognize Nationalist China in order to assure

11. Recent House reforms have made it more difficult for a committee chairman to attain the dominance that Mills had achieved in 1971. Committee procedures have been opened up and democratized. On Ways and Means the chairman's power has been diluted by an increase in the committee's size and the establishment of formal subcommittees, actions that Mills had resisted during his chairmanship.

Senate ratification of the peace treaty. Anticipation of similar congressional pressure on Okinawa strengthened the U.S. military in intragovernmental debates and contributed to pressure on the Japanese government to be flexible on base arrangements and assume greater regional security responsibilities as part of the reversion package.

In U.S. politics Wilbur Mills was the nearest equivalent to a senior Japanese cabinet member who leads a competing faction. Possessed of a separate power base, he was a rival baron with whom the President had to negotiate if they were to work in harmony. Once Mills felt that their textile collaboration of 1969 and 1970 had taken a turn unacceptable to his interests and convictions, he acted on his own. Similarly, Ministers Fukuda and Miki left the Tanaka cabinet in July 1974 when—after the LDP suffered a setback in the upper house elections—they felt their interests, and their party's interests, were no longer served by their continued membership. And for Miki, of course, this action bore fruit when he succeeded the discredited Tanaka the following December.

Fukuda and Miki were, of course, major Diet members and LDP leaders. And it is the balance among LDP leaders (and among parties within the Diet) that determines the composition of the ruling cabinet. The Diet also exercises significant, behind-the-scenes restraining power on government policy through the extensive consultations typically conducted before legislation is formally submitted. These primarily involve LDP Diet members, but the general preference for a working consensus also gives opposition members some marginal legislative power through their membership on particular Diet committees.

Once issues reach the formal decision stage, however, debate—though often heated—tends to have more ceremonial than substantive significance. The Diet generally enacts legislation as submitted by the cabinet and the bureaucracy, with the ruling party voting as a bloc. Thus it has not usually exercised the kind of power that the U.S. Congress can exert through floor votes on appropriations, the details of particular legislation, confirmation of senior appointees, and ratification of treaties. But there have been recent exceptions to LDP solidarity—the abstention of eighty-eight party members in the ratification vote on the China aviation agreement in 1974; the resistance of the party's right wing to ratification of the nonproliferation treaty a year later. And the declining relative position of the LDP in the Diet may enhance the leverage of the legislature and its committees even if the party continues to dominate the cabinet.

The Diet, moreover, exercises an indirect influence on Japanese foreign policymaking through its ability to call ministers to account. The major Japanese daily newspapers tend to play up such questioning—reporting it daily, in detail, with a slant frequently critical of the government and its officials. Ministers tend to respond by speaking cautiously. And their tendency toward caution in action is reinforced as well. Indeed, almost any step taken in U.S.-Japanese relations is colored by concern about and anticipation of Diet reaction and interpellation, and how it will be reported in the press.

Staffs of Political Leaders

A final area where Japanese policymaking institutions differ from American is in the paucity of major staff officials and offices serving the prime minister or the cabinet as a whole. In the United States, the president has a White House staff of several hundred and an executive office staff numbering several thousand—the "institutionalized presidency." This includes numerous politically appointed White House assistants who have specific substantive issue mandates domestic and foreign, and a welter of councils, staffs, and offices with a wide range of policy leadership and coordination functions. These officials and units stand outside of the cabinet departments, and frequently stand between cabinet officers and the president.

There is nothing parallel to this in Japanese government. Nor, for foreign policy, has any Japanese premier had an aide remotely like the president's assistant for national security affairs—a central U.S. foreign policy figure in the sixties and early seventies—or his supporting staff of foreign policy professionals operating outside of and above departmental bailiwicks. The Japanese prime minister has some staffing outside the ministries. There is the Cabinet Secretariat of nearly two hundred officials, as well as a small number of private secretaries on detail from the ministries to assist the premier in particular issue areas, including foreign policy. But most of the Cabinet Secretariat staff handle routine matters (including internal security), with only a few focusing on international matters. And the private secretaries are relatively junior. Generally, the only senior political aides whose allegiance is mainly to the premier are the chief cabinet secretary and his deputy. The term *kantei* (prime minister's official residence) is used to refer to the small political circle personally loyal to the premier.

If Japan has no counterpart to America's large presidential staffing, one reason is that the United States has nothing parallel to the Japanese cabinet. The most important policy issues in Tokyo tend to be handled and decided not by the prime minister acting alone but ceremonially by regularly convened cabinet meetings and in practice by an ad hoc group including the premier, the chief cabinet secretary, ministers in charge of the issues at hand or with recognized prerogatives for influencing them, and, frequently, one or more of the major LDP officials. No such collegial decisionmaking constrains the U.S. president's personal authority. Since Eisenhower's administration, the full cabinet has met infrequently and considered major current policy business very rarely; it has not even a ceremonial, ratification function. The closest approximation to the Japanese cabinet in American government, rather, is the senior circle of foreign policy advisers who attend National Security Council (NSC) meetings—the secretary of state, the secretary of defense, the national security assistant, the chairman of the Joint Chiefs of Staff, and the director of the Central Intelligence Agency.[12] They are important, however, not because of their formal membership on the council; after all, the usually peripheral vice president is also a member. Rather, their substantive responsibilities sometimes make them the group that meets regularly with the president on critical foreign policy matters. (An example was the "Tuesday lunch" of Lyndon Johnson, which brought together the secretaries of state and defense, the national security assistant, and sometimes the CIA director, the JCS chairman, and the president's chief press aide.) But the president has greater flexibility than a Japanese premier to operate according to his preferred style. Richard Nixon preferred to talk foreign policy overwhelmingly with one man, Henry Kissinger. Nixon emulated Presidents Kennedy and Johnson in using the National Security Council as a base, even a cover, for the operations of the national security assistant and his staff. This gave the

12. The NSC, established in 1947, now has four formal members: the president, the vice president, the secretary of state, and the secretary of defense. The JCS chairman, the CIA director, and the director of the Arms Control and Disarmament Agency are statutory advisers to the council. The president's assistant for national security affairs is the council's chief staff official. Its primary official role is to offer the president integrated advice on issues combining defense and general foreign policy considerations. Its actual role has varied according to the preferences and styles of particular presidents. (See Richard Moose, "White House National Security Staffs Since 1947," in Keith C. Clark and Lawrence J. Legere, eds., The President and the Management of National Security [Praeger, for Institute for Defense Analyses, 1969], pp. 55–98; and I. M. Destler, Presidents, Bureaucrats, and Foreign Policy [Princeton University Press, 1972 and 1974], especially chap. 5.)

president an independent capability to monitor and coordinate the operating foreign policy agencies, and to provide analyses and sometimes to manage negotiations independently of the operating agencies. In Nixon's first term, dependence on the national security assistant and staff reached new heights.

For a Japanese premier such a strong separate staff is not possible. The constitutional framework and governmental traditions do not provide for it, and the cabinet—being chosen for factional balance—does not offer an appropriate base for it. White House aides are, in Japanese terms, "members of the president's faction"—their loyalty is to him. But both the Japanese cabinet and the central ruling party organization lack such coherence, because the Liberal Democratic party upon whose support the premier's tenure depends is not a cohesive central organization but a coalition of factions.

But if strong central staff organizations tied to political leaders are less possible in Japan, leaders are also less likely perhaps to perceive a strong need for them. For the LDP leadership group is composed of men with long governmental experience. Not only have they served in the Diet but, in many cases, their political careers were preceded by long service in the government bureaucracy. Thus they move into their current positions with long-standing patterns of relationships both among themselves and with influential senior bureaucrats. In the United States, however, it is typical for presidents (and frequently cabinet members) to come into office without prior experience in federal executive positions. They have little sense for how one gets action out of the federal bureaucracy, and thus feel a particular need to do what their authority and large staff organizations notably permit—to bring in their own people, loyal to them, to ride herd on the federal establishment. This is a major element in the somewhat differing roles and influence of the career bureaucracies in the two countries.

The Bureaucracies

A glance at the postwar course of U.S.-Japanese relations reveals the pervasive influence of career officials and permanent bureaucratic institutions. Pentagon resistance delayed the negotiation of the 1951 peace and security treaties and affected their substance. The State Department country desk and the U.S. embassy in Tokyo, working closely with civilian and military members of the Defense Department, dominated Okinawa reversion policy in the critical 1966–68 period. Their Gaimushō counterparts in Tokyo played a substantial role during this same period, as the sole agency capable of interpreting the evolving U.S. position on the Okinawa issue. And MITI bureaucrats repeatedly prevailed over Japanese political leaders in setting the government's stance in the textile negotiations.

None of this is to deny the leading and frequently dominant roles that political leaders can play. In both Japan and the United States, major initiatives for change tend to grow out of the interests and actions of senior political figures. And major issues can be resolved only when political leaders settle on a particular resolution or, at minimum, acquiesce in it. In the United States, presidential dominance of the bureaucracy has recently been highlighted by the Nixon-Kissinger foreign policymaking system. And political leaders frequently prevail in Japan as well. Donald C. Hellmann's study of Japanese decisionmaking leading to the 1956 peace agreement with the Soviet Union, for example, chronicles the futile efforts of the leading Gaimushō officials to prevent its negotiation.

But from this case Hellmann draws a more general conclusion—that "the peace agreement of 1956 marked the passing of an era. Unlike the pre-war period the Japanese Foreign Office proved incapable of directly competing with the ruling party in the making of policy. As intended in the 1947 Constitution the Prime Minister and his party were in control—the old gave way to the new, the politician replaced the bureaucrat."[13]

It is true that no contemporary Japanese career bureaucracy has power approaching that of the prewar military services, and party politicians are infinitely more powerful. Yet bureaucratic influence in Japan is considerably greater than Hellmann's language implies. This is due in part to the weaknesses in political leadership institutions, but even more to the sheer volume and complexity of international transactions, which can only be managed by large bureaucratic institutions. The power-dwarfing of the Japanese bureaucracy emphasized by Hellmann

13. *Japanese Domestic Politics and Foreign Policy: The Peace Agreement with the Soviet Union* (University of California Press, 1969), pp. 141–42.

seems to have been the exception rather than the rule.[14] And American
bureaucracy, while weakened by the Nixon-Kissinger system, was never
so reduced in power as appearances made it seem.[15]

The Soviet-Japanese peace agreement issue was so unusual, moreover,
that it is hardly surprising that Hellmann's conclusion could not be automatically applied to Japanese policymaking toward the United States.
For Soviet relations were outside the mainstream of postwar Japanese
foreign policy—particularly in the period before regular diplomatic relations were reestablished. The agreement had more symbolic importance
than substantive impact on major Japanese interests and policies, foreign
or domestic. And since there was no regular embassy channel in operation, the Gaimushō was deprived of the types of leverage it derives
from its inside role. Thus it stands to reason that the politicians would
be less constrained.

One of the sources of bureaucratic power is the size of the institutions
involved. This is both effect and cause of the complexity of foreign
policymaking in each country, and it clearly limits the ability of political
leaders in both countries to control all that goes on. In the Japanese
executive branch there are about 1 million public servants; the U.S. total
is about 2.5 million. The proportion of these working on foreign policy is
small, but the absolute numbers are considerable. By a liberal estimate,
there are close to 10,000 Japanese bureaucrats with foreign policy responsibilities, including 2,600 in the Ministry of Foreign Affairs, a large
percentage of MITI's 6,600 officials, and others from such institutions as
the Finance Ministry, the Defense Agency, the Economic Planning
Agency, and the Ministry of Agriculture and Forestry.[16] In the U.S.

14. See Shigeo Misawa, "An Outline of the Policy-Making Process in Japan," in
Hiroshi Itoh, ed. and trans., *Japanese Politics, An Inside View: Readings from Japan*
(Cornell University Press, 1973), pp. 12–48.

15. See Destler, *Presidents, Bureaucrats, and Foreign Policy*, chap. 5; and
Chester A. Crocker, "The Nixon-Kissinger National Security Council System,
1969–72: A Study in Foreign Policy Management," in National Academy of Public
Administration, *Making Organizational Change Effective: Case Studies of Attempted Reforms in Foreign Affairs*, Appendix O to the Report of the Commission on
the Organization of the Government for the Conduct of Foreign Policy (Government
Printing Office, 1976).

16. See Haruhiro Fukui, "Bureaucratic Power in Japan," in Peter Drysdale and
Hironobu Kitaōji, eds., *Japan and Australia: Two Societies and Their Interactions*
(Oxford University Press, forthcoming); and Jinjiin Ninyokyoku [Personnel Agency,
Employment Bureau], "Shōwa 45-nendo ni okeru ippanshoku no kokka kōmuin no
ninyō jōkyō chōsa hōkoku" [Report on government employment, 1970] (n.d.;
processed).

government, 12,604 Americans were employed by the State Department at home and abroad in 1974, another 9,346 in its sister agencies (the Agency for International Development, the Arms Control and Disarmament Agency, and the United States Information Agency), an estimated 15,000 by the Central Intelligence Agency, and 987,236 as civilian workers on military matters for the Department of Defense.[17] To all these must be added the many other officials whose day-to-day business is primarily international—in the White House national security and international economic policy staffs; and in the international arms of departments with predominantly domestic missions such as Treasury, Agriculture, Commerce, and Labor.

Controlling all these officials would obviously be a formidable task for political leaders even if this were their paramount objective. In fact, of course, these leaders have competing priorities as well—relations with other senior officials; partisan political success in elections; particular high-priority issues they feel they must handle personally. Thus bureaucratic management gets only a fraction of their time. Yet national policy is, in many areas, the sum of the countless day-to-day operational decisions and actions officials take at various bureaucratic levels. To the extent that top leaders (and subordinates responsive to their interests) cannot ride herd on these many decisions and actions, they must, in practice, yield power to institutions over which they reign but cannot completely rule.

On those issues that they can personally oversee, moreover, government leaders depend on bureaucracies for a range of services and skills— information about current issues and the broader political and economic variables that affect decisions on these issues; expertise and experience in dealing with these issues; communications processes and channels linking their own to foreign governments. If leaders cannot go elsewhere for these resources, they must go to bureaucrats; they will thus tend to see the facts of issues as bureaucrats see them, and their policy decisions will tend to reflect bureaucratic preferences. Moreover, in all policymaking systems bureaucrats will have standard policy-influencing roles and authorities—whether established by law, regulation, or custom— that political leaders will disregard at their peril. And they have one

17. Senate Committee on Government Operations, *Organization of Federal Executive Departments and Agencies* (Government Printing Office, 1975); and Harry Howe Ransom, *The Intelligence Establishment* (Harvard University Press, 1970), p. 87.

further advantage vis à vis politicians: their narrower roles and interests and group loyalties allow for a single-mindedness in promoting their views and interests that politicians, who must respond to a broader range of interests and groups, cannot normally match.

Thus, the size of bureaucracies and the nature of their established skills and services assure that they will have significant foreign policy impact in both countries. In Japan, permanent governmental institutions are further strengthened by the way officials are recruited and the unusual prestige of the career public servant. In institutions like the Foreign Ministry (and, above all, the Finance Ministry), the professional group that enters under highly competitive qualifying examinations is considered—and considers itself—an elite. Moreover, entry into these elites is virtually impossible except at the beginning of one's career. Once in, an elite bureaucrat rises through the organization until he retires, generally after holding a responsible senior position. This reflects a broad characteristic of modern Japanese society. Social mobility from generation to generation is very great, but if birth does not determine status, success in school and examinations generally does. How one enters which organization is the major determinant of one's ultimate accomplishments.

In the U.S. bureaucracy, too, most bureaucrats are careerists who will devote all—or the bulk—of their working lives to government service. Their prestige in the society, however, is several notches lower than that of their Japanese counterparts.[18] And in the U.S. government, a significant role is played by the "in-and-outers," those mobile individuals, usually with professional bases outside government (in law or academia, for example), who take official positions for limited periods, perhaps two to five years. They are frequently identified politically with the party in power, or personally with high officials of the administration. And they occupy not only a large proportion of positions in the political layer (assistant secretaries upward) of each department, but also some of the positions—both senior and junior—on general policy planning or analysis staffs that serve the White House assistant for national security affairs, the secretary of state, and the secretary of defense.

The Japanese government is very different. There, aside from the political minister and the generally insignificant parliamentary vice

18. An exception is the military. As a reaction to the wartime experience, members of Japanese Self-Defense Forces have very low prestige in their society, much lower than that of American military officers and servicemen. Civilian officials of the Japan Defense Agency also have less prestige than their Pentagon counterparts.

ministers, the top positions in the ministries are filled by career officials. So also are the (generally very small) staff advisory and coordinating units that serve the premier and the cabinet. And the Japanese politicians who lead the bureaucrats tend also to be a rather stable grouping, drawn from among the senior LDP Diet members and thus changing but slowly year after year. The political figures brought in by a U.S. president, however, are likely to be less known to their colleagues and subordinates, less predictable in their policy views and personal capabilities.

The comings and goings of such in-and-outers at both the near-cabinet and the staff level make the U.S. government a far more open and fluid place than the Japanese. Consequently the U.S. government has a considerably weaker institutional memory, at least at the level of those who have substantial influence over policy.

The Gaimushō and State

In the United States and Japan all *foreign* policy issues concern the State Department and the Gaimushō (Foreign Ministry), and each is in fact involved in most such issues. As the major action channels of foreign policymaking within the bureaucracies, the two share many organizational and behavioral characteristics typical of foreign offices. The differences between them reflect mainly the larger political systems within which they operate.

The Foreign Ministry's influence over Japanese policy is derived overwhelmingly from its inside role—as the operating agency that handles diplomatic relationships; as the source for the bulk of information, analysis, and policy proposals on which the cabinet must make its decisions. The U.S. State Department has similar levers for influence, but nothing like the Gaimushō's near-monopoly of them. State has very strong competitors in intelligence, policy analysis, and policy implementation. By contrast, neither the LDP party organization, nor the Diet and its committees, nor the Cabinet Secretariat possesses sufficient information, or analytic or operational resources, to challenge the Gaimushō.

The two foreign offices are similarly staffed. The dominant role in each is played by an elite corps of officials recruited in their twenties or early thirties. These officials rise (and expect to rise) through the ranks to reach senior positions—including ambassadorships—prior to retirement. In the U.S. State Department, this elite is the approximately three thousand Foreign Service officers. In Japan, it is the nearly six hundred Foreign Ministry officials with Higher Foreign Service Examination

(HFSE) certificates, and the seventy-five or so with the near-equivalent prewar Higher Civil Service credentials.[19]

The differences between the two personnel systems are differences in degree; in sum, however, they make the Gaimushō a considerably purer example of the closed bureaucratic organization. Major U.S. ambassadorships and Washington positions at the bureau (assistant secretary) level and above are often filled by in-and-outers; so—though less frequently—are more junior staff jobs. This almost never happens in Japan. Internally, the U.S. Foreign Service is also more overtly competitive. Those judged as best are promoted more rapidly earlier in their careers than are their peers, and an elaborate performance evaluation system provides the formal basis for promotion decisions. The Gaimushō lacks such a structured performance evaluation system. In fact, the elite services of the Gaimushō are promoted almost automatically, with each "class" group entering the service together raised in rank simultaneously. Lateral entry into the U.S. Foreign Service at the middle and upper ranks is exceptional, but it does happen, particularly in cases where specialized talents are required; in the Japanese foreign service, it is virtually unheard of. These relative differences—when added to the smaller size of the Japanese Foreign Ministry—give the Gaimushō a stronger cohesiveness and corps spirit.

The predominance of the business of managing bilateral relations tends to strengthen the geographic subunits of both foreign offices. In State, the regional bureaus prefer to treat policy toward particular countries and areas as "their" business, and tend to control it unless the White House, departmental leaders, or strong competing departments or offices assert an active interest. In the Gaimushō, the same phenomenon holds, but without the counterweights of the U.S. system. There is nothing in the Japanese Foreign Ministry like the large "seventh floor" staff (office of the secretary of state and his major subordinates and staff) that exists in the U.S. State Department. Officials outranking the regional chiefs are fewer in number, and coordinating staffs very limited. Structurally, the senior career official in the Gaimushō is the vice minister, who works directly under the political minister. He is supported by two deputy vice ministers. Beneath this top triumvirate are the bureaus, which are either geographic (like the American Affairs Bureau) or functional (like the Economic Affairs Bureau). Each bureau is in turn divided into divisions. Bilateral issues are generally assigned to the geographic

19. Fukui, "Bureaucratic Power in Japan," p. 7.

bureaus, whereas multilateral problems are assigned to the functional bureaus. Nor is there any strong staff for overall planning and coordination, though the Treaties Bureau does get involved in a wide range of issues as the general legal counsel and adviser for the entire ministry. Thus, the Foreign Ministry is notably decentralized. The bureaus and divisions are "the basic units of decision and action"; their chiefs enjoy a "large measure of freedom, within the limits defined by the rule of seniority, to map out their courses of action with regard to any specific policy issue at hand."[20]

Heads of these bureaus and divisions naturally tend to give priority to their policy interests, and the interests of their clients (which are usually the foreign countries with whom they deal daily). Such loyalties are kept within bounds, however, by rotation of career officials among geographic and functional divisions, and among different parts of the world in their overseas assignments. Similar rotation policies are practiced in the U.S. State Department, though this does not prevent many officials from becoming identified with particular regions or countries for considerable portions of their careers.

Finally, each career service has a similar "organizational essence." In each, "the view held by the dominant group of the organization" as to its appropriate "missions" and "capabilities"[21] stresses the day-to-day management of relations with foreign governments and the shaping of government policy insofar as it affects those relations. Foreign service officers view themselves as diplomatic professionals trained (mainly by practical experience) in the art of dealing with foreign governments, and the art of understanding such governments. They tend to equate wisdom in foreign policy with careful, undramatic reliance on their expertise. On issues of policy substance, however, it is the generalist who is valued over the specialist.

In the conduct of normal, routinized, and invisible foreign relations, State Department and Gaimushō bureaucrats have played dominant

20. Haruhiro Fukui, "Policy-Making in Japan's Foreign Ministry" (paper prepared for delivery at a conference on Japan's foreign policy, at Kauai, Hawaii, Jan. 14–17, 1974; processed), p. 17. Interestingly, John Creighton Campbell reaches similar conclusions about the Japanese budget process, finding its "subsystems" to be "very independent . . . at least when compared with the United States." (Contemporary Japanese Budget Politics [University of California Press, forthcoming].)

21. This concept is developed in Morton H. Halperin with the assistance of Priscilla Clapp and Arnold Kanter, Bureaucratic Politics and Foreign Policy (Brookings Institution, 1974), p. 28.

roles, usually with skill and self-assurance. They have given priority to the bilateral security and economic relationship, and laid much of its legal and political groundwork. So long as issues fall within their jurisdictional bailiwicks, they are generally handled with reasonable efficiency and orderliness according to well-established operational procedures.

But most important foreign policy issues cannot be so neatly and exclusively treated. In practice, the foreign offices must share responsibility with two types of competitors—with politicians as issues become domestically visible, or important to powerful home interests; with other bureaucracies having security and economic responsibilities as issues affect these responsibilities.

Relations with Political Leaders

On the critical question of relations with the political leaders and groups ultimately responsible for foreign policy, foreign office officials in each country are inevitably ambivalent. As professionals, they tend to see political leaders as ignorant meddlers in complex diplomatic issues. But as practical men, they realize that their ability to influence foreign policy depends heavily on their ties with the political leadership, since neither career group has—or is likely to develop—a strong domestic constituency. They particularly need the help of political leaders on the really big issues, for these involve not only domestic politics, but usually also interagency relationships which foreign office people have difficulty managing without support from political executives.

The U.S. State Department has been regularly found wanting by presidents and their White House aides.[22] The Gaimushō seems to have done considerably better in its relations with LDP politicians. It can hardly exclude them from issues where they have political stakes. Nor can foreign office officials always thwart policies that they oppose, as their 1956 failure on the Soviet peace agreement demonstrated. But though it is politicians, not bureaucrats, who play the prominent—and frequently dominant—parts on the politically most important issues, formal deference by the bureaucrats leaves room for substantial actual impact. Since there is no base for a strong, competing central staff at the

22. For the classic account, see Arthur Schlesinger, Jr., *A Thousand Days* (Houghton Mifflin, 1965), pp. 406–47. For an analysis of the major ways presidents have found State to be unresponsive, see Destler, *Presidents, Bureaucrats, and Foreign Policy*, pp. 154–60.

political level, the Gaimushō can, if it is skillful in reading and accommodating factional politics, maintain considerable influence through the operational support it provides to the foreign minister and the premier, and through its day-to-day responsibilities for implementing foreign policy and managing foreign relations. On China policy in 1972 and 1974, for example, key Gaimushō officials were cooperatively and supportively involved, shaping many of the critical details of Japan's new relationships with Peking and Taipei. The contrast with the State Department's noninvolvement in Nixon's basic China policy turn of 1971 is striking, though State's China desk played a significant support role thereafter.

On issues involving Japan, however, State's relative weakness vis à vis the political leadership has frequently been offset by the asymmetry of the bilateral relationship. Prior to the Nixon years, U.S.-Japan issues were of distinctly subordinate interest to American political leaders, whereas they were vital to Japanese political leaders. These issues tended to be as neglected in the U.S. media as they were dramatized in the Japanese. For these reasons (and also because on matters Japanese the White House and State were usually in basic agreement), Japan issues tended (again before Nixon) to be "left pretty much in the hands of the experts," particularly the "middle-level bureaucrats in both the State Department and Defense Department" with "a continuing interest in U.S.-Japanese relations."[23] Arthur Schlesinger, Jr.'s forty-page chronicle of Kennedy administration complaints about State, for example, dealt at no point with Japan. In Tokyo, however, U.S. relations were politically crucial to LDP leaders and controversial in domestic politics. This made influence over these issues by Japanese political leaders greater than was the norm. Comparing relations with political leaders, then, the Gaimushō's relatively greater strength is counterbalanced by the far greater political importance of U.S.-Japan issues in Tokyo.

Interagency Relations

Considerable differences also exist between the two foreign offices in their dealings with other bureaucracies with interests in particular areas

23. Priscilla A. Clapp and Morton H. Halperin, "U.S. Elite Images of Japan: The Postwar Period," in Akira Iriye, ed., *Mutual Images: Essays in American-Japanese Relations* (Harvard University Press, 1975). See also I. M. Destler, "Country Expertise and U.S. Foreign Policy-making: The Case of Japan," in Morton A. Kaplan and Kinhide Mushakōji, eds., *Japan, America, and the Future World Order* (Free Press, 1976).

of foreign policy—though the same broad factors affect both governments.

The day has long passed when foreign offices could hope to monopolize all dealings with foreign governments. Well under half of the officials attached to U.S. embassies are State Department personnel; MITI and Finance officials are prominent on Japanese embassy staffs in major countries. And international conferences and missions on subjects such as defense, trade, finance, and agriculture bring senior officials and specialists from domestic agencies in the two governments into frequent contact.

Still less can State and the Gaimushō exclude other agencies from influencing basically domestic issues that have some foreign policy content. The line between international and domestic matters is hard to locate; the overlap is pervasive. In the economic area, problems such as international energy supply and consumption, regulation of exchange rates, and trade (in general and in particular commodities) are all matters of major consequence to agencies that cannot effectively carry out their domestic responsibilities without substantial influence over international matters. Similarly, decisions and actions on security issues affect the roles and capabilities of military organizations, whose leaders naturally become involved in these matters. In general, a foreign office's influence tends to wane on issues where its officials lack expertise, where groups with strong domestic interests and ties to other agencies (or to politicians) become engaged, and where the matter at stake is of major concern to agencies that are responsible for domestic policy.

ECONOMIC ISSUES. In foreign economic policy the Japanese Foreign Ministry faces formidable competition from two major ministries, Finance and International Trade and Industry.[24] In the 1969–71 negotiations on the financial terms of Okinawa reversion, for example, the Gaimushō, like the State Department, had great difficulty influencing either the progress or the outcome of the talks, though they were essen-

24. The discussion of these two ministries draws substantially on Philip H. Trezise with the collaboration of Yukio Suzuki, "Politics, Government, and Economic Growth in Japan," in Hugh Patrick and Henry Rosovsky, eds., *Asia's New Giant: How the Japanese Economy Works* (Brookings Institution, 1976); Fukui, "Bureaucratic Power in Japan"; Yōnosuke Nagai, "MITI and Japan's Economic Diplomacy" (paper prepared for delivery at a conference on Japanese foreign policy, at Kauai, Hawaii, Jan. 14–17, 1974; processed); Campbell, *Contemporary Japanese Budget Politics;* and I. M. Destler, Hideo Sato, and Haruhiro Fukui, "The Textile Wrangle: Conflict in Japanese-American Relations 1969–71" (1976; processed), chap. 2.

tial to the implementation of the Sato-Nixon agreement in 1969. They were dominated instead by the Finance Ministry (with its senior official Yūsuke Kashiwagi acting as a de facto one-man negotiating team) and the U.S. Treasury Department (with Anthony Jurich, special assistant to Secretary David M. Kennedy, acting as Kashiwagi's counterpart). Similarly on the textile negotiations, it was MITI that usually played the lead bureaucratic role. Especially during the last and critical phases of the negotiations in the fall of 1971, a few MITI officials working directly under the new MITI minister, Tanaka, almost completely monopolized the action on the Japanese side. The Gaimushō made only weak efforts to get into the act.

The Finance Ministry is the elite agency of Japan's bureaucracy, responsible for macroeconomic policy and the government budget. Thus, it combines in form, and to a considerable degree in practice, the powers of the U.S. Treasury Department, Office of Management and Budget, and Council of Economic Advisers. Until very recently its basic (and unusually consistent) domestic economic policy orientation was to combine a low-interest, quite expansionist monetary policy with tightness on the fiscal side. This not only proved an effective formula for facilitating rapid economic growth, but meshed nicely with the ministry's role of budgetary gatekeeper. In years when the revenue-expenditure balance seemed likely to prove too repressive, Finance preferred tax reduction to increased public spending.

In foreign policy views, the ministry tends to be loosely divided between a group centered in the International Finance Bureau and more domestically oriented officials elsewhere. On balance, Finance has been more internationalist than MITI, and its relationship with the Gaimushō has frequently been cooperative. It has opposed sharp increases in Japan's defense capabilities because of the possible impact on the budget, paralleling the Gaimushō's opposition to such expenditures on the grounds of likely adverse diplomatic repercussions. The two ministries were allied in supporting import liberalization against the opposition of MITI and Agriculture. They have tended to cooperate in international financial negotiations to their mutual benefit, with Finance—as in other countries—clearly the lead agency. But on economic aid, Finance Ministry officials have been strongly restrictive, directly at odds with Foreign Ministry—and MITI—officials who would like to expand such aid and soften its terms.

The Gaimushō-MITI relationship has been generally much less amicable, with their rivalry deeply rooted in the prewar period. In the twenties and thirties the Gaimushō faced aggressive competition from MITI's predecessor, the Ministry of Commerce and Industry. In fact, "reformist" Commerce bureaucrats (such as future Premier Nobusuke Kishi) often worked hand in glove with radical army officers against Foreign Ministry moderates to whittle away the latter's authority over the management of the overseas territories in northern China and Southeast Asia.

After the war was over, though the military suddenly ceased to be a significant force, the renamed Commerce bureaucracy not only survived but prospered beyond earlier dreams. And the preoccupation of the successive postwar cabinets with economic expansion at home and abroad has worked to MITI's advantage in the interministry rivalry.

The role of the Ministry of International Trade and Industry is to promote and strengthen Japan's industrial development and foreign trade. The policy stands of MITI bureaucrats tend to follow rather directly from this role; their solicitude toward Japanese domestic economic interests leads to frequent, predictable differences with Gaimushō officials. In dealings with the United States, the Foreign Ministry will almost always be the advocate of trade concessions, with MITI urging a tougher stance.[25] Until very recently, the dominant view of MITI officials was that the Japanese economy remained weak and vulnerable. Its development, therefore, needed to be promoted by encouraging those industries and sectors with the best growth prospects, and protecting this development from overseas threats (such as excessive imports or possible domination by American capital investment). And in practice this spilled over into protecting the interests of slow-growing industries as well. At times, MITI officials have viewed international economic policy as simply an extension of domestic economic policy: seeing Japan's national interest as, essentially, the highest possible gross national product; arguing that foreign policy issues can be clearly divided into political and economic categories, with the latter to be resolved on technical grounds by specialists such as themselves. And these officials have felt that special protection for Japan was justified because they saw their country as

25. But MITI's concern with the domestic economy can lead to its advocacy of diplomatic concessions as well—in the oil crisis of late 1973, for example, MITI was inclined to favor concessions toward the Arabs on Israel to assure the flow of oil; Gaimushō officials were reluctant because of fear that it would damage what they considered most important, Japan's international prestige and reputation and the relationship with the United States.

weak; as one of them put it, "We cannot be optimistic about measures taken for unconditional free competition between Gulliver and the Lilliputians."[26]

Within MITI, however, there are spokesmen for a more internationalist policy orientation. The ministry is organized under the minister (a politician) and the vice minister (a career official), who are supported by a small secretariat. The line bureaus of the ministry, such as Heavy Industry, and Textiles and General Merchandise, are responsible for broad industrial sectors; the International Trade Bureau deals with foreign commerce. There is chronic tension on international issues between the line bureaus, which are the heart of the organization, and the International Trade Bureau and the secretariat. These latter tend to be responsive to a broader range of policy considerations, and their stances on issues often approach those of the economic sections of the Foreign Ministry. This tension led one ranking MITI official to note: "MITI is no Goethe, but it is a unique government agency that has 'two souls.' One is nationalism and the other internationalism. Other agencies, such as Foreign Affairs and Defense, only have internationalism. Agriculture and Construction have only nationalism. MITI has both. When the wave of internationalism becomes too strong, nationalism asserts its identity, saying, 'What is my raison d'être?' "[27]

The ministry's influence on Japanese foreign policymaking derives, of course, from its influence on domestic economic policymaking. The concept of MITI as an all-powerful headquarters for "Japan, Inc." is clearly exaggerated. Nevertheless, MITI undoubtedly had a broad, many-faceted influence on Japan's postwar economic course in general, and even more on the day-to-day actions of particular firms. This influence has declined as the Japanese economy has become progressively decontrolled, with industries less and less dependent on MITI for specific actions approving imports of goods and technology, or foreign exchange transactions. And as this has taken place MITI has become somewhat more internationally oriented, as if seeking to compensate in the foreign sphere for its decline in power domestically. But the ministry's power on particular issues remains closely related to its technical expertise on the Japanese economy, and to its network of relationships with Japanese businessmen. These relationships are important in securing information,

26. Naohiro Amaya, quoted in Nagai, "MITI and Japan's Economic Diplomacy."
27. Quoted in Daizō Kusayanagi, "Tsūsanshō: Tamesareru sutā kanchō" [MITI: Star agency on trial], Bungei shunjū, August 1974, p. 114.

and in gaining cooperation from businessmen on problems they must help to solve. This gives MITI a card to play in the larger political arena that the Foreign Ministry does not possess—the support, or threatened opposition, of business interests who are a major supporting group of the ruling party. This MITI-business relationship is strengthened by the frequent movement of ranking MITI bureaucrats to high-level positions in major industries after their retirement from the bureaucracy.

The types of stands taken by Finance and MITI, and the insistence of specialist agencies that policy issues are technical ones requiring their expertise, have clear parallels in American foreign economic policy-making. But if the U.S. State Department faces competition comparable to the Gaimushō's, it is not always as certain and consistent from whence the competition cometh. A larger number of institutions is involved, and their power waxes and wanes. The senior departmental competitor is Treasury, which is generally supreme in international monetary policy, but lacks Finance's macroeconomic dominance and its budget role. Instead, government spending is managed by the Office of Management and Budget, which is part of the president's executive office, and Treasury and OMB share the lead in national economic policy with the Council of Economic Advisers and the independent Federal Reserve Board. The balance of national economic policy influence depends significantly on the strengths, interests, and presidential relationships of politically designated executives in these organizations.

Multilateral trade negotiations are coordinated by the Office of the Special Representative for Trade Negotiations, which participates also in trade policy deliberations along with State, Commerce, Agriculture, and other departments. Since 1971, trade policy has also been coordinated to some degree by the staff of the White House Council on International Economic Policy (CIEP), whose formal writ covers all foreign economic matters. Interestingly, the Treasury's role on general trade policy has usually been minor, though recently strong secretaries like John Connally and George Shultz have made their marks in this area, and the department has particular trade regulation responsibilities—like that for countervailing duties.

The Treasury Department's international staff is quite small, totaling somewhat over two hundred. Its senior responsible official for monetary questions is the under secretary for monetary affairs; below him is the international office headed by an assistant secretary. A major concern of the department through the sixties and seventies has been the protection and improvement of the U.S. balance of payments. Treasury also, for historical reasons, has primary responsibility for U.S. policy vis à vis the multilateral development banks, though the Agency for International Development—an autonomous unit within State—retains responsibility for the shrinking bilateral aid program.

If Treasury thus differs from the Finance Ministry, it is even harder to find an American counterpart for MITI. The Commerce Department played a parallel role in the textile negotiations, but its leverage has not been comparable on other product issues, let alone other matters related to foreign policy. The Commerce Department's international staff numbers about thirteen hundred persons, concentrated particularly on export promotion services to U.S. businessmen, and on specialized problems of regulating trade with communist countries. On broader trade and investment policy issues, Commerce tends to be protectionist, responding to the interests of U.S. firms that feel threatened by international competition. But in general, Commerce is one of the weakest of the executive departments, and its role in determining U.S. economic policy is far more modest than its name implies. A stronger agency on issues relevant to it is the Department of Agriculture (USDA), with wide-ranging impact on domestic crop production and international trade. And in contrast to its Japanese counterpart, USDA in general is internationally oriented, reflecting the strong interest of U.S. agriculture in world markets.

Coordination of foreign economic policy is a recurring problem in the American bureaucracy, with the CIEP one in a series of imperfect organizational approaches. When coordination has been strong, it has generally come from individuals based in foreign policy agencies (State or the NSC staff) or economic policy institutions (mainly Treasury). In the Nixon administration, for example, strong leadership in this area came from economic policy czars like John Connally and George Shultz when it came at all.[28]

---

28. In the Kennedy and Johnson administrations a staff approach was employed: the president had a deputy special assistant for national security affairs whose mandate covered foreign economic policy and major overlapping political issues. In the late Eisenhower administration, Under Secretary of State Douglas Dillon proved an effective foreign economic policy czar operating from this line position. The Ford administration established a cabinet-level Economic Policy Board in September 1974 to coordinate foreign and domestic economic policy, and the CIEP has been subordinated to the new structure. But the Kissinger State Department has been unusually assertive on economic issues, and friction has been frequent between it and the domestic economic advisers and institutions.

Because of the concentration of authority in key ministries, the Japanese government has had neither the coordinating offices and committees that exist in the United States, nor any comparable shifting of power among individuals and institutions. There is no Office of the Special Trade Representative in the Kantei; no cabinet Council on International Economic Policy to coordinate (or at least try to coordinate) government activity in this sphere. But the absence in Japan of a body above the ministerial level does not prevent considerable coordination between ministries. On most noncontroversial matters, relevant divisions and bureaus in different ministries do cooperate with one another and coordinate views successfully enough. For instance, the Second North American Division in the Foreign Ministry's American Bureau maintains regular contact with the First Overseas Market Division in MITI's International Trade Bureau regarding economic relations with the United States. Moreover, the Japanese tendency toward consensus decision-making[29] may help to compensate for the lack of a supraministerial coordinating mechanism. This is not to deny that once a serious conflict does arise between ministries, it may be harder in the Japanese system to keep it under control or for top policymakers to resolve it. For smooth working relations within ministries are frequently accompanied by strong, sometimes bitter rivalry between them.

SECURITY ISSUES. In security matters it is the U.S. government that features strong career organizations with continuing major roles and responsibilities. The weight of these bureaucracies is illustrated (though not caused) by those in regular attendance at the National Security Council, including the secretary of defense, the director of central intelligence, and the chairman of the Joint Chiefs of Staff. For Americans, the blending of diplomatic, military, and intelligence activities has been the overriding problem in the formulation of postwar foreign policy, particularly on those issues that get the most sustained high-level attention. And control of the military services (and sometimes the CIA) has been perceived as the most crucial challenge to government foreign policy leaders.[30]

There is nothing comparable to the U.S. national security structure in postwar Japanese foreign policymaking. In fact, the weakness of the

29. Consensus decisionmaking is treated on pp. 101–08, below.
30. For detailed treatment of the roles and interests of the armed services and other security agencies with an influence on foreign policy, see Halperin, *Bureaucratic Politics and Foreign Policy*, chap. 3.

military establishment today is as remarkable as its dominance was in the thirties and early forties. After the war the Japanese military establishment was promptly liquidated by the occupation authorities. And the 1947 constitution prohibited, in the famous Article Nine, the nation's remilitarization and engagement in acts of war. But this constitutional proscription was modified in practice (and under pressure from the United States) to allow the development of substantial Self-Defense Forces (SDF) and progressively more sophisticated armament. Today the Defense Agency overseeing these forces is a reasonably large organization and a bureaucracy in itself. The management of nearly 250,000 troops and an annual budget of about $3.6 billion is a very substantial operation.[31] Compared to the formidable defense and security establishment of postwar America, however, Japan's Defense Agency and SDF do not look impressive at all. Moreover, there is no important foreign intelligence organization even remotely comparable to the American CIA. The Cabinet Research Office (Naikaku Chōsa-shitsu), the closest Japanese analogue, has been a very modest operation, interested predominantly in intelligence-gathering on communist bloc nations, especially the Soviet Union, China, and North Korea.

The difference between the politics of national security policymaking in the two governments is well illustrated by the Okinawa reversion case. In the United States, the key bureaucratic concern was the interests and stands of the military services, particularly the Army. Unless the military were prepared to go along, U.S. officials could not even discuss the question seriously with the Japanese government. Gradually, the U.S. military came to believe that reversion (1) was probably inevitable, and (2) could be accomplished in a way that would not damage the U.S. security position in the Far East. Only because of this accommodating military position was President Nixon able to decide on reversion in 1969 without precipitating a major bureaucratic (and, in consequence, congressional) fight. On the Japanese side, however, the Defense Agency was essentially out of the picture, even on issues like whether Japan would assert a security stake in Korea and Taiwan. These were all taken care of by the responsible segments of the Foreign Ministry—the North American Affairs and Security divisions of the American Affairs Bureau in cooperation with the Treaties Bureau. The critical politics in Japan on this issue was not that inside the government, but the broader national controversy

31. *Asahi nenkan* [Asahi almanac], *1974.*

over security policy and the potential impact of Okinawa on this controversy.

Conclusions

In its general structure and institutions, the Japanese government differs from the American in several important respects. There is the basic difference between parliamentary and presidential systems, and thus between prime ministers and presidents, with the particular impact on the former caused by the structure of Japan's ruling party and the character of the opposition. There is the related difference in staff support for political leaders and bureaucracies, with the Tokyo government featuring few of the high-level coordinating staffs or the in-and-out officials who are found in abundance in Washington. There are differences —which reflect postwar policy priorities and constraints—in the identity and influence of the major institutional actors in the two main policy spheres—economics and national security. And there are differences between the broader national communities interested in foreign policy, most notably the continued polarization between ruling and opposition parties in Tokyo.

These differences are varied and sometimes subtle, yet they are typical of the variation one might expect between any two large governments. Yet miscalculation based on misunderstanding of these differences helped bring crisis in security treaty revision, then later in the textile negotiations. In both cases, Americans overestimated the ability of the prime minister to control the issue.

In the first instance, what was underestimated was the leverage the opposition could exercise on a politically controversial matter. The decision to negotiate a new security treaty requiring Diet ratification, and the plans for an Eisenhower visit to cement and symbolize the new relationship, both assumed that Premier Kishi could handle his domestic politics. They assumed he could use his Diet majorities to get the treaty ratified in a way that would vindicate and strengthen the conservative leadership, upon whose continued rule American policy hopes rested. But popular opposition to the treaty and to Kishi was strong, and the combined effect of his and the opposition's tactics led the premier to a situation where he could get the treaty ratified in time for Eisenhower's visit only by violating procedural norms, which undercut his legitimacy as a democratic leader. The outcome was the humiliation of both national leaders.

On textiles, the major miscalculation involved an overestimation of Sato's power within the cabinet and the conservative establishment. Sato was pressured by the Nixon White House to accept the American position on the terms of an agreement, and he agreed to do so. It was almost two years, however, before he could bring his government to carry out his wishes. He replaced one minister of international trade and industry with a man he thought more amenable, only to find that he had to replace this second minister eighteen months later. He sought to negotiate outside of official channels, and to convey all sorts of indirect signals of his intentions and his sincerity to both Americans and Japanese. But he met resistance from both the MITI bureaucracy and the Japanese textile industry and its supporters in the Diet, resistance dramatized by a national press that considered Japanese rejection of American proposals a long-overdue exercise of "autonomous diplomacy."

The White House response was to blame Sato personally—he had promised but had not delivered. A wiser reaction would have been to reevaluate the usefulness of pressing a Japanese premier to make promises he was likely to prove unable to keep. Sato was certainly not blameless—he seems to have dealt with the White House in a way that led Nixon to believe he could deliver. Kishi bore even more responsibility for the crisis in 1960, since it was his government that had pressed for the new treaty in the first place and pushed it through the Diet. But in both cases, American misreading of the politics of Japanese policymaking was a major contributor to a serious U.S.-Japan crisis.

American policymaking on Okinawa avoided such overestimation of the premier's power. Indeed, those who led in bringing the U.S. government around on the issue were moved by a sense of the vulnerability of Sato and the ruling Liberal Democratic party on the issue. These Americans feared that unless reversion on mutually acceptable terms were negotiated before the initial ten-year term of the security treaty expired in 1970, a new crisis threatening the ruling regime and the U.S.-Japanese alliance would arise. Because of this fear, the U.S. government proved willing to make substantive concessions aimed at clearing Sato's domestic path, rather than assuming that the premier could prevail at home with such terms as he signed onto. For example, Sato could probably have been brought to accept—as a price for reversion—a status for U.S. bases on Okinawa different, and more favorable to the U.S. military, than that of bases on the main Japanese islands—a status allowing greater flexibility for their military use, conceivably even the storage of nuclear weapons there. He was not pushed this far because responsible officials—including President Nixon—saw that what counted was not getting the maximum in specific concessions but an agreement that Sato and his successors could live with at home, one that would therefore really resolve the Okinawa issue. And special status for Okinawan bases would have meant, at minimum, a continuing domestic controversy for years to come.

Had the same American restraint been applied to the textile negotiations, much strife would have been averted. Yet the overestimation of Sato's power was only one of many political miscalculations by both sides in that unfortunate episode. And policy mistakes arising from misinterpretation of the politics of policymaking in the other capital have been frequent in other bilateral cases as well. This suggests the need for a general analysis of misperceptions in U.S.-Japanese relations, a look at some recurrent ways that officials in one capital have tended to misunderstand and misconstrue events and actions in the other capital. That is the purpose of chapter 4.

CHAPTER FOUR

Misperceptions across the Pacific

"LOOKING BACK on the mass of evidence that was available at the time," wrote journalist A. Merriman Smith a year later, "it becomes all the more unbelievable that Eisenhower thought he could go to Japan in June, 1960."[1] But apparently he did think so, and so also did American diplomats who advised him in the days and weeks before his plane was scheduled to land. A bit over nine years later, another Republican president was convinced that a Japanese premier would deliver him a stringent textile agreement. And fifteen months after that, politicians and bureaucrats in Tokyo were convinced that Congressman Wilbur Mills would not be negotiating a textile limitation agreement if he did not have White House acquiescence.

In these, as in all instances of relations between governments, officials in one capital had to make judgments about what would transpire in the politics of the other. They had to interpret what their counterparts had said and were doing, and predict how they might subsequently behave. They had to make certain assumptions about the broader political arena abroad and the abilities of particular leaders to prevail in that arena. They had to make at least some crude calculations as to how particular negotiators would respond to different types of personal negotiating styles and appeals. Often their perceptions and calculations were reasonably accurate, and seldom did their errors have such serious consequences as the three cited above. Yet misperceptions have been frequent enough in U.S.-Japanese relations to pose continuing problems for the relationship, and at times very serious problems.

One way of attacking the problem of misperception is to strike at one of its causes—lack of basic knowledge of one another's systems. To provide such information was one of the major purposes of chapter 3. But it

1. *A President's Odyssey* (Harper, 1961), p. 209.

is useful also to analyze misperceptions as they have actually occurred, to explore and attempt to categorize what kinds of mistakes are most frequently made by officials in reading the other government. And doing so requires consideration not only of political and institutional complexities and differences of the sort already introduced, but also of difficulties rooted in the two nations' quite different cultures. For a look at episodes of misperceptions in recent U.S.-Japanese relations suggests that they fall rather clearly into two general categories. The first type is those that arise inevitably in relationships between any two major democratic countries with complex and differing political and institutional structures. These flow directly from the existence of bureaucratic and broader political divisions and struggles within the countries, and seem to be characteristic of U.S. relations with European allies as well. The second type finds its causes in those divergent cultural values and styles peculiar to the U.S.-Japan relationship—for example, in the particular role that consensus plays in decisionmaking in Japan and the ways it is sometimes misconstrued by Americans.

Misperceptions Rooted in Politics as Usual

In his study of Anglo-American relations Richard E. Neustadt finds that crises between counterpart officials follow a recurrent pattern of "muddled perceptions, stifled communications, disappointed expectations, and paranoid reactions. In turn, each 'friend' misreads the other, each is reticent with the other, each is surprised by the other, each replies in kind."[2] This pattern he finds in dealings between two countries where the cultural and the language differences are markedly small, but where officials (as everywhere) are preoccupied with domestic and bureaucratic politics in their respective home capitals. This suggests that politically based misperceptions are endemic in relations between any two large countries.

In U.S.-Japanese relations, this kind of misperception may arise when actors in one country fail to recognize the existence of political divisions and conflicts in the other, seeing the target government as if it were a

2. *Alliance Politics* (Columbia University Press, 1970), p. 66. For application of this formulation to the 1969–71 textile negotiations, see Morton H. Halperin, "Comment," *Foreign Policy*, no. 14 (Spring 1974), pp. 155–56; and Yōnosuke Nagai, "Dōmei gaikō no kansei" [Trap of alliance diplomacy], *Chūō kōron*, January 1972.

unified, rational actor making a series of carefully calculated decisions (for example, "the Japanese" are trying to make us do x). Or officials may recognize that the other side also has its domestic political complexities and divisions, but then interpret them in terms of the particular features of their own political system. A third source of misperception is the particular interests and stakes of actors in one country, which may limit and distort their perception of events abroad.

Seeing the Other Government as Unified

Writing about official misperception, Robert Jervis concludes that, in general,

actors see others as more internally united than they in fact are and generally overestimate the degree to which others are following a coherent policy. The degree to which the other side's policies are the product of internal bargaining, internal misunderstandings, or subordinates' not following instructions is underestimated. Seeing only the finished product, they find it simpler to try to construct a rational explanation for the policies, even though they know that such an analysis could not explain their own policies.[3]

And because they see a particular action as a deliberate and calculated attempt by the foreign government to influence the behavior of their own, they tend sometimes to overreact, creating or increasing tension between the two countries.

This type of misperception was present in two decisive episodes during the slide toward war in 1941. The first was in July, when in response to the movement of Japanese troops into southern Indochina, President Franklin D. Roosevelt issued a "freezing order" which led ultimately to an embargo on U.S. oil exports to Japan. This embargo, in turn, forced Japanese leaders to choose either to make political and military concessions to the United States to negotiate its removal, or to strike out militarily to gain control of alternative oil sources before their reserve stocks became too depleted for full-scale military operations.

How united was the U.S. government on the embargo issue? It was, in fact, sharply divided. In ordering a freeze on Japanese assets in the

3. "Hypotheses on Misperception," *World Politics*, no. 3 (April 1968); reprinted in Morton H. Halperin and Arnold Kanter, eds., *Readings in American Foreign Policy: A Bureaucratic Perspective* (Little, Brown, 1973), pp. 134–35. On this same point, see Graham T. Allison and Morton H. Halperin, "Bureaucratic Politics: A Paradigm and Some Policy Implications," in Richard H. Ullman and Raymond Tanter, eds., *Theory and Policy in International Relations* (Princeton University Press, 1972) (Brookings Reprint 246).

United States Roosevelt was taking, he apparently thought, a middle course that explicitly rejected the immediate oil embargo desired by U.S. "hawks" like Treasury Secretary Henry Morgenthau and Assistant Secretary of State Dean Acheson. The chief of naval operations also opposed an embargo, fearing it would lead to a war with Japan before U.S. forces were ready to fight it. Whether the freezing order would in fact bring about an embargo depended on "how it was administered";[4] there were "weeks of wavering" about whether the U.S. government should "be lenient or severe in the issue of licenses to use 'frozen' dollars to pay for Japanese purchases."[5] But Japanese leaders seem to have concluded almost immediately that the freezing order was part of a coherent policy, essentially the total oil embargo which they had long feared. Hawks argued that this made it essential to press ahead with war plans for securing Southeast Asian oil before Japan's two-year oil stocks were too much depleted; "doves" were moved to redouble efforts to negotiate a modus vivendi. The Navy, which had been opposed to risking war with the United States, was now moved by the impending oil squeeze to harden its position, thus depleting the ranks of the doves in Tokyo.[6] No one there seems to have recognized the extent of the division and uncertainty within the U.S. government and the opportunity this might have offered to secure further oil in significant quantities if specific applications for export licenses were astutely contrived. Of course, Japanese officials' limited understanding of the U.S. government, and the lack of sympathetic U.S. officials with whom to work, would have made such an approach difficult.[7]

Four months later, President Roosevelt similarly overestimated *Japanese* unity at a particularly crucial point. As December approached, the Japanese government was divided in both its views and its lines of activity. Military forces were preparing steadily for war; Premier Hideki Tōjō and Foreign Minister Shigenori Tōgō—supported by the emperor

---

4. Dean Acheson, *Present at the Creation* (Norton, 1969), p. 24.

5. Herbert Feis, *The Road to Pearl Harbor* (Princeton University Press, 1950), p. 242.

6. See Kōichi Kido, *Kido Kōichi nikki* [Kōichi Kido diary], vol. 2 (Tokyo: Tokyo University Press, 1966), p. 896; and Teiji Yabe, *Konoye Fumimaro* [Fumimaro Konoye] (Tokyo: Jiji Press, 1958), pp. 154-55.

7. In fact, Acheson suggests that the way, presumably accidental, that the Japanese actually tested the freezing order played into the hands of Americans like himself who wished to use the freeze to enforce an oil embargo. (*Present at the Creation*, pp. 25-27.)

and his entourage—were striving to achieve some eleventh-hour U.S.-Japan agreement acceptable to the military that could avert a conflict. On the morning of November 26, Roosevelt was considering what response the United States should make to the most promising of Japan's proposals for a short-term modus vivendi; he had even drafted proposals of his own not too far from those Tokyo had put forward. Then he received a telephone call from Secretary of War Henry Stimson, a hawk. Stimson was passing on an intelligence report of Japanese troops heading south of Formosa. According to Roosevelt's biographer,

The President fairly blew up—"jumped into the air, so to speak," Stimson noted in his diary. To the President this changed the whole situation, because "it was evidence of bad faith *on the part of the Japanese* that while they were negotiating for an entire truce—an entire withdrawal (from China)—*they* should be sending *their* expedition down there to Indochina." Roosevelt's truce formula died that day. In its stead, Hull drew up a ten-point proposal that restated Washington's most stringent demands.[8]

In fact, "the Japanese" were pursuing no single coherent policy; the charge of "bad faith" presumed a unity that was absent. But the President's misperception triggered a hardening of the U.S. negotiating position that ended any chances for a peaceful settlement.

Another U.S. overestimation of the unity and purposiveness of Japanese policymakers came thirty years later, in March 1971. The Japanese textile industry unveiled its unilateral plan for moderate restrictions on exports to the United States, and the chief cabinet secretary announced that this plan made further intergovernmental negotiations on the subject unnecessary. A U.S. official deeply involved in the issue said he believed this was "the first time the Japanese had unilaterally broken off a negotiation with the United States since December 7, 1941"; he implied, once again, deliberate deceit, with "the Japanese" suddenly invoking their own desired solution as the Americans were still negotiating in good faith for another sort of outcome in a very different channel. And President Nixon himself seems to have held Premier Sato directly responsible for the industry's actions. In fact, however, Sato and other high Japanese officials had played only very limited and passive roles in the events leading to the plan's adoption by the textile industry; the driving force came from the unusual alignment of that industry with Congressman Wilbur Mills.

8. James MacGregor Burns, *Roosevelt: The Soldier of Freedom* (Harcourt Brace Jovanovich, 1970), p. 157. Emphasis added.

In the late sixties and early seventies, the "Japan, Inc." image held by many Americans reinforced their tendency to view the Japanese government as more united and purposive than it really was. For example, there was widespread exaggeration of the extent to which the Japanese government effectively controlled the development of its domestic economy and international trade.[9] And throughout the textile negotiations, U.S. officials repeatedly blamed "Japanese arrogance" or "delaying tactics" for Japanese actions that were unresponsive to the U.S. desire for an agreement. But in many cases, minimal, temporizing responses to U.S. proposals were caused rather by the sharp divisions among Japanese officials and industrialists involved.

Seeing the Other Government as Parallel to One's Own

A more sophisticated pattern of misperception arises when officials project assumptions derived from their own political framework onto the politics of the other country. They recognize political complexities and divisions in the counterpart government, and yet still err by assuming that the details of the other country's decisionmaking are like those at home.

This form of misperception is so natural that it is particularly difficult to avoid. For the process of policymaking in Japan is in many ways similar to that in America; each government is (as Neustadt says of America and Britain) "constitutional in character, representative in form, limited in scope, confined by guarantees of private right . . . and legitimatized by the symbols of popular sovereignty."[10] If misperceptions frequently arise between British and American leaders due to misreading of fine details or nuances where those two systems diverge, they seem even more likely in U.S.-Japanese relations. Thus, "intellectual conditioning as well as governmental gamesmanhip makes it extraordinarily difficult to transcend one's own frame of reference and to avoid assuming, by analogical reasoning, that the frame of reference of counterparts in Tokyo is comparable to the political environment in Washington, and vice versa."[11]

9. See Philip H. Trezise with the collaboration of Yukio Suzuki, "Politics, Government, and Economic Growth in Japan," in Hugh Patrick and Henry Rosovsky, eds., *Asia's New Giant: How the Japanese Economy Works* (Brookings Institution, 1976).

10. *Alliance Politics*, p. 79.

11. Michael H. Armacost, "U.S.-Japan Relations: Problems and Modalities of Communications," *Department of State Bulletin*, Jan. 15, 1973, p. 68.

Perhaps the most prominent postwar misperception of this type has been Americans' overestimation of the Japanese premier's power. In the textile case (where this mistake proved most costly), the United States not only sought commitments at summit conferences, but Presidential Assistant Henry Kissinger repeatedly tried to achieve a breakthrough by negotiating directly with the premier's personal office, the Kantei. Such efforts could have worked only if the Kantei were able to make prompt decisions, as the White House sometimes could, before cabinet or bureaucratic consensus had jelled. Its powers were not parallel, so the result was further White House frustration. White House misperception may have been fueled, however, by the repeatedly expressed Japanese desire to negotiate on textiles with someone other than Secretary of Commerce Maurice Stans. Sato himself signaled the White House on this point on at least three occasions. And some Japanese felt that moving Stans to one side on the issue might lead to significant U.S. substantive concessions. Thinking in terms of their own system, they apparently assumed that Stans's Commerce Department portfolio and industry constituency were the main sources of his hard line. In fact, Stans was—like most American cabinet officials—heavily dependent on the President. His views and actions generally reflected the President's political objectives, as was particularly likely on any "special issue" to which the President gave high priority. Thus, though Stans was replaced as U.S. negotiator in the fall of 1970, the U.S. negotiating position changed only marginally.[12]

And one of the greatest political miscalculations in postwar U.S.-Japanese relations occurred when Tokyo political leaders acquiesced in the import control plan that Japanese industry leaders had negotiated with Congressman Mills, in the expectation that President Richard Nixon would acquiesce also. Here too projection of homeland political assumptions onto the other system was an important source of error (though some important American actors misjudged this one as well). In Japan, with a parliamentary system dominated by the LDP, the pre-

12. A similar misperception in the other direction occurred in June 1970, when MITI Minister Kiichi Miyazawa came to Washington to negotiate with Stans, accompanied by Foreign Minister Kiichi Aichi. Kissinger sought to work around the former and strike a deal with the latter. He was right in assuming that the foreign minister would be more receptive than the MITI minister to U.S. interests. But he was wrong in assuming that Aichi could negotiate around Miyazawa as Kissinger was operating around Stans. Textiles was clearly within the organizational jurisdiction of the MITI, and the foreign minister could not simply bypass the MITI minister.

mier and his cabinet seldom view the Diet and its committees as independent competitors. And to the degree that Japanese actors did recognize that separation of powers made Mills something of a rival baron to Nixon, it was assumed that their mutual dependence would prevent either from risking a major public fight. Mills would not move without being sure the President could live with the arrangement; Nixon would not break with Mills on the issue because his Ways and Means Committee controlled so much of the President's priority legislation. And Mills—very much a widely consulting, consensus-style legislative leader —personally assured those Japanese who asked that he did have reason to believe the White House would go along. Thus, they were shocked when Nixon denounced the deal. To the President, however, Mills's action amounted to an attempt to undercut him politically and to challenge his basic constitutional prerogative of negotiating agreements with foreign governments.

The Stakes of the Beholder

In government, "where you stand depends on where you sit."[13] Officials' "comprehension of the other [government's] actual behavior is a function of their own concerns."[14] Moreover, "decision-makers tend to fit incoming information into their existing theories and images . . . actors tend to perceive what they expect."[15] This universal tendency for individuals to perceive the world in terms of their own day-to-day concerns and expectations, from their own vantage points, in part reflects political interests—officials see events in the context of their particular stakes in the policy actions to which such events may be relevant. They view the world from particular "perspectives." But it reflects also the apparent need for each human mind to view specific events within broader conceptual frameworks which change but slowly. Specific events or signals are perceived not independently, as pure new facts; they are interpreted —sometimes distorted—so that they may fit in with what the mind already knows.[16]

13. Graham Allison, *Essence of Decision: Explaining the Cuban Missile Crisis* (Little, Brown, 1971), p. 176.
14. Neustadt, *Alliance Politics*, p. 66.
15. Jervis, "Hypotheses on Misperception," p. 115.
16. For an extensive analysis of these cognitive phenomena and their relation to foreign policymaking, see ibid.; and, in particular, John D. Steinbruner, *The Cybernetic Theory of Decision: New Dimensions of Political Analysis* (Princeton University Press, 1974), especially chap. 4.

Once again the textile case offers illuminating examples. In the spring of 1969, the Japanese reaction to U.S. pressure for comprehensive export controls was uniformly negative. To State Department officials, who felt that such thoroughgoing restrictions were unnecessary, this was evidence that they were unattainable; they concluded that less stringent trade restrictions should therefore be sought. But Commerce Department officials who were committed to the comprehensive approach had a rather different reading. As one of them told the press, "The first thing the Japanese say to new negotiations is no. But this is just their way of opening."[17] Several months later, after Japan's Minister of International Trade and Industry Ohira had agreed to send a technical mission to Washington to discuss the textile problem, American officials differed again as to whether he had also agreed that the mission would discuss potential solutions. Predictably, Commerce bureaucrats (who had developed a proposal that the talks include discussion of solutions) argued that Ohira had acceded to this; their State Department colleagues believed he had acceded to no such thing.

The Japanese government made similar miscalculations. In the fall of 1970, with intergovernmental textile negotiations stymied and with restrictive import quota legislation making progress on Capitol Hill, the Japanese government needed to judge how likely the legislation was to pass, in order to determine whether they needed to makes concessions in order to prevent the bill's enactment. Gaimushō (Foreign Ministry) officials, who favored compromise to avert a further increase in general U.S.-Japanese tensions, judged that Congress was likely to pass the bill, and that Nixon was likely to sign it. Their MITI counterparts, who did not want to be pressured into major concessions on textiles, argued the opposite conclusion: that the "Christmas tree phenomenon" (the tendency of quota bills to attract a large number of restrictive amendments favoring various domestic interests) would either lead to congressional failure to enact the legislation, or force President Nixon to veto it. Thus for MITI officials the situation did not require Japan to soften its negotiating position.

In the treaty revision case, a look at the particular vantage points and stakes of major American actors helps to explain why "Eisenhower thought he could go to Japan in June 1960." The White House was anything but unaware of the street protests in Tokyo against the new secu-

17. *Daily News Record* (New York), March 24, 1969, p. 16.

rity treaty and the means Premier Nobusuke Kishi had used to force Diet action. Within four days of the controversial lower house vote on May 19, Secretary of State Christian Herter cabled Tokyo on the President's behalf raising the possibility of postponing the trip to late July or early August, so that Eisenhower's arrival would not coincide with final Japanese ratification of the treaty on June 19. The question of postponement was raised again, with considerably greater force, after the car carrying Press Secretary Hagerty's advance party was surrounded by demonstrators at Haneda airport on June 10. Eisenhower certainly wanted to go to Japan. It was to be the major Asian stop in his extended "journey for peace," his quest for diplomatic and goodwill gains abroad and a vindication at home in the form of a Republican victory in the 1960 election. Already his Moscow invitation had been withdrawn in the wake of the U-2 fiasco; the last thing he wanted was a second public rebuff, particularly one that would appear as backing down before communist pressure. But there was also an awareness in the White House and the State Department, expressed in a cable to the embassy on June 10, of the "need to face squarely the possibility of the grave damage which could result at home and abroad from either failing to make certain of an orderly visit or unwisely persisting in the visit."[18] There was also some concern within the administration that the fall of the Kishi government might be inevitable "regardless of whether the President visits Japan," and consequently with "why the prestige of President Eisenhower and the United States should be so deeply committed to so precarious and uncertain a cause."[19]

Given such recognition of the complexity of the situation, why did Eisenhower persist in his plans? A crucial reason was that he perceived the situation, in the final analysis, through the eyes of the U.S. embassy in Tokyo and Ambassador Douglas MacArthur II. There was no lack of information flowing through other channels—in the twenty-eight days before Kishi's eleventh-hour withdrawal of the invitation, events in Japan made the front page of the New York Times sixteen times. But for interpretation of what this all meant and how the United States should respond, the President depended, not surprisingly, on the ambas-

18. Assistant Secretary of State J. Graham Parsons, "Chronology of Ambassador MacArthur's Meetings with Prime Minister Kishi and Other Japanese Government Officials Prior to Postponement of President's Visit" (memorandum to Secretary of State Christian Herter, June 27, 1960).

19. New York Times, June 16, 1960.

sador. And while MacArthur did raise the question of postponement with Japanese leaders when instructed to do so, he accepted and supported, time after time, Kishi's determination to proceed.

The ambassador's position and his personal stakes made him far more an advocate and promoter of the trip than an objective evaluator of whether it should take place. On the day in May that Herter's cable arrived suggesting possible postponement, MacArthur was arguing vehemently (and for public effect) with the Japan Socialist party leader who had just delivered him an open letter to Eisenhower asking postponement.[20] Not surprisingly, he cabled back that "for President to take initiative in postponing his visit to Japan" would be a "great mistake" and "could be mortal blow for Kishi."[21] And not only did his personal identification with the success of the trip encourage him to persevere; he saw U.S. interests as tied very closely to the Kishi regime. This reflected not just the normal identification of a diplomat with the leaders with whom he deals, but the fact that the new security treaty—the prime accomplishment of his ambassadorship and of U.S.-Japanese relations since the occupation—had been negotiated with that regime and was being defended by that regime. Thus—in a turbulent political situation impossible to predict with certainty—his perceptions and recommendations reflected these priorities and preoccupations, and merged above all with the hope that—with steadfastness and perseverance—the President could make a triumphal visit that would vindicate the United States and the Kishi government. Positive evidence was highlighted—the press was giving signs it would put aside its animosity toward Kishi ("whom they hate blindly") and "soon begin to call on Japanese people to welcome President warmly."[22] Negative evidence was minimized—though "Japanese security authorities were very inadequate in handling Hagerty arrival," the fault was partly that of "White House and Embassy security people" who did not press the Japanese hard enough about the specific arrangements.[23] As late as a day before the massive, violent encounter between demonstrators and police that led to Kishi's withdrawal of the invitation, the ambassador reported and endorsed the Japanese

20. Ibid., May 25, 1960.
21. Cable no. 3825, U.S. Embassy, Tokyo, to Secretary of State (eyes only), May 25, 1960.
22. Cable no. 4082, U.S. Embassy, Tokyo, to Secretary of State, June 8, 1960.
23. Cable no. 4139, U.S. Embassy, Tokyo, to Secretary of State (eyes only), June 11, 1960.

government's assurances that "the security measures that they have instituted plus changes in the climate of public opinion" offered "reasonable assurances" of a successful visit.[24] The result of all this perseverance, of course, was the humiliating eleventh-hour cancellation which the embassy, the President, and the Kishi government wanted least of all. In retrospect, the postponement suggested in late May would have been far preferable, but it was not vigorously pursued because an ambassador both set on the visit and staked to the Kishi government perceived sticking to the plan as the politically necessary course.[25]

Like other examples of misperception cited here, the U.S. mistake in persisting with the trip can be explained by the sort of political interplay within governments present in any bilateral relationship, by politics as usual. But there also are deep cultural differences between Japan and the United States, which are both reflected and reinforced by their two very different languages. And these too have affected the perceptions and expectations of officials as they looked across the Pacific.

Misperceptions Rooted in Cultural Differences

In its relations with Japan the United States faces a wide cultural gap not present in its dealings with other major allies. An assistant secretary of state pinpointed one key element of the problem:

Perhaps it is fair to say that both Americans and Japanese are poorly prepared for cross-cultural understanding. We both developed, in rather isolated cir-

24. Parsons, "Chronology." For more on how officials' interpretations of particular situations are typically "biased in the direction of supporting plans that had been built on the basis of other considerations," see Joseph de Rivera, The Psychological Dimension of Foreign Policy (Merrill, 1968), p. 71.

25. The perceptions of the embassy and Washington were also substantially colored by the "shared images" of a bipolar, cold-war world that shaped American attitudes generally. Kishi was anticommunist, his opponents were communists and socialists and vehement critics of the American connection. Thus MacArthur, like most Americans, exaggerated the extent of foreign instigation in the antitreaty, anti-Kishi movement ("Moscow and Peking are committing all their available reserves to present internal struggle in Japan to defeat security treaty" [Cable no. 4082, U.S. Embassy, Tokyo]). He concluded that "the very survival of Japanese democracy" depended on thwarting the campaign by "minority groups" against Kishi, the treaty, and the visit (paraphrased in Parsons, "Chronology"). And in language that foreshadowed a widespread official interpretation of another Asian nation's internal crisis, he warned that "backing down to Communists will create domino reaction in free Asia" (Cable no. 4082, U.S. Embassy, Tokyo). On the concept of "shared images," see Morton H. Halperin with the assistance of Priscilla Clapp and Arnold Kanter, Bureaucratic Politics and Foreign Policy (Brookings Institution, 1974), chap. 2.

cumstances, relatively free from entanglements with other cultures and encroaching nations. We have both grown up in societies that until recently have emphasized cultural homogeneity as the desirable goal of national and human existence. It was the other fellow whose duty it was to understand us, if such understanding was even considered relevant, or necessary, or possible.[26]

The line between what is political and what is cultural is not easy to draw. But certain characteristics of Japanese and American policy behavior appear to be based on deep-rooted cultural values and patterns of interpersonal relationships; thus they are not adequately explained by the structures of the two political systems. And these lead to certain types of misperceptions that appear peculiar to the U.S.-Japan relationship (though some of them may also appear in Japan's dealings with other Western countries).

Consensus

American business leader Donald Kendall, frustrated in his attempt to mediate the controversial textile issue, concluded that consensual decisionmaking in Tokyo was the main barrier to smooth U.S.-Japanese relations. "So long as this basic decision-making remains predominant in Japan, U.S.-Japanese economic (as well as political) relations will continue to require a great deal of understanding on both sides, because Japan can never make a timely shift in policy."[27] Decisions either take too long, or they are not made. Many other Americans have had difficulty getting timely, responsive action out of the Japanese government.

This emphasis on consensus is, in part, a product of Japanese values and expectations about how human relations within groups should be maintained. Japanese culture attaches great importance to avoidance of direct confrontation. As a noted psychiatrist puts it, "The Japanese hate to contradict or to be contradicted—that is, to have to say 'No' in the conversation. They simply don't want to have divided opinions in the first place."[28] To Americans, a decision by a majority overruling a minor-

26. Testimony by Assistant Secretary of State John Richardson, Jr., in *Japan-United States Friendship Act*, Hearings before the Senate Commitee on Foreign Relations, 93:2 (Government Printing Office, 1974), p. 66.

27. Interview confirmed in letter to Hideo Sato, from Donald Kendall, Jan. 16, 1976. For a description of Kendall's textile experience, see pp. 137 and 138, below.

28. Takeo Doi, "Some Psychological Themes," in John C. Condon and Mitsuko Saito, eds., *Intercultural Encounters with Japan: Communication—Contact and Conflict* (Tokyo: Simul Press, 1974), p. 22. Students of Japanese culture sometimes stress the impact of a crowded environment on social relationships: the existence of a large population on small islands, secluded from the rest of the world, limited until recently

ity is legitimate, and the minority is supposed to adhere to it even if its views and needs are not accommodated. To Japanese, maximum effort should be made to involve and accommodate a potentially dissident minority in the process of decisionmaking; something decided by a majority and imposed without such an effort at accommodation is viewed as arbitrary and overbearing. Americans also believe, formally, that hierarchical rank gives its holders the right to make decisions and have them obeyed. By contrast, Japanese values emphasize the obligation of a senior officeholder to take due account of the views and sensitivities of his subordinates, even where this borders on rubber-stamping their recommendations.

These Japanese values lead logically (and practically) to a preference for broad participation as organizations debate their objectives and means of attaining them. They also lead to heavy reliance on substantive initiatives from persons lower in the hierarchy. When excessive delay can be avoided, and when the interests of those involved can in fact be accommodated by a policy accepted (though not necessarily preferred) by potential dissidents, then implementation can be remarkably smooth since those who must carry out the decision already understand and are committed to it.[29] And even where decisions are made by smaller

---

in geographic and social mobility even within those islands, seems to have induced Japanese to make special efforts to avoid friction and confrontation among themselves, particularly within the groups and communities where they would be spending their entire lives.

29. Richard Tanner Johnson and William G. Ōuchi, in "Made in America (Under Japanese Management)," *Harvard Business Review*, September–October 1974, pp. 61–69, discuss the advantages of a consensus, participatory management style within particular business firms. "Contrary to what many Westerners think, the Japanese system does not demand that all participants 'sign off.' Those who affix their seals to the document containing the decision are indicating their consent, which is not the same as their approval. Each participant is indicating satisfaction that his point of view has been fairly heard, and while he may not wholly agree that the decision is the best one, he is willing to go along with and, even more, to support it. In this manner, the Japanese sidestep the nearly impossible task of obtaining unanimity." (Ibid., p. 66.) Thus, the fact that he is consulted may bring a Japanese participant to acquiesce in a decision about which he retains substantive reservations, whereas had he not been consulted he might well have resisted. A related means by which the consensual style sidesteps the unanimity problem is through standards, also consensually determined, by which the parties "qualified" and "eligible" to influence a given issue are separated from the "unqualified" and "noneligible." These standards are usually based on seniority, general achievement, or specific responsibility and competence.

circles, there is often exceptionally broad consultation and information-sharing across jurisdictional and organizational lines. Japanese business and government leaders, for example, seem much more aware of important decisions being taken in each other's spheres than is the case in the United States, where the government-business relationship is more an adversary one.

There are also, however, very practical and pragmatic political reasons for Japanese leaders to apply a consensual style to broader political issues. In any society there are certain types of issues on which interests and opinions are so sharply and deeply divided that leaders risk major unrest if they initiate decisive actions on them. Decisions that are taken have to be based on compromise supported by at least an apparent consensus. Most frequently, decisions are avoided or deferred as long as the circumstances permit. In postwar Japan this has been true of many foreign policy issues—as well as some more basic constitutional issues.

In the United States, postwar disagreements on foreign policy issues have seldom been strictly along party lines. Majorities on foreign policy issues tend to be ad hoc, and U.S. senators and congressmen habitually cross party lines in their votes. In Japan, by contrast, the Liberal Democratic party is assured of the needed votes in every major legislative battle. If the rule of majoritarianism were strictly followed, the views of a large portion of the Japanese populace would be ignored. Their reaction would be to question the very legitimacy of the system and the ruling regime, as many Japanese did when Kishi used his numerical majority to push the revised security treaty through in 1960. Thus in a one-party dominant system like that of postwar Japan, pragmatic concern for democracy dictates that a pure and simple majoritarianism be tempered by considerations for minority interests and opinion.

The Japanese emphasis on consensus procedures in arriving at decisions can be thus attributed in part to the divisive nature of certain foreign policy issues and the lack of prior substantive consensus on them. And this applies not only to national political divisions, but those within the government as well. Japanese policymaking institutions are exceptionally closed. Bureaucratic and political elites are self-contained and slowly changing; issues tend to be dominated, where feasible, by organizational subsystems of middle-level specialists. But the cohesiveness of particular groups means that conflict between them can be notably bitter—as between MITI and the Gaimushō on textiles.[30] Consensus decisionmaking is a means of bridging these internal gaps. The existence of political as well as cultural roots for consensus decisionmaking is suggested also by its presence in other countries. In the United States even policies with full presidential sponsorship are much more easily implemented, much less subject to assaults, if they are backed by a broad coalition inside and outside the executive branch—indeed, they often cannot succeed without one. Similarly, bureaucrats must establish broad interagency participation and agreement if they are to pursue policy courses requiring a wide range of official actions, and to maintain the broad working-level communication and trust essential to effective operations. Thus, an analysis of U.S. policymaking in the early postwar period stressed the "strain toward agreement," the "need to build a consensus that includes, as it were, one's enemies as well as one's friends."[31] And in cases like Okinawa, efforts to build such consensus have been successful.

Nor should one assume that the Japanese preference for consensus means that policymaking on controversial issues is always immobilized by the need to get incompatible actors to agree. Shigeru Yoshida virtually dictated his policy on the 1951 peace treaty and the accompanying security treaty. His times were indeed quite exceptional and afforded him much greater freedom of action than any other postwar premier has enjoyed. In 1956, however, his successor Ichiro Hatoyama accomplished the peace settlement with the Soviet Union despite strong and sustained opposition of many of his colleagues in the Liberal Democratic party as well as that of the Foreign Ministry. And Nobusuke Kishi, of course, breached the rule of consensual decisionmaking by pushing the revision of the U.S.-Japan Mutual Security Treaty through the Diet.[32]

30. Chie Nakane argues that the traditional emphasis on vertical interpersonal relationships in Japan often militates against horizontal coordination and harmony between organized groups, such as government ministries and political party factions (*Japanese Society* [University of California Press, 1970]).

31. Warner R. Schilling, "The Politics of National Defense, Fiscal 1950," in Warner R. Schilling, Paul Y. Hammond, and Glenn H. Snyder, *Strategy, Politics, and Defense Budgets* (Columbia University Press, 1962), p. 23.

32. In those cases where the Japanese government makes major policy departures, it seems to operate very much as the American government operates in such cases: A small, ad hoc group develops, usually combining political and career officials; and this group has considerable day-to-day latitude in what steps to take and whom to consult, provided that due regard is paid to the major interests involved. (See Haruhiro Fukui, "Foreign Policy Making in Japan: Case Studies for Empirical

Nonetheless, on issues involving deep conflicts among interests, decisions do often come more slowly in Japan than in the United States. On textiles, for example, it was President Nixon who decided the basic U.S. negotiating stance, ignoring or overriding substantial opposition in the process, maintaining his position until finally successful. In Japan, however, political leaders and senior bureaucrats were repeatedly deferring to their colleagues, to business leaders, and to subordinates. They seemed unwilling to force a position on them, reluctant to move toward decisive action to settle the issue until the other interested parties, including especially the textile leaders, were "on board." The premier, the MITI minister, senior officials, business leaders—all deferred strong moves time and again because a consensus had not jelled.

Strong action on textiles was, of course, easier for Nixon than for Sato. The President was aligned with the most interested party—the textile industry. In Japan, decisive action meant going against that industry's interests. This maximized the political risks for any Japanese politician who stepped forward and proposed such action, and encouraged all to seek the protection of collective responsibility. Yet cultural styles and expectations were clearly a factor, also, in Sato's reluctance to press his ministers too forcefully for particular solutions, despite his deep personal stake in reaching a textile accord. Conversely, perceived breaches of the principle of consensus created ill feelings between Sato and the Japanese textile industry and damaged the prospects for agreement. Sato believed that industry concessions were vital to serve the overriding Japanese interest in the U.S. relationship. He felt that the industry was not behaving properly—was putting its selfish interests above the interests of the collectivity—when it failed to come around after he personally emphasized the need for agreement. The textile leaders, on the other hand, suspected that Sato had made secret concessions about which they had not been consulted, which they saw as a major breach in the proper procedure for handling such issues.

The value placed on consensus in Japan is reflected also in the effort

---

Theory" [paper prepared for delivery at 1974 meeting of the Association for Asian Studies; processed]). This pattern is very similar to that of the "ad hoc groups" which a recent senior participant describes and recommends for the management of important *United States* foreign policy issues. (See the testimony of Francis Bator, deputy special assistant to President Johnson for national security affairs, in *U.S. Foreign Economic Policy: Implications for the Organization of the Executive Branch*, Hearings before the House Committee on Foreign Affairs, 92:2 [GPO, 1972], p. 114.)

to avoid having obvious winners and losers on issues, and in the reluctance of officials in leadership positions to visibly move out front and summon support overtly in the public arena, or even in private cabinet meetings. Even Tanaka as MITI minister, who forced a textile agreement on his bureaucracy in a notable departure from the consensus style, continued to voice his resistance to such an agreement in press conferences—and even, apparently, in cabinet meetings—until long after he had determined to force through a solution on U.S. terms. And unlike Kishi in 1960, Tanaka was able to handle his issue without overriding textile quota opponents in a winner-loser fashion. Rather he bore the brunt of a *national* loss that many Japanese now felt essential to put an end to the issue. By so doing Tanaka gained politically from textiles, whereas Kishi undercut his legitimacy by winning on the security treaty and was forced to resign.

This Japanese emphasis on consensus often irritates American negotiators, for such decisionmaking necessarily becomes time-consuming and sometimes produces minimal, temporizing decisions. Americans are likely to attribute these unsatisfactory results to political weakness or conscious delaying tactics. In November 1970, for example, MITI and Foreign Ministry officials had to revise the Japanese stance on textiles after the second Sato-Nixon summit, where the premier had endorsed a rather specific restriction formula. But they were unable to get textile industry representatives to acquiesce in even a considerably looser formula. So rather than presenting a proposal over industry opposition, MITI Minister Miyazawa and Foreign Minister Aichi cabled Ambassador Nobuhiko Ushiba a summary of the MITI-industry discussions and representative positions. When Ushiba presented this "position paper" at the first session of the resumed talks Peter Flanigan, the U.S. negotiator, was taken aback. He expressed extreme unhappiness with the failure of the Japanese government to take a clear stance. And there were many other instances in the talks when Americans were frustrated by Japanese delays and failure to come up with a counterproposal; these tended to be attributed to a conscious central decision to avoid or delay an agreement—an outcome, of course, that some Japanese actors did seek.

Japanese consensus values can also cause American officials to misread Tokyo politics more generally. In the crisis of 1960, much of the intense, widespread anti-Kishi feeling in Japan grew from the premier's breaches of consensus values—his forcing the treaty through the Diet, his ignoring or disregarding of public sentiment. But Ambassador Mac-Arthur interpreted the domestic confrontation as an essentially two-sided contest in which one side or the other, Kishi or the antitreaty coalition of the left, would have to prevail. Thus his cabled reports emphasized how "democracy in Japan now stands at crossroads," and his exhortations to Japanese moderates to do battle with the left stressed that "as a believer in Christian principles he saw no possibility of compromise between right and wrong."[33] Given such an interpretation, it was hardly surprising that MacArthur saw potential disaster if the leftist parties and demonstrators achieved any of three objectives—preventing Eisenhower's visit, forcing Kishi's resignation, reversing ratification of the treaty. In fact, they achieved two of them. But the result was not the fundamental setback for U.S. interests that MacArthur feared, for Kishi was replaced by a more moderate LDP premier, Hayato Ikeda, who stuck by the treaty and still won electoral endorsement and general domestic support. This middle-road solution reflected consensus values in several ways. By the end of May there was an overwhelming sentiment in Japan that Kishi would have to go because his "arbitrary" and "undemocratic" behavior had violated procedural norms; many LDP members and adherents shared in this view. But this did not mean most Japanese wanted or expected the Socialists to come to power; indeed, after the demonstrations took a violent turn, there was a reaction against the left as well. Similarly, MacArthur's cold-war-style, right-and-wrong formulation was at variance with the substantive Japanese consensus for minimal involvement in the ideological confrontation, a consensus that included supporters of the security alliance with the United States as well as opponents. Under all of these circumstances, what was necessary for resolving the crisis was that it be defused, which required Kishi's departure from power and a public deemphasis of security and ideological issues by his successor.

Related to the emphasis on consensus is the tendency of the Japanese to formulate their stands on issues during—rather than before—negotiations; they tend to *adapt* themselves to initiatives taken by others. And even when they initiate a negotiation, they have difficulty presenting particular proposals until there is not only domestic consensus but a basis for telling what the other side will accept. In contrast, Americans tend to emphasize initiatives and direction and work for agreement on

33. Cable no. 4081, U.S. Embassy, Tokyo, to Secretary of State, June 8, 1960, and an Embassy cable of June 11, 1960, as paraphrased in Parsons, "Chronology."

a specific proposal they set forth at the outset of negotiation.[34] On Okinawa, Sato made a specific request for home-level, nuclear-free reversion by 1972 only after several years of bilateral interaction on the issue; in the textile case, the U.S. government developed a specific substantive proposal very early and insisted on it throughout the dispute with very little modification.

These contrasting styles—Americans taking the initiative and Japanese adapting—may seem complementary. But the Japanese, in trying to accommodate the other side's position, expect their negotiating counterparts to respond in kind. They may be driven to strong resentment and resistance by efforts of the other side to force a settlement from a position of superior strength, just as they resent breach of consensus or "tyranny of the majority" in their domestic system. Exactly this sort of resistance arose repeatedly on the textile issue. However, in the case of Okinawa—where the Japanese were doing the asking—this difference in styles of negotiation worked to the advantage of both sides. The slow emergence of the Japanese position on specific terms gave American actors sympathetic to reversion time to bring their government around; indeed, the consensus on possible terms that was emerging in Washington fed importantly into Japanese decisionmaking and the consensus that emerged there.

Amae and Sincerity

Another cultural source of misperception in U.S.-Japanese relations is the Japanese psychological and cultural orientation known as *amae*. Essentially, *amae* refers to the attitude and expectations of the inferior or weaker party in a relationship of dependence with a superior party.

34. Kinhide Mushakōji calls the American style one of *erabi* (choosing) and the Japanese one of *awase* (adapting) (*Kokusai seiji to Nihon* [International politics and Japan], [Tokyo: Tokyo University Press, 1967], pp. 155–75). This difference in style is related to divergent attitudes toward the environment. Japanese culture shares with some non-Western cultures an emphasis on harmony with external environments, be they human or natural. Man is supposed to adjust or adapt himself. In Western society, on the other hand, man is supposed to control and change his external environment for his own purposes. For development of this contrast, see ibid.; Charles A. Moore, ed., *The Japanese Mind: Essentials of Japanese Philosophy and Culture* (Honolulu: University Press of Hawaii, 1967); and Hajime Nakamura, *Ways of Thinking of Eastern Peoples: India-China-Tibet-Japan* (Honolulu: University Press of Hawaii, 1964). Certainly the American tendency to emphasize initiatives and direction and the Japanese tendency toward passive adaptation derive also from the asymmetry of the power relationship between the two countries. The asymmetric relationship seems to reinforce this difference in cultural style.

It involves an assumption that the stronger will have indulgence for the weaker party, that the stronger will recognize an obligation to take care of and protect the weaker without requiring a reciprocal obligation.[35] Americans, by contrast, tend to think of relationships in terms of reciprocity—particularly when the parties are formally equal.

Amae explains in part why leaders in Japanese organizations may feel obligated to their followers. Leaders of the textile industry, for example, had to take care of the interests of the smaller firms, whereas the latter had no reciprocal obligation to place their demands within the framework of the overall interests of the industry. That kind of expectation sometimes carries over into international relations. The United States fits into the role of the superior partner vis à vis Japan, the older brother from whom much has been received and from whom much continues to be expected. Prime Minister Sato, for example, was apparently indulging in *amae*-type optimism when he hoped, on several occasions, that Nixon would be sympathetic to his domestic predicament on textiles. He seems to have assumed that Japan's patron, the United States—perhaps even Richard Nixon personally—would somehow accommodate Japan's and Sato's political needs because the United States was the stronger party. To Nixon, however, what was right and proper was that Sato should *reciprocate* politically for Nixon's agreement to return Okinawa.

Closely related to *amae* in Japanese society is the importance placed on demonstrating sincerity. The spirit in which a person approaches another is likely to be as important in achieving a favorable response as the substance of what is sought. Two people in a negotiating situation may not agree at first, but once one of them can demonstrate that he is sincerely doing his best to accommodate the other's interests, the other person will be inclined to reciprocate his sincerity by making reasonable concessions. Particularly if the former is the weaker of the two, the latter is more likely to make such concessions. This contrasts with Americans' tendency to place emphasis on what each party actually concedes.

In early summer 1941, Ambassador Kichisaburō Nomura and Secretary of State Cordell Hull were engaged in talks seeking a political accommodation that might arrest their countries' move toward war. On July 12, Japanese leaders were discussing how to respond to Hull's stiff counterproposal, which had included an oral statement indicating that

35. See Takeo Doi, *The Anatomy of Dependence*, trans. John Bester (Tokyo and New York: Kodansha International, 1973).

recent public statements of the Japanese foreign minister might pose "an insurmountable roadblock to the negotiation." Tōjō, then war minister, suggested to his colleagues that they should keep negotiating with America even if there seemed to be little hope. "Naturally the Oral Statement is an insult to our *kokutai* [national essence] and we must reject it. . . . But what if we *sincerely* tell the Americans what we hold to be right? Won't this move them?"[36]

In the postwar era, the most dramatic public example of the Japanese *amae* mentality and sincerity cult was the acceptance of Article Nine of the constitution of 1947 authored by the American occupation authorities. This renunciation of war and arms was founded, for many Japanese, on faith in the power of Japanese sincerity to dissuade potential aggressors from attacking. They felt such sincerity in pursuit of world peace would be rewarded by understanding from cooperative "peace-loving" nations of the world, who would help protect Japan not only by refraining from themselves committing aggression, but also by defending her—if necessary—with their own troops and arms through the United Nations peace-keeping machinery.

Such faith appeared increasingly naive to Americans becoming inured to the cold war. Many Japanese political leaders and senior foreign policy bureaucrats were also skeptical. The problem, as with less sweeping manifestations of this style in interpersonal negotiations, was that the other side might perceive it as an indication of weakness. When MITI Minister Ohira accepted Commerce Secretary Stans's proposal of July 1969 to hold "technical discussions" on the textile issue between expert representatives of the two countries, he apparently did so as a demonstration of his sincerity and willingness to give consideration to Stans's political needs even though he was convinced the Americans did not have a good substantive case. He apparently hoped that Stans's face would be saved and America's "unreasonable" push for controls would be significantly modified. For the Americans, however, the predominant interpretation was that now that the Japanese had conceded something, they were likely to concede more if pressure were maintained. Some considered the "technical discussions" label to be a face-saving device for Ohira and believed (incorrectly) that the discussions as carried out would include consideration of U.S. proposals.

On several occasions Prime Minister Sato acted as if he felt a demon-

36. John Toland, *The Rising Sun: The Decline and Fall of the Japanese Empire, 1936–1945* (Bantam, 1971), p. 97. Emphasis added.

stration of sincerity on his part could bring American concessions on a resolution of the textile impasse. One dramatic example was in June 1970, when MITI Minister Miyazawa flew to Washington for three days of private talks with Stans. Sato's method of making his "utmost efforts" to resolve the issue was not to intervene directly in the substantive debate within Japan for major modification of Japan's negotiating position in the direction Washington desired. Instead, he dispatched his foreign minister, Aichi, to join Miyazawa in Washington, and sent with Aichi a personal message to Nixon expressing Sato's desire to be helpful to the President on this issue and indicating he was doing all that he could. When Miyazawa did not concede on the substance, however, American leaders were not particularly mollified by Sato's letter or the fact that he had sent Aichi also; indeed, they do not seem to have understood his message at all.

An effort to demonstrate sincerity can even provoke bitter American reaction if found wanting on substantive grounds. In March 1970 a Japanese aide-mémoire on textiles was transmitted to the American government in an effort to break the impasse. It was, for those Japanese officials in Tokyo (and at the Washington embassy) who pressed it, a sincere effort to be as responsive to American needs on the issue as the politics of the issue in Japan would allow. It arrived at the Commerce Department, however, during a meeting of the Management-Labor Advisory Committee on textiles, an active, assertive group of textile industry and union leaders who had pressed for restrictive U.S. proposals and were frustrated by the lack of results. They angrily denounced the document as "arrogant" and unhelpful, because it did not come close to their terms on substance, and it suggested a U.S. Tariff Commission investigation of the extent of import-induced injury to the American textile industry. The Tariff Commission had been unsympathetic to the industry's case in the past and the committee members could only assume it would continue to be.

Haragei Bargaining

Related to the emphasis on sincerity is the frequent Japanese preference for sorting out issues by gut, nonverbal (*haragei*) bargaining, a time-consuming talking around a problem until a consensus begins to develop and each participant can work out his own individual way to adapt to it. *Haragei* can also be used to signal resistance, as MITI bureaucrats did during the 1969–71 negotiations when they emphasized "maintaining a spirit of confidence" between the government and the textile industry—meaning that the former should not act against the latter's wishes. However used, *haragei* reflects a cultural difference: "Americans do not grasp the fact that language plays an unusual role in Japan. Americans set great store by the literal meaning of words; Japanese are much more interested in the relationships and impressions that go unspoken."[37] According to Masao Kunihiro, "the art of *haragei* is very much a Japanese technique of communication. . . . In the use of this word there exists a feeling of a community of emotions, that is, a desire to be given special consideration (again related to *amae*) since the other man is considered to be your friend, a member of your group."[38] The problem, as Kunihiro goes on to explain, is that *haragei* communication works well only among members of an intimate group brought up in the same culture. Thus in cross-cultural dealings this style of communication often causes confusion or misunderstandings.[39]

In the pre-Pearl Harbor negotiations, Japanese leaders who were anxious to avoid war with the United States proposed a summit conference between President Roosevelt and Premier Fumimaro Konoye. They believed that agreement could be reached if such high-level person-to-person talks were "carried out with broadmindedness." Konoye apparently thought that if he personally met with Roosevelt and was able to convey his "gut" situation and sentiments (*hara o waru*),[40] his weaknesses and needs as a human being, the President would somehow understand his (and Japan's) position and seek a way to accommodate it. But the proposal was not accepted. President Roosevelt seemed in-

37. Bernard Krisher, *Newsweek*, Aug. 6, 1974.

38. Masao Kunihiro, "U.S.-Japan Communications," in Henry Rosovsky, ed., *Discord in the Pacific: Challenges to the Japanese-American Alliance* (Columbia Books for American Assembly, 1972), p. 167.

39. *Haragei* is not limited to Japan. A similar type of communication exists elsewhere among people of homogeneous background, including the United States. Here again the difference is in the realm of degree. And even in Japanese domestic politics, *haragei* does not work where very deep conflicts of interest or opinion exist, as between the Liberal Democratic party and the Japan Communist party.

40. In 1956, Ichirō Kōno, one of the most powerful LDP leaders, conducted direct personal negotiations with Premier Nikita Khrushchev in Moscow without the help of a Japanese interpreter. His rationale was that the language barrier could be overcome by the mutual trust generated if he "opened his heart." Prime Minister Hatoyama's Russian trip that followed also had a *haragei* flavor, though to a lesser degree.

clined to meet Konoye, but did not push the matter in the face of strong
skepticism among his key advisers: Secretary of War Stimson, who wrote
in his diary that "the invitation to the President is merely a blind to try
to keep us from taking definite action"; Secretary of State Hull, who
seems to have recognized that Konoye might be personally sincere, but
"doubted the Premier's capacity to bring the military into line." So the
Americans insisted that the summit must be preceded by "a meeting of
minds on essential points," and in turn, Japanese military leaders—who
felt they had yielded a good deal in acquiescing in the idea of a summit
meeting—saw Washington's coldness as new evidence of the futility of
negotiating with the Americans.[41]

Prior to his departure for Washington for his second summit textile
discussion with President Nixon in October 1970, Prime Minister Sato
reportedly stated: "Since Mr. Nixon and I are old friends, the negotiations will be three parts talk and seven parts *haragei*."[42] Although the
premier was not sure he could make all the substantive concessions the
Americans were demanding, he apparently believed that something
would be worked out if only he personally talked to Nixon again. A personal meeting, a chance to convey his gut situation as one man to another, might help Nixon understand why he had been unable to deliver
on his promise of a year earlier, so the President would not think Sato
had designedly deceived him. For Nixon, however, what mattered was
the terms of settlement; he refused to engage in any *haragei*-style discussion, insisting instead on Sato's personal endorsement of an explicit
American five-point proposal as the basis for agreement.[43] And when
Sato assented and then failed to deliver, further damage was done to
relations between the two men and the governments they headed.

41. Feis, *Road to Pearl Harbor*, pp. 258–60; Burns, *Roosevelt: Soldier of Freedom*,
pp. 134–37 and 144; Toland, *Rising Sun*, pp. 102–10.

42. Kunihiro, "U.S.-Japan Communications," p. 167.

43. Keidanren President Kogorō Uemura apparently made a similar mistake
when he visited the United States in October 1970 to sound out major U.S. officials
and business leaders on textiles prior to this second summit. He thought discussions
conducted on general terms might lead to a way out of the textile impasse and
apparently concluded that just because he emphasized a "spirit of mutual concession"
and the Americans did not particularly object to it, they were actually prepared to
make necessary concessions. For the Americans the "spirit of mutual concession" had
no serious substantive implications. But for Uemura, who was used to *haragei*
communications, a tacit understanding of such a general posture was very important.
Consequently, he advised Sato to resume the negotiations.

Form versus Substance

In his 1973 foreign policy report to Congress, President Nixon chided Tokyo for placing such emphasis on Washington's having undertaken major policy changes in 1971 on China and international trade without prior consultation with Japan. A "mature alliance relationship," Nixon wrote, "means seriously addressing the underlying causes, not the superficial public events."[44] Such a relatively gentle rebuke might have been accepted quite calmly—or dismissed as mere verbiage—by a Western nation. But Japanese reacted as if they had been slapped. "The underlying thought of the statement," one ranking Japanese official said, "is 'what matters is the substance not the form.' For Japanese, where 'face' is involved, the form is as important and sometimes more important than the substance."[45]

In Japan, officials and politicians pay considerably greater respect to formal jurisdictions than do their American counterparts. To bypass those with formal responsibility for all or part of an issue is to humiliate them, whether they be subordinates or superiors or those in other offices. So formal prerogatives are carefully observed, even while active informal networks make it possible to move issues forward. If due respect is paid to an official's position, he may well not insist on exercising his substantive prerogatives.

One manifestation of this emphasis on form arose in mid-1945 when the Suzuki cabinet was trying to bring about Japan's surrender on terms that could be considered honorable. What really mattered to them—and to Japanese more generally after the surrender—was not so much the "substance" of imperial divinity and sovereignty, but rather the "form" of maintaining the imperial institution. Thus there was remarkably little resistance from his loyal subjects when the emperor, following occupation orders, renounced his divinity and was then reduced in the new constitution to the status of merely a "symbol" of national unity.

On the Okinawa reversion issue, American officials recognized the importance of form to the Japanese and were able to meet this need. The form of the decision that Japanese wanted—home-level reversion— was understood early in the game as the probable political requirement in Japan. Those in the U.S. government who recognized this were able

44. *U.S. Foreign Policy for the 1970s: Shaping a Durable Peace: A Report to the Congress by Richard Nixon* (GPO, 1973), p. 104.
45. *Newsweek*, Aug. 6, 1974, p. 35.

to put the substantive terms important to Americans into a home-level package suitable in form to Tokyo. The issue of nuclear weapons was left unresolved until the November 1969 summit meeting because it was feared that their removal might not be negotiable within the Washington bureaucracy; yet their retention would breach the form, since nuclear storage was not allowed on Japan's main islands. So it was left to the President to make a separate decision on nuclear storage; by the time he did, the balance of argument was clearly against it and his decision reflected this. (Of course, Japanese concern about nuclear weapons had strong substantive roots as well.)

In the textile negotiations, however, Japanese emphasis on form led to confusion and misunderstanding. At a bilateral Geneva conference in November 1969, the Japanese delegates insisted that any textile restraint agreement must maintain the form of "objective proof of injury" to the U.S. industry caused by imports. So they placed particular emphasis on establishing multilateral machinery for injury investigation, but gave signals that this would be rather flexibly applied. In fact, a directive from Tokyo on November 19 specified: "Even if proof of injury was absent, a Working Group consisting of the four Far Eastern countries might still consider some sort of export control, including the creation of a 'trigger mechanism' to alleviate the potential threat of imports to the United States industry."[46] However, the Americans wanted to first make sure that such a working group would in fact act favorably on American proposals for import restrictions. They either did not understand—or thought it insufficient—that if the United States accepted the Japanese-proposed form, the latter would feel they had an obligation to take American substantive interests fairly into account.

The issue became more complicated when, two months later, the Japanese government was unable to follow through on its suggestions that formal American concessions would lead to substantive Japanese ones. In mid-January 1970, the newly designated MITI minister, Miyazawa, suggested that once the United States presented information purporting to prove injury to the U.S. textile industry from imports, Japan might consider it as establishing actual injury even if the evidence was

---

46. This is described further in I. M. Destler, Hideo Sato, and Haruhiro Fukui, "The Textile Wrangle: Conflict in Japanese-American Relations 1969–71" (1976; processed), chap. 6. The "trigger mechanism" was a device by which sharp rises of exports in particular textile categories would automatically bring quantitative restrictions into play.

not convincing. The Americans did submit detailed injury materials, but Japanese actors who were strongly opposed to concessions on substantive grounds withheld their assent, and Miyazawa was unable to make the positive response he had suggested.

In December 1970, however, American concessions on matters of form came close to settling the issue. The U.S. negotiators accepted the format of an agreement (export ceilings based not on individual product categories but on groups of categories) that the Japanese government had developed, but proposed changes in its details that would make its practical effects very close to what the Americans had persistently sought. The Sato government responded positively, and the two sides moved to the verge of agreement. Had the White House not then toughened its stance under industry pressure, the textile issue might have been settled at this point.

As these examples indicate, attention to form is closely related to consensus decisionmaking. Respect for form includes efforts to assure that all relevant actors are properly consulted. It can also include adoption of a principle important to certain policy actors ("objective proof of injury" on textiles), but with adjustments in its practical application that result in an actual outcome at variance with their preferences. In both cases, attention to form gives potential dissidents a face-saving way out: they have a chance to participate in the decision; they win acceptance of their principle. And just as consensus and form are closely related, both are linked to *haragei* and *amae*. *Haragei* minimizes unnecessary verbal exchanges that might lead to confrontation; consensus is thereby approached as contestants feel each other out, read one another's minds. *Amae* facilitates *haragei*-type communications, particularly if one side (or both) reveals its weaknesses to the other. And the emphasis on consensus and form can fulfill an *amae* expectation of weaker parties that others will at least listen to them and seek to accommodate them. Moreover, by eventually conforming to the general sentiment of the group, dissidents can enhance their *amae* expectation that the group will take care of their interests more generally, in other ways.

None of these cultural patterns is unique to Japan; they probably exist in some form in all societies. But their particular importance to Japanese means that Americans dealing with that country need to be especially sensitive to these procedures and expectations, just as Japanese need to recognize that such sensitivity will not always be present in international negotiations. On most of the instances noted here, for example, accurate American perception of Japanese attention to form proved productive. This was not, of course, always the case, and none of the differences in cultural style highlighted here will necessarily prove the decisive barrier to an agreement in any given case. But they are relevant and potentially important factors in all such negotiations. Officials will ignore them at their peril.

Universalism and Cultural Arrogance

Not all culturally based misperceptions and misunderstandings have Japanese roots. Indeed, the very idea that when the two cultures differ it is the Japanese who are unusual reflects a general American cultural tendency that creates continuing problems in dealings with Japan, and with other countries as well.

Many students of American foreign policy have pointed out the tendency of Americans to believe that the policies they pursue reflect not just U.S. interests, but universal interests—if not of all countries, at least those that are allied with the United States. Thus American officials and political leaders are inclined to believe either that people in other countries share U.S. perceptions of common threats and common goals, or that they need to be persuaded that American policies fully reflect their own interests. On cold-war-related issues in particular, Americans have tended to resist the notion that allies have distinct sets of interests, or that the conceptual framework of leaders in other countries may be markedly different from their own.

In postwar U.S.-Japanese dealings, the guardian-ward relationship offered unusual opportunities for the expression of such universalism. During and after occupation, Americans saw their country as the benefactor of Japan, and on many security or economic issues Japanese in turn relied on the United States either to protect their interests or to speak for them in international forums. To many Americans, the occupation had reformed Japan along the lines of American values. This belief led some Americans to treat Japanese with condescension. One manifestation of this sense of superiority was the notion that "our military leaders somehow had a better grasp of the potential threats to Japan than the Japanese themselves";[47] those who did not share U.S. perceptions were militarily naive and required educating. And the popular criticism of the 1960s, that the Americans were shouldering a dispropor-

47. George R. Packard, "A Crisis in Understanding," in Rosovsky, *Discord in the Pacific*, p. 120.

tionate burden of the "common defense," implied that the magnitude and shape of U.S. security efforts in Asia served Japanese interests as much as American.

All of these characteristics were further reinforced by postwar Japanese reticence in articulating any clear conceptions of national security interests, let alone conceptions distinct from the Americans'.

Intertwined with this universalism is a cultural arrogance, historically familiar, that assumes—explicitly or implicitly—that the values and practices of one's own culture are the standard by which others' behavior should be judged. In American foreign relations, this has given rise to a messianic belief that the United States was setting an example for all peoples. In the words of one Japanese analyst, Americans who had pioneered in creating a new world felt "their faith and values were the best in the world, and the values of different cultures were regarded as inferior."[48] And for many Americans, he might have added, others' inferiority was the greater the more they deviated from the American standard.

When cultural arrogance becomes acute and focuses on distinctions based on ethnic origins, it is appropriate to call it "racism." Racism is hardly an exclusively American characteristic; many ethnic or larger groups, including Japanese, conceive of themselves as superior to certain other groups.[49] But American racism can cause particular difficulties because of (1) American power and (2) American universalism, which tends to mask for Americans some aspects of such racism even as it makes it particularly unpalatable to others. Such racism was particularly evident in the anti-Japanese immigration legislation early in this century, and in public campaigns against the sale or purchase of Japanese textiles and other products in the postwar period. Nor has it entirely

---

48. Hiroshi Kitamura, *Psychological Dimensions of U.S.-Japanese Relations,* Occasional Papers in International Affairs, no. 28 (Center for International Affairs, Harvard University, 1971), p. 21. Stanley Hoffmann emphasizes a different aspect of Americans' cultural biases: "Americans, whose history is a success story, tend to believe that the values that arise from their experience are of universal application, and they are reluctant to recognize that they are tied to the special conditions that made the American success possible." ("The American Style: Our Past and Our Principles," *Foreign Affairs,* vol. 46 [January 1968], p. 363.)

49. Japanese racism is important for understanding that country's relations with groups and nationalities to whom Japanese have tended to feel themselves superior— for example, Koreans. But because the typical Japanese attitude toward Americans since World War II has been closer to the opposite, it does not bear on the bilateral relationship the way that U.S. racism does.

disappeared; many observers saw racism in the way Maurice Stans approached the textile issue and felt that the Nixon administration's handling of the issue was more brutal than would have been the case had a European power been the target.

Americans' cultural arrogance can lead to underestimation of Japanese capabilities—as many American officials did prior to World War II. And when Japanese perform well by American standards, as on the world economic scene in the late sixties and early seventies, this refutation of American notions of superiority provides a ready market for explanations that the Japanese succeeded because they were somehow unfair, or did things in some fundamentally different way—charges never without some supporting evidence as cultural differences mean, by definition, some playing by different rules. Hence, many Americans have conceived of "Japan, Inc." as an integrated government-business economic juggernaut moving relentlessly forward to capture larger and larger shares of world markets, with even an aura of unstoppability. Thus an American cabinet official could say in 1971: "The Japanese are still fighting the war, but it is no longer a shooting war." And the recurrent concept of a "yellow peril," usually reserved for Chinese because of their large numbers, is applied also to Japan.

Reflecting the shallowness of American cultural exposure to Japan, such stereotyping is susceptible to quick change. Thus Japanese can be docile and hard-working, or relentless and inscrutably overpowering in economic enterprise; or they can be deceitful and untrustworthy, essentially impossible to deal with except through direct coercion. President Nixon, who came to office generally sympathetic to Japan and her conservative political leaders, reacted to Sato's failure to deliver on the textile issue by holding up Japan and Japanese cultural traits to contempt and ridicule.[50]

Language Differences

Underlying all of the differences in cultural values and styles, all of these causes of misperception, is the language barrier. Not only do America and Japan not share a common tongue; their two languages represent very different ways of thinking, in two very different civilizations. Reminiscing about the textile dispute in January 1973, former Premier Sato remarked that "if only Japan and the United States had a

50. See, for example, Marvin Kalb and Bernard Kalb, *Kissinger* (Little, Brown, 1974), p. 255.

common language things would have worked out smoothly." Whether this is true for that case is doubtful, but Sato's observation is a very apt general illustration of the sense of frustration, of communications difficulty, that American and Japanese officials often feel because they must talk through interpreters.

Interestingly, there are few decisive examples of mistranslation in the postwar period.[51] In 1941, after U.S. cryptographers broke the Japanese diplomatic codes, American mistranslation of the Japanese internal communications that U.S. leaders had gained access to seems to have exacerbated that deepening crisis. And after the Allied powers issued the Potsdam Declaration of July 1945 on the terms of Japanese surrender, Premier Suzuki's ill-worded response had the effect of converting a wait-and-see decision by a divided Japanese cabinet into an apparent rejection.[52] But on the textile negotiations, what Sato apparently meant to suggest—that his difficulties with Nixon were mainly the result of the errors of his translator at their first summit meeting—does not seem in fact to have been the case.[53] And occasionally, language differences can

51. Packard cites one moderately important case: "When Japanese Foreign Minister Takeo Fukuda visited Washington in September 1971, he held a press conference at which he was asked whether Japan would support the U.S. position on China at the United Nations General Assembly meeting that fall. His answer was 'not for the time being.' The interpreter missed the nuance of 'for the time being' and rendered the answer as a flat 'No' in English. Newspapers across the U.S. played the story as if Japan had harshly rebuked the United States. Later, it turned out that Japan did support the United States position at the U.N." ("A Crisis in Understanding," pp. 125–26.)

52. For many prewar examples, see Toland, *Rising Sun*, especially pp. 153–57. The Potsdam misunderstanding arose when Premier Suzuki spoke with Japanese reporters about the government's reaction to the Allied message. He was actively seeking some route to peace, and the cabinet had decided to withhold any response for the time being. Unfortunately, Suzuki characterized the official stance toward the declaration by using the word *mokusatsu*, whose literal meaning is "treat with silent contempt." The news agencies broadcast this language in their reports, and interpreters (Japanese as well as American) translated it directly. Thus, one week before Hiroshima, American leaders concluded that the Japanese government was set against surrender whereas in fact there was considerable support for it. However, the misperception was not so much a result of mistranslation as of Suzuki's poor choice of words. (See William Craig, *The Fall of Japan* [Dial, 1967], pp. 67–68; Herbert Feis, *The Atomic Bomb and the End of World War II* [Princeton University Press, 1966], p. 109; Robert J. C. Butow, *Japan's Decision to Surrender* [Stanford University Press, 1954], pp. 143–49; and William J. Coughlin, "The Great *Mokusatsu* Mistake," *Harper's*, March 1953, pp. 31–40.)

53. For the general story, see chap. 2, above. It receives detailed treatment in Destler, Sato, and Fukui, "The Textile Wrangle," chap. 6.

be used consciously to mutual advantage—as in the 1967 summit communiqué, where the English text pointed to Okinawa reversion within a "few years" (a general phrase chosen to avoid the impression of imminence), and the Japanese rendered the phrase as "*ryo-san-nen*," literally "two to three years," to satisfy reversionist sentiment in Japan.

But more general language problems pervade U.S.-Japanese relations. Americans sometimes underrate such problems because they expect, generally, to deal in English and have others do so. Theirs has long been a predominant world language, and the power position and relative autonomy of the United States are such that Americans have never been forced to cope with another culture on its terms as the price of survival. But since relatively few Japanese know English, this means that Americans are in fact restricted in their informal contacts to a small circle, and those Japanese end up shielding them from broader exposure to their society even as they make possible what communication in fact occurs.

In bilateral negotiations, of course, the language problem is generally handled through the use of interpreters. But this creates subtle problems of its own. In U.S.-Japanese negotiations, it is particularly important for officials to try to perceive both the political and cultural framework of their negotiating counterparts. But ironically, speaking through an interpreter tends to relieve an official at a negotiation from the pressure to do so—he speaks in his own language, and it is his interpreter's job to make his meaning clear. The principal negotiators, on both sides, are thus likely to be much less attentive and sensitive to subtle messages than they should be. And the negotiating sessions tend to be exceptionally formal and impersonal, hampering the development of mutual trust and sympathy. Such mutual trust, of course, is hardly all that is required for agreements. Resolving difficult bilateral issues is not a simple question of winning over one's negotiating counterpart, but the far more complicated one of reaching a position that can be viable in two complex national (and bureaucratic) political arenas. But relationships of personal trust can be very helpful in developing solutions, and the language barrier all too often stands in the way.

Conclusions

Whether rooted in political or in cultural differences, the misperceptions of officials in each government have frequently led them to oversimplify the politics of the other country, and in ways that rendered effective negotiations more difficult. In many cases, expectations were unjustifiably high—Eisenhower would be able to visit Japan; Nixon would respond sensitively to Sato's *haragei* approach on textiles. In other circumstances, the perception was overly negative—"the Japanese" were irrevocably determined on war in November 1941; Japanese unresponsiveness on textiles reflected calculated delaying tactics rather than problems in achieving domestic consensus. But whether optimistic or pessimistic, these misinterpretations almost always made issues harder to resolve.

Too hopeful assessments postponed the facing of tough political problems by allowing an official to indulge in wishful thinking. The other country's officials and institutions might yet behave according to his domestic needs, eliminating or reducing any need for politically painful adjustments of his own. Thus Sato in the fall of 1970 postponed serious domestic political bargaining on textiles until after he saw his "old friend" Nixon, who would understand his political predicament and somehow accommodate it. Extremely negative interpretations, on the other hand, made agreement seem less attainable than it really was, and therefore reduced the incentive to search for political accommodation. If the dominant thrust of the other government's policies appears totally contrary to that of his own, then the quest for common ground seems hopeless; an actor will not then propose initiatives that are politically risky at home in order to test the international waters. Thus Roosevelt backed away from his modus vivendi proposal in 1941; he was not going to embark on a touchy political course at home if the Japanese seemed bent on making war anyway.

If such misperceptions have pervaded U.S.-Japanese relations, why did they not pose insuperable obstacles on an issue as difficult as Okinawa? Misperceptions were not entirely absent: Gaimushō officials, for example, underestimated more than once the extent of the concessions the U.S. government might make in order to accommodate Japanese domestic politics. And the state of bargaining on Okinawa reversion within the U.S. government often made American officials reluctant to communicate important information to their Japanese counterparts, thus limiting their understanding of where Washington stood on the issue and where it was heading. In 1966–67, internal discussions were closely held lest State and Pentagon civilians' attitudes toward reversion be revealed before military acquiescence was in sight. In 1969, the issue of nuclear weapons was reserved for separate presidential decision, so State Department negotiators were unable to discuss a solution of the question in the presummit negotiations. Thus Japanese officials were kept in the dark on a vital issue. Yet a satisfactory resolution was nonetheless achieved. Why?

One reason is that the misperceptions involved were not fundamental. Foreign Ministry men and other Japanese activists may not always have known exactly where the U.S. government was on this issue and where it would ultimately stand, but they understood, increasingly, who the key American actors were, what the critical arguments among them were, and how Japanese officials might influence the outcome by when and how they raised the issue. And since in their misperception they generally erred on the side of moderate pessimism, they brought pressure to keep Japanese political doors open to less desirable solutions if the U.S. government could not be moved beyond them. In this case, the slow process of consensus decisionmaking worked to their advantage, helping prevent a premature hardening of the Japanese stand. At the same time, their American counterparts were pressing in Washington for flexibility in considering Japanese political constraints. Thus neither government got locked into a position until mutually acceptable terms of agreement were beginning to emerge. On textiles, by contrast, both sides moved—because of intense domestic pressure—to fixed (and irreconcilable) positions long before any possible basis for mutual understanding had been established.

Part of the problem, on textiles, was that on neither side did those dominating policy place priority on understanding the politics of the issue in the other capital and making reasonable adaptations to it. Instead, they responded overwhelmingly to politics at home, holding to positions that would minimize their domestic and bureaucratic political vulnerability even though these positions were unacceptable across the Pacific. Thus the misperceptions that helped to exacerbate the textile crisis and to inhibit careful calculations of what outcomes might be politically viable in the other country were caused, in part, by the lack of serious concern about the politics of the other country's decisionmaking in the first place.

Thus, though misperception and misunderstanding seriously complicated resolution of the textile case, they did not cause the dispute, nor do they explain, by themselves, why it proved so intractable. The intractability, rather, was rooted in the domination of decisionmaking on both sides—particularly the American side—by men who not only were primarily concerned with what was good domestic and bureaucratic politics on the issue (this is not untypical, and is true in a sense of Okinawa as well), but who also failed to give much weight in their political calculations to the demands of politics on the other side of the Pacific. Such considerations, however, are part of the broader question of the overall political management of controversial bilateral issues.

CHAPTER FIVE

The Interplay of National Systems

CHAPTER 4 explored how politics in each capital can cause officials to misconstrue actions taken in the other, and how cultural differences create further problems of misinterpretation and misunderstanding. Yet the problem faced by officials who seek to resolve difficult bilateral issues is still more complex. For they must deal not just with the other system, but within their own at the same time. It was not enough that Japanese politicians and bureaucrats were astute in moving the U.S. government to negotiate a revised security treaty in the 1950s, if miscalculation of their own domestic scene meant that it produced a crisis in 1960. Nor could State Department officials in 1969 apply their Japan expertise very effectively on the textile issue as long as they were disregarded or overruled on the major policy decisions at home. For a particular settlement formula can win acceptance, and can endure, only if it can command enough political support within both the Japanese and the American domestic systems to be adopted, ratified if such is required, and implemented.[1]

Yet though these systems are in important respects inward-looking and relatively self-contained, they do not operate independently of one another. Actions of officials in one capital have varied effects on the politics of decisionmaking in the other—sometimes bringing agreement nearer, sometimes retarding it. Some such effects are consciously de-

---

1. How much support is enough for such purposes is a question without easy answer. The only fair response is that "it depends"—on the nature of the issue, the actors and institutions involved, the relevant policymaking procedures, the overall distribution of power. Frequently, broader consensus will be required in Tokyo than in Washington. This is true for cultural reasons, and also because of the lesser power of the prime minister, and the greater political visibility (and controversiality) of bilateral issues in Japan.

signed, but many come from signals originating in one country that influence the other without any particular intention that they do so. How then does the interplay of the two systems develop? Is there a pattern in the *initiation* of issues, in how they rise to prominence within one of the governments? How do they then become bilateral policy problems, of live concern in both capitals? Once an issue rises to importance, what are the patterns of *interaction* between national policymaking systems? What sorts of impacts do actions, proposals, and other communications and signals from one country have on the politics of the issue in the other? What is the effect of the asymmetry of impact—the fact that events in the United States have far more impact on Japanese policymaking than vice versa? Finally, what are the routes to *resolution* of issues? What role is played by informal *transnational alliances* in which actors from both countries work together to achieve particular negotiating outcomes? And what *official channels* are employed to negotiate U.S.-Japan issues, to what effects?

Issues do not, of course, move neatly through clearly delineated stages of initiation, interaction, and resolution. Interaction occurs continuously, with initiation and negotiation toward resolution two of its particular forms. And though the three postwar cases stressed in this study led eventually to negotiated resolutions, such is not always necessary or possible. Nevertheless, an analysis organized around these questions can shed further light on the politics of bilateral relations and the problems of officials who must manage them.

Initiation of Bilateral Issues

Each of the cases highlighted in this study was pressed by a politician seeking to enhance or solidify his position. Sato raised Okinawa as a candidate in the 1964 contest for the presidency of the Liberal Democratic party; Nixon embraced textiles as a competitor for the Republican presidential nomination in 1968. And security treaty revision—though an almost inevitable Japanese objective flowing out of the unbalanced treaty of 1951—first rose to become a live issue in 1955 when Premier Hatoyama "badly needed something in the nature of a diplomatic stunt to lend glamour to his new government." Thus, he sent three powerful ruling party leaders to Washington "to sound out Dulles' reaction to a revision of the security pact,"[2] which was widely resented in Japan as an "unequal treaty." After Dulles responded negatively, Hatoyama devoted his prime diplomatic energies to reaching a peace agreement with the Soviet Union. But the initiative was resumed in 1957 by Kishi, who had used his role as one of Hatoyama's emissaries on the 1955 trip to advance his own domestic political objectives.[3]

In the security treaty case, Hatoyama could gain little domestically unless he could get something from the Americans. Thus when he was rebuffed, he stepped back. Politicians who seize issues for campaign purposes, however, can often score gains in the electoral contest merely by advocating a change; they do not need a positive response from the other capital. On neither textiles nor Okinawa, in fact, was it in the aspiring leader's interests to think too carefully about whether the goal was politically attainable in the other country. Indeed, both Okinawa and textile quotas were available as domestic political issues precisely because they did not appear within reach to current leaders. In both cases, however, the aspirant soon won his office, reiterated his commitment, and thus reinforced his political stakes in attaining it. In each case the issue ultimately reached the point where failure to resolve it threatened to, or did, damage the broader relationship.

In the textile case, moreover, U.S. bureaucratic and domestic politics determined not only the priority given the issue, but how it was initially pursued and who would pursue it. Quotas were sought through international negotiations not because the Japanese were known to be receptive (they were not), but because the U.S. Congress was believed un-

2. Asahi Shimbun Staff, *The Pacific Rivals: A Japanese View of Japanese-American Relations* (Weatherhill/Asahi, 1972), pp. 231–32.

3. Of course, not all U.S.-Japan issues arise out of political leaders' needs for isues to ride. Some, like the differences in approaches to the oil crisis that began in 1973, stem from externally triggered events with unavoidable impact on both nations. Others appear more or less accidentally—like the reemergence of the nuclear weapons issue following the LaRocque statement of September 1974. Moreover, the fact that a politician exploits an issue does not necessarily mean that he lacks convictions on it. Sato certainly believed strongly in Okinawa reversion, particularly after his trip to the islands in the summer of 1965. But Nixon's convictions on textiles were hardly of comparable depth, nor did they reflect any deep national commitment on the issue. And the difference between the two cases in the type of domestic political interests involved affected the prospects for resolving them. The "low politics" roots of the textile issue in the United States undercut the legitimacy of the U.S. initiative in Tokyo, whereas the political urgency of reversion in Japan provided the principal impetus for American policy changes on that issue.

likely to enact restraints on textile imports without adding other products as well. Secretary of Commerce Maurice Stans was assigned negotiating responsibility not because he knew how to negotiate with Japan (he did not), but because he was committed to the objective, loyal to the President, and acceptable to the U.S. textile industry.

And just as politicians were in the vanguard on all three issues, foreign office officials were counseling restraint. There were several reasons— State Department coolness on textiles, for example, was partly a product of a disinclination to give such priority to that kind of issue. But a common strand was the diplomats' relatively greater sensitivity to the constraints of the other country's politics, which made them reluctant to force issues. Their concern for the bilateral relationship made them fear that pushing an issue prematurely would lock the two governments into positions that might prove irreconcilable and could not be changed because of domestic political forces, with textile-type crisis the consequence.[4]

Initiatives with strong political roots pose particular risks for the U.S.-Japanese relationship unless handled with exceptional skill. For they commit key actors in one government to an objective that can develop a lot of domestic political steam, leaving them little room for compromise, when there is no assurance that the other political system can arrive at a consensus on a solution acceptable to the initiators. Thus the initiating politician can find himself out on a limb. Premier Sato's ultimate success on Okinawa came after years of uncertainty; by 1969 he was a hostage to American leaders' willingness and ability to deliver a reversion package he could accept. President Nixon's ultimate success on textiles came only after the unacceptability of his demands in Japanese politics left him vulnerable to the alliance between Wilbur Mills and the Japanese textile industry which confronted him in March 1971.

A problem important to one country's foreign policymakers becomes a bilateral issue when the seriousness of their political concern is communicated to the other country in such a way that its officials must consider the issue and take some stance, however tentative, on it. Some

---

4. And such a deadlock can damage their roles as negotiators; giving them a task of mediation that they cannot successfully perform undercuts their credibility both at home and abroad. Officials thus caught in the middle risk losing the action to others more committed to the substantive goal. And they appear to officials in the other government either as unable to speak for their own government, or as unable to move that government in the direction required for agreement.

bilateral communication to this end is consciously directed by officials in the first country toward those in the other. But most Japanese-American communication on major issues is carried out not by purposive messages from one country's officialdom to the other's, but by *indirect communication*—a wide range of signals that pass from actors in one country to those in another without being explicitly directed or channeled to them.

The Okinawa issue, for example, became of concern to responsible American officials in the mid-sixties because of a particular form of indirect communication. Official Americans watching events in Japan and Okinawa had concluded that the issue was heating up politically, that it could not be postponed very much longer without substantial risk to the security relationship. They reached these conclusions from their reading of Tokyo's media, public statements and press conferences of political figures, from U.S. embassy reporting, and from other sources. There was also *informal direct communication* between Japanese and American officials from the early sixties: the discussions that President Kennedy's special commission held with Japanese officials in 1961 and 1962; consultations with Japanese officials by Ambassador Edwin Reischauer and his successor, U. Alexis Johnson; recurrent State Department–Gaimushō (Foreign Ministry) discussions in Washington and Tokyo.[5]

Such informal communication elicited a constructive U.S. response because those official Americans vitally interested in Japanese political developments were a relatively small group, whose members generally believed that continued conservative rule in Tokyo was crucial to the alliance, and that both the conservatives and the alliance would be threatened if Japan's territorial grievance remained unassuaged. By the time the 1967 Johnson-Sato summit conference approached, the issue had been a live one in both governments for over a year, and officials negotiating preliminary drafts of the summit communiqué knew that it would have to be treated in a way indicating some movement toward Japanese objectives.[6]

5. *Informal direct communication* is thus distinguished from *direct and formal communication*, involving either actual negotiations or the conveying of official stands from one capital to the other.

6. The favorable orientation of State and Defense civilians did not, of course, assure strong positive action by President Johnson. Sato seems to have perceived this well, and realized that he had to communicate effectively to Johnson not just that he wanted reversion—this no one doubted—but that he regarded its near-term attainment as very important. He needed to signal that he thought a serious bilateral crisis

The textile issue also became binational through indirect communications—flowing this time in the other direction. Candidate Nixon's commitment to new quotas was reported in Tokyo, as was Democratic presidential candidate Hubert Humphrey's parallel promise. Reported also were postinauguration public statements by Nixon and Stans, a major Stans speech on the subject to U.S. textile manufacturers, the views of other quota proponents (and opponents) in the United States, leaks from intragovernmental strategy meetings in Washington, and above all Stans's April trip to Europe where he sought support in restricting exports from Japan and other prime Asian producers. Broad Japanese attentiveness to any significant U.S. policy initiative toward their country assured that this news would appear frequently on the front page. Stans initiated direct and formal communication on the issue with Japanese when he went to Tokyo in May to convey personally the President's interest in quotas; the fact that he, a cabinet member, was heading a large interdepartmental mission was intended as a strong signal of U.S. seriousness that would encourage Japanese concessions. But the months of publicity that preceded his visit had spurred a fierce resistance campaign, mounted by Japan's textile industry, but drawing on a deep resurgence of nationalism as well. And Japanese wishing to resist "unreasonable" American trade demands could find hope in many of the signals they received, for the general trade policy community in Washington was clearly cool toward the initiative, as was the State Department. Even Stans's signal could be used against him—and was. Opponents of quotas in both countries expressed the view that the Nixon administration was making a lot of noise in order to impress the U.S. textile industry with the effort it was making; if Japan resisted firmly, the administration might then abandon or modify its initiative, emphasizing to the textile lobby how hard it had tried.

The Politics of Interaction

For an important issue to be seriously considered, it must rise to prominence in both governments. In so rising, however, it is likely to

---

might develop if progress toward reversion was not made, and thus that American actors needed to give serious consideration to meeting his needs in order to maintain a harmonious security relationship in the future. This priority Sato was able to communicate effectively through use of a private emissary, and though Johnson did not move as far as he might, sufficient progress was made to keep Sato on top of the issue at home.

engage a wide range of actors and interests in each country. On any given day, such actors will be saying and doing a variety of things with potential impact on the issue. They produce a welter of signals that pass from governmental and private actors in one country to actors in the other. Many of these signals are not intended as U.S.-Japanese communications, but rather are directed toward domestic targets. Thus the very process by which an issue gets taken seriously has the simultaneous effect of complicating its resolution—by plunging it into domestic political controversy that spills over into the international arena.

Moreover, even those signals meant to be bilateral communications are often not received as intended by the senders. For reception of signals is inevitably colored by the general policy views and concepts of the receiver, and by his specific interests and stakes in the issues the signal affects. The reception of signals between Japan and the United States is further clouded by cultural differences.

Sources of Signals within One Country

Signals are a product, of course, of the politics of decisionmaking in the country where they originate. If this politics were controlled by a dominant central actor, then each governmental action or signal could be assumed to be based on careful calculation as to how the articulation of an issue, the shape of a proposal, the means of its delivery, and the selection of a receptor in the other country could maximize the chances of a favorable response. Sometimes the behavior of a government approaches this—as in, apparently, the U.S. opening toward China in 1969–71. But usually the politics of policymaking in the initiating country is sufficiently competitive and complicated to preclude central control over communications. Individual actors may still calculate (and argue about) how best to communicate with the other side. But the sum of signals actually conveyed will not add up to a particular tactical plan.

One example of how governmental politics can produce particularly counterproductive signals was the set of decisions leading to Maurice Stans's April 1969 textile trip to Western Europe. Almost all U.S. actors felt, in retrospect, that this trip had been a mistake, feeding resistance and bitterness among Japanese resentful of the effort to create a unified Western front against them, making it politically impossible for Japanese leaders to make even a marginally helpful response to Stans's initiative. Moreover, the effort was unsuccessful in lining up European support. It resulted, however, not from any carefully planned textile negotiating strategy, but from a sequence of actions and pressures having little to do with Japan. In February 1969, before Stans assumed responsibility for the textile issue, President Nixon announced during a European visit that his secretary of commerce would follow him shortly to discuss trade issues that the President had not treated personally. Stans presumably welcomed this opportunity, since he was seeking the lead administration role in trade policymaking. In the six weeks between the trip's announcement and its taking, however, the secretary was losing his battle for general trade policy primacy but winning the textile mandate. Moreover, the administration had not developed very many other trade proposals, and the Europeans—still absorbing the tariff cuts negotiated in the Kennedy Round of the mid-sixties—were not very interested in further liberalization. Thus, once he got to Europe, textiles was what Stans emphasized—it was the issue for which he had responsibility, and on which he knew what he wanted. (And the initial means through which the administration sought quotas—a multilateral trade agreement among all significant textile importers and exporters—required that the issue be raised at an early stage with the Europeans.)

Twenty-eight years earlier, Japanese leaders sent a similarly unintended signal across the Pacific when they decided in July 1941 to move troops into southern Indochina. The action was not particularly designed to influence the United States. Rather, it was a response to Germany's invasion of Russia, which forced decision on the issue of whether Japan should join in attacking the Soviets. Japanese decisionmakers all favored some form of expansionist policy, and all were concerned that the country not "miss the bus" by failing to exploit the rapidly changing world situation to enhance Japan's security and position. In this context, the Indochina move was a limited step, one unlikely to bring major bloodshed because Vichy France (which ruled Indochina) would have to acquiesce. But Washington nevertheless received it as a strong signal that Japan was moving ahead with aggressive policies, and it led to the freezing of Japanese assets and—through that—to the embargo on oil.[7]

The decisions that led to Stans's textile trip to Europe focused mainly on other issues—how the new administration would deal with Europe on trade policy; who within the administration should become the leading trade policy figure. And the signals it conveyed to Japanese actors were largely indirect and unintended—reported through Japanese newspaper headlines to attentive readers. Similarly, Japan's decision to move into Indochina was not made in the framework of Japanese-

7. See pp. 91–92, above.

American relations. But domestic politics can also produce inappropriate bilateral signals even when actors are focusing directly on the issue at hand, and even when the communication is an official, intergovernmental message. Japan's March 1970 aide-mémoire on textiles,[8] for example, was triggered by two Japanese embassy officials in Washington who feared a complete breakdown of the dialogue on the issue unless Japan signaled a serious willingness to compromise. So they flew to Tokyo and succeeded in getting the aide-mémoire drafted and conveyed through diplomatic channels. But because the politics of the issue in Japan prevented major concessions, the aide-mémoire's substance was only a marginal improvement from the American point of view. And it was received in Washington not as a constructive initiative on which to build, but as what a U.S. industry leader called "the latest Japanese rebuff." Even State Department officials did not consider it very helpful at that point in the negotiations.[9]

In each of these examples, what was communicated proved counterproductive because officials' minds and pressures were mainly elsewhere —on domestic policy bargaining, on other foreign policy issues. The signals that were conveyed were compromises—the March 1970 aide-mémoire—or the result of bureaucratic happenstance—Stans's European textile visit. Yet each did affect, and negatively, the receptiveness of the other government to compromise. Could this have been anticipated? How, more generally, do signals from one country affect decisionmaking in the other?

The Impact of Signals in the Recipient Country

Signals from one country influence another, of course, through its politics. They may affect conceptions of what is at stake, or beliefs about the prospects, costs, or consequences of particular courses of action.

---

8. See p. 111, above.

9. A parallel—and far more consequential—occasion when an appropriate American signal was not sent because of domestic political pressures was in the Potsdam Declaration of July 1945 calling for Japanese surrender. To encourage this result, Secretary of War Henry Stimson and Under Secretary of State Joseph Grew argued that the declaration should include language suggesting Allied willingness to accept a continued role for the emperor under a "constitutional monarchy" following "policies of peace." Such language was included in the draft Truman took to Potsdam, but removed there partly because of contrary views of other officials, and mainly because Truman and Secretary of State James F. Byrnes felt that a publicly flexible attitude toward the emperor would appear as appeasement at home and engender strong U.S. domestic opposition. Of course, the United States did in fact accept retention of the emperor though he was required to renounce his divinity.

They may inject a closely held issue or proposal into the public arena. In these and other ways, they influence how officials must confront an issue in their own government, and often affect their leverage within that government as well.

ASYMMETRY OF IMPACT. In U.S.-Japanese relations, a key factor in how signals from one country affect the other is the asymmetry of the relationship. United States policies are far more important to Japan than vice versa; the same U.S.-Japan issues that are buried (or unreported) in the *New York Times* and the *Washington Post* make the front page of the *Asahi shimbun*. Thus, for example, every stage of the Okinawa reversion negotiations was closely followed in Japan, but these negotiations were barely noticed in the United States except by those with a particular interest. The main cause of the unbalanced relationship is the disparity in power and the (relatively) one-directional dependence during the postwar period; a further contributing factor is the unusual attentiveness of Japanese to how they are thought of in the United States (and in other major countries).

Thus the words and actions of U.S. policy figures have had far greater impact on Japanese politics than those of Japanese leaders have on American. Maurice Stans's statements and activities of early 1969 triggered emotional public resistance in Tokyo, but this resistance was not even prominently reported in the United States. Presidential visits, actual or aborted, are major political events in Japan; relatively few Americans are even aware of it when a Japanese premier comes to Washington. The Washington remarks of Japanese and American officials after high-level talks there seldom cause political problems for the Americans; the Japanese are usually confronted with them when they return to Tokyo.

Sometimes this asymmetry exacerbates difficulties, as it did on the textile issue. On Okinawa, however, it worked to the advantage of those favoring reversion. Limited U.S. attentiveness meant that reports of how the issue was heating up in Japan came mainly through persons sympathetic to the case for reversion. And American apathy made it possible for U.S. officials handling the issue to keep it largely out of the public arena. They feared that early public exposure would arouse potential opposition to reversion, activating an alliance between the military and conservative senators that could block a reversion treaty on any terms acceptable to Japan. But if public airing of the issue could be delayed, they could negotiate quietly with the military and work out a practical solution, a reversion package satisfying military base needs.

CHANGING THE BALANCE OF INFLUENCE. On controversial bilateral issues, the two governments tend to be divided between those inclined to make negotiating concessions and those who favor a more adamant stance. The internal debate is seldom simply a division between "hawks" and "doves," but on major issues there tends to be a group of moderates within each government who feel there are limits to how much the other government can concede, who wish to reach a settlement relatively soon, who feel a solution is possible on terms acceptable to the national interest, and who see mutual accommodation as the way to achieve it. Those favoring a tougher stance, by contrast, tend to place the substance of what is at stake (for example, how much control of textile trade) above the immediate need to resolve the issue. They typically prefer holding to a strong position, buttressed if possible by unilateral action. Often they believe that if such a stand is maintained the other government will come to understand its seriousness and yield to it, whereas modifying their own position will be seen as a demonstration of weakness, encouraging the other country not to make reciprocal concessions, but to hold fast and await further softening. And if the other government will not yield to firmness, they prefer no negotiated solution, and perhaps will press for unilateral action to achieve their ends (for example, textile quota legislation).

Behind these rationales are particular domestic orientations. Thus moderates tend to be foreign office officials and others who value international negotiation and accommodation; those taking a harder line will often reflect bureaucratic or private interests with major stakes in the substance of an issue—the U.S. military on Okinawa, both textile industries in 1969–71. But whatever the roots of their positions, much of the internal debate turns on how the other government is likely to behave, and how the actions of one's own can affect it. Officials whose predictions are borne out, whose intergovernmental initiatives bear fruit, tend to strengthen their credibility and influence at home. Those whose prove wrong or unsuccessful tend to be weakened.[10]

10. Of course, evidence will seldom be conclusive, and officials will if at all possible interpret it in ways consistent with their previous stands and arguments. In fact, either a tough or a conciliatory stand in one country is likely to be viewed by each faction in the other as a confirmation of its own assumptions. A concession, for example, will be seen by hawks across the Pacific as a reward for standing firm, and they will argue that more firmness will bring further concessions. Doves will likely see it as proving the possibility of agreement if their side reciprocates, but argue that failure to reciprocate will not win further concessions but rather undercut advocates of compromise in the other government.

In major deteriorations of bilateral relations, the typical pattern has been for each government's actions to undercut the moderates in the other. Allison and Halperin provide an interpretation of what each side's moderates needed—and did not get—in 1941.

In the months leading up to Pearl Harbor, competing groups in Japan and the United States needed different actions from each other's government in order to accomplish their objectives. In Tokyo those who opposed war with the United States needed to be able to show that the United States would not interfere with Japanese expansion by cutting off sources of scrap iron, oil, and other materials. They also needed the United States to avoid actions which would have enabled their opponents to argue that war with the United States was inevitable. . . .

. . . Roosevelt, who sought to avoid [a Pacific] war, . . . had to resist pressures within the government from those who wanted to go to war with Japan. At the same time he did not want to so demoralize them that they would resign or reduce their efforts to prepare for the war with Germany which he believed was necessary. Thus Roosevelt's purposes required that Japan avoid: (1) flagrant violations of international law, (2) linking up with Germany in ways that made it impossible to resist arguments that war with Japan was a part of the war against the Fascist alliance, and (3) threats to the British or Dutch colonies which could be seen as a threat to the Allies in Europe. . . .

In this context Japan moved to occupy all of French Indochina. This Japanese move . . . was incompatible with what Roosevelt needed from the Japanese government. He no longer felt able to resist the pressures to take some sort of action against Japan.[11]

And after he responded with the freezing order, which led to the oil embargo, "the Japanese leaders opposed to war did not have what they needed from the United States to pursue their objective."[12]

Similarly, the deletion of language about a role for the Japanese emperor from the Potsdam Declaration weakened the position of Japanese moderates favoring immediate surrender (Lord Keeper of the Privy Seal Kido, Premier Suzuki, Foreign Minister Tōgō, Navy Minister Yonai, and Emperor Hirohito himself), because they needed to be able to argue that yielding would not lead to utter destruction of the nation and its institutions.

The textile dispute was similarly characterized by failures of moderates on either side to get actions from their government that would

11. Graham T. Allison and Morton H. Halperin, "Bureaucratic Politics: A Paradigm and Some Policy Implications," in Richard H. Ullman and Raymond Tanter, eds., *Theory and Policy in International Relations* (Princeton University Press, 1972), pp. 66–67 (Brookings Reprint 246).

12. Ibid., p. 67.

strengthen moderates on the other side. One example of this was the failure of business executive Donald Kendall to win unambiguous Japanese support for the textile compromise he proposed in March 1970. Fearing the opposition of the U.S. textile industry and its governmental allies, Kendall and those working with him carefully limited their communications with Washington officials prior to his departure for Tokyo. They seem to have hoped that Kendall's personal relationship with President Nixon would make him credible as a negotiator in Tokyo, and that a strongly positive reaction from Japanese leaders might in turn strengthen his ability to win approval of his proposal in Washington. But though his plan bore marked resemblance to a recent Japanese official statement, Kendall was still unable in Tokyo to get the affirmative signal he sought, for reasons of Japanese domestic politics. Both government and industry leaders there were sympathetic to the plan, but each was reluctant to take the political heat of endorsing it first, particularly since U.S. commitment to the plan was uncertain. This undercut Kendall's ability to make the only argument at home that stood a chance of success—that his proposal was negotiable whereas the official administration stand was not.

By contrast, progress in resolving issues can be achieved when one government's actions serve to strengthen moderates on the other side. Thus, in the 1967 summit communiqué on Okinawa reversion, Premier Sato—who wanted to accommodate U.S. military needs insofar as domestic politics allowed—was given U.S. concessions sufficient to maintain his credibility at home as one who was, if gradually, achieving results. Thus during the last phase of the textile negotiations, Ambassador-at-Large David Kennedy and Minister of International Trade and Industry Kakuei Tanaka, both of whom wanted a settlement, were sensitive to one another's needs to maintain leverage at home.

Actors on one side can also seek to change the balance of decision power in the other government by trying to alter the views of key individuals. One major effort to do so on the Okinawa issue was the Kyoto conference of January 1969 sponsored by Japanese scholars who served as informal advisers to Sato on the question. Among those invited were two long-time American military leaders, General Maxwell Taylor and Admiral Arleigh Burke. The meeting was perceived by Japanese sponsors and participants as a vehicle for conveying the sincerity of Japanese feelings against nuclear weapons. They hoped their arguments would influence the American participants decisively toward a nonnuclear solution to the Okinawa problem and that the opinion of these participants, in turn, would have a direct impact on the decision process in Washington. This conference is often identified in Japanese accounts as a landmark in communication between Japan and the United States on the issue of Okinawa reversion, as the means by which popular Japanese feelings were conveyed effectively to Americans such as Taylor and Burke that perhaps led to significant modification of their views.[13] Whether this conference had any real effect on American thinking is a matter of debate. The record of the proceedings of the conference indicates very little movement by the American participants between the first and last meetings of the conference. It is even likely that they saw the conference as a means of educating Japanese participants about the relationship of Okinawa to Asian security needs and the state of opinion in Washington.

LIMITING OR WIDENING THE POLITICAL ARENA. Officials in one country can also affect policymaking in the other by influencing who knows in detail about an issue or a proposal, and thus the range of actors able to involve themselves. Kendall kept his compromise textile plan secret to prevent the U.S. industry from attacking it before he could mobilize support in Tokyo. But not only was he frustrated by the failure of Japanese moderates to lend active support; he was also undercut when four days after he brought it up there, it was leaked by dissident Japanese officials to the Tokyo press and thence to the textile press in the United States. This aroused American industry leaders and their governmental allies, ending any chance that the Nixon White House would put its weight behind the compromise.[14] A similar fate befell a compromise proposed at about the same time by Henry Kissinger. Its leak was apparently inadvertent, but nonetheless led to its being attacked (though more obliquely than Kendall's) in the United States and thereby undermined.

Another example of how action by one country's leaders can broaden the policy arena in the other was President Eisenhower's decision to visit Japan in 1960 to celebrate the new era in U.S.-Japanese relations. By increasing the visibility of the revised security treaty, by providing a target for demonstrations, and by threatening to strengthen Kishi in the

13. See, for example, Asahi Shimbun Staff, *Pacific Rivals*, pp. 228–29 and 11–13.
14. The leak had similar impact in Tokyo, subjecting those Japanese government and industry leaders sympathetic to the plan to vehement attack from smaller textile firms who saw their interests being sacrificed.

Japanese leadership struggle, the scheduled visit broadened the controversy in Japan, leading to the crisis of June.

Because exposure of a negotiating stand or a compromise proposal frequently subjects it to domestic attack, responsible officials usually favor keeping information on a particular negotiation closely held. American officials sought to keep the Okinawa issue out of the public arena lest a potentially popular case against reversion develop, encouraging resistance by the U.S. military before the issue could be negotiated within the bureaucracy. And they were notably successful in preventing leaks—partly, of course, because of limited public interest in the issue.[15] But Japanese-American cooperation in keeping the arena limited would have availed little unless broader support could eventually be secured— ultimately the U.S. government had to seek public backing in order to secure Senate ratification of a reversion treaty, and military interests had to be accommodated lest their Senate allies act to block it. And on textiles, even those secret efforts to negotiate an accord that were not leaked to the press were unsuccessful because they lacked necessary political backing in one country or the other. In the end, agreement was reached by negotiators who largely kept their dealings out of the press —but only because Tanaka was able to win broad enough acceptance of Japanese capitulation in the political and business community to counter textile industry opposition.[16]

IMPOSING A FAIT ACCOMPLI. Policy actors in one country frequently take unilateral action aimed at changing—in their favor—the range of possible outcomes on a bilateral issue. Thus the Japanese textile industry pushed to increase its exports to the American market while the negotiations were under way, since (according to standard international practice) these higher levels would then become the base from which any quota limits were calculated. Thus (far more consequentially) nations seek to strike decisive blows in war, as Japan sought at Pearl Harbor and the United States achieved through the two atomic attacks.

15. There seems to have been only one important Okinawa leak, a *New York Times* article of June 3, 1969, that revealed a U.S. negotiating position not yet officially raised with the Japanese. Not only did this not trigger significant political trouble at home; it also seems to have had little effect on the Japanese. They already knew that the Nixon administration might well take the position reported, which was sympathetic to the Sato government's needs. But at this stage, the premier wanted more than hints. He needed assurances, and such could hardly be provided by a newspaper account that U.S. officials could write off as incomplete or misleading.

16. The Japanese textile industry was also compensated for the limitations on its exports by large-scale governmental aid.

Due to the asymmetry of power and impact, it has generally been the U.S. side that has been successful in imposing faits accomplis that fundamentally changed the politics of decisionmaking in the other country—most notably through the Nixon shocks of July and August 1971. The opening to Peking undercut the Taiwan-oriented Sato government and led to its replacement a year later by a new LDP mainstream coalition committed to restoring relations with the mainland. The import surcharge and floating of the dollar ended Japanese resistance to revaluation of the yen. And these, together with the September ultimatum threatening unilateral import quotas, helped end Japan's two-and-a-half-year domestic stalemate on textiles by creating a new political climate where it was possible for the new MITI minister, Kakuei Tanaka, to win support for textile concessions.

The effectiveness of such shocks is due in part to the role that the outside intervenor can sometimes play in Japanese politics. Commodore Perry's "black ship," or *kurofune*, has become a symbol of the ostensibly unwanted, but irresistible, external force that can produce policy change in Japan. The stress on consensus in Japan can result in inaction, in stalemate. But if an outside force brings a change in the situation that all Japanese must contend with, a new policy can sometimes be put across domestically as a means of coping with the new outside challenge. A relatively modest example of a *kurofune* was Wilbur Mills's intervention in the textile controversy in early 1971. Because of Mills's pressure—and his threat to move on restrictive legislation by March unless an alternative could be arranged—the fractious Japanese textile industry was able to agree on and proclaim the export restraint program that so angered President Nixon.[17]

This phenomenon suggests why the sorts of tough steps usually opposed by moderates are sometimes effective. But for such actions to bring significant Japanese policy changes, certain preconditions seem

17. Of course, here again the difference between Japanese and other nations' decisionmaking is one of degree. In any government where power is dispersed and opinion and interests diverge, action is easier taken if in response to an external initiative that cannot be ignored. As an extreme example, Pearl Harbor could be characterized as a classic *kurofune* for the United States. For an Anglo-American relations case, see Richard E. Neustadt's account of how, in the Skybolt crisis, each nation's defense chief failed to take preventive action because it would be politically easier for him to win agreement within his government on a substitute strategic weapon for the British if the other took the initiative. (*Alliance Politics* [Columbia University Press, 1970], pp. 45–47, and 106–09.)

necessary. First, the action or threat of action must be unambiguously decisive, believed to be more or less irrevocable, a genuine fait accompli. On textiles, the President's threat to impose quotas on October 15, 1971, unless an agreement were negotiated brought forth the desired Japanese response, whereas his earlier, oft-repeated warnings that Congress would legislate massive trade restrictions did not. Second, within the new set of alternatives that Japanese decisionmakers face, accommodating the outside intervenor must have strong advantages over continued resistance. This criterion was met in the fall of 1971 on both exchange-rate adjustment and textiles, not least because U.S. actions seemed to be threatening the foundations of the postwar economic relationship upon which Japan depended. Third, there must be those within the Japanese system already favorable to accommodation, who are well-placed to use the *kurofune* as a rationale for doing what they wanted done anyway. Thus MITI Minister Tanaka seems to have determined on settling the textile issue on whatever terms he could get before any of the Nixon shocks, though he skillfully concealed this determination and allowed outside pressures to help clear his path. An earlier U.S. threat of unilateral action on textiles might not have brought a bilateral agreement, since Tanaka's predecessor was less ready to make major substantive concessions.

But the broader problem with such shock tactics is that they threaten, in real though hard-to-measure ways, the assumptions of mutual reliability and relative predictability upon which a continuing alliance depends. Their effectiveness rests on their inexorability—they cannot be altered whatever major interests the other country has at stake. But if officials in the target country believe this, they must believe there are times when the country imposing the fait accompli will disregard the alliance. This may then impel them to reduce their stakes in that alliance.

Nor should it be assumed that the effects of such tactics are calculated carefully by those who employ them. No available evidence (except ex post facto rationalizations) indicates any serious advance consideration of the impact of the China shock on Japanese domestic politics or foreign policy; and while elements of the August 15 economic decisions were pointed directly at Japan, those who shaped them did not have detailed knowledge of the politics of the country whose policies they wanted to change. Only the textile shock seems to have been employed in a calculated way, since the inclination of Tanaka to settle was apparently known to Ambassador David Kennedy in advance. The handling of both of the economic shocks, however, reflected a feeling among American policymakers that more diplomatic approaches to these issues had met with continued frustration; there was a widespread belief that the time had come to force the Japanese to yield.

Resolution of Issues

To this point the analysis of initiation and interaction has highlighted the negative effects of signals from one country on decisionmaking in the other, or the accidental nature of much of the impact whatever the results. Why then can the U.S.-Japan relationship still be considered, on balance, a success? Is it simply luck that has prevented domestic and bureaucratic political pressures from moving the two governments in irreconcilable directions?

One force in the success of the postwar relationship was the compatibility of interests as perceived by Japanese and American leaders. For Japanese, unready to face squarely their own security problems, American strategic protection and hegemony were useful if seldom applauded. And if Americans could work out reasonable base arrangements, Japanese rearmament became, in practice, a postponable goal for the United States, the oft-reiterated need for enhanced free world military strength notwithstanding. Similarly, postwar U.S. economic dominance and world leadership meshed nicely with the Japanese need for expanding overseas trade while maintaining protectionist controls at home.

But while these large compatibilities made cooperation far easier, they hardly assured it. Immediately after the occupation, the Dulles-Pentagon emphasis on Japanese rearmament (a product of their global interests and priorities) was both insensitive and unsuited to strengthening alliance-oriented Japanese leaders at home. The softening of this emphasis led to the new security treaty, but that treaty triggered a major crisis in Tokyo (the product of complex political interplay there). While Okinawa, the emerging security problem of the sixties, was wisely foreseen and astutely managed, it was followed by the bitter, prolonged, unforeseen wrangle over textile quotas in which both governments acted as brokers for their textile industries. Before it was settled, there were the major shocks on China and trade policy where the United States acted as if the Japanese alliance hardly existed.

Obviously the relationship has been prone to crises. But there have also been bridges between the two systems that have helped to resolve them. One contributor to maintaining tolerable U.S.-Japanese relations is informal *transnational alliances,* ongoing relationships based on overlapping interests and mutual support that link particular policy actors in Japan and the United States.[18] A second, somewhat intertwined institutional force bringing order to the politics of the relationship is the official negotiating channels which are employed on specific issues.

Transnational Alliances

In their broadest sense, transnational alliances include any relationship in which actors within the U.S. and Japanese systems collaborate to achieve particular policy outcomes desired by both. At minimum, such allies take compatible positions in their respective internal policy struggles and maintain general mutual awareness of these positions; at maximum, they strive consciously to strengthen one another's leverage and credibility at home, and conspire actively to put across particular negotiated solutions in the two systems.

The first important transnational alliance after the occupation developed in the fifties between U.S. officials specializing in Japan, on the one hand, and Gaimushō and LDP leaders on the other. It was rooted in acceptance by these Japanese of the priority of the U.S. relationship, and the Americans' conviction that the benefits of the relationship— Japanese and East Asian security, tolerable U.S. base arrangements

18. The term *transnational* is drawn from the work of Robert O. Keohane and Joseph S. Nye, Jr. In *Transnational Relations and World Politics* (Harvard University Press, 1972), p. xi, they define "transnational relations" as "contacts, coalitions, and interactions across state boundaries that are not controlled by the central foreign policy organs of government." They distinguish between "transnational interactions" involving "nongovernmental actors" and "transgovernmental interactions" which take place "between governmental subunits across state boundaries," but they also use "the broad term transnational relations" to include both (ibid., p. 383). More recently, they have concluded (with particular reference to *organizations*) that this dual usage of "transnational" is "unnecessarily confusing," and have opted to "restrict the term 'transnational' to nongovernmental actors" ("Transgovernmental Relations and International Organizations," *World Politics,* October 1974, p. 41). But to adopt this restriction here would leave us without an adjective to apply to those particular "alliances" which include *both* governmental and private policy actors. These have been particularly important in the cases we examine. Thus we employ the term *transnational* in the original, broader Keohane-Nye sense. Indeed, we have found it useful to broaden the term still further to allow inclusion of political leaders and foreign office officials in particular transnational alliances, as long as they are employing mutually supportive relations with actors in the other country to strengthen themselves in policy debates at home.

—rested on continuing conservative rule in Tokyo. Thus the U.S. ambassador, while pressing the Japanese government for concessions on specific issues, would simultaneously resist what he saw as inappropriate and counterproductive efforts in Washington to force the security relationship into the NATO mold, since these subjected conservative leaders to opposition attack.

The prime accomplishment of this alliance, the security treaty of 1960, reflected both its strengths and its limitations. It won U.S. accession to a unique security relationship, in which the United States made the security commitment Dulles had withheld in 1951 without either a fully reciprocal Japanese commitment or NATO-type rearmament. But because of its relatively narrow membership, the alliance contributed to misinterpretation and underestimation of the domestic controversy that arose in 1960. As opposition to the Eisenhower visit increased, Japanese scholars independent of the government but particularly concerned about American relations sought to win U.S. embassy acceptance of their view that the visit should be postponed.[19] But the ambassador, a victim of his own narrow interpretation of the event, rejected the message and denounced its purveyors. As Reischauer characterized the "broken dialogue" at the time, "almost all Japanese intellectuals who had contact with Americans showed an almost pathetic eagerness to explain the 'true situation' to their American friends."[20] But their official friends, at least, did not seem to be listening.

Since 1960, however, lines of communication and dialogue have been notably strengthened and broadened—though those between Americans and Japanese opposition groups remain weak and thin. In part the strengthening has been the result of conscious efforts to develop a range of conferences and forums, from the cabinet-level ministerial meetings to less august bilateral gatherings of businessmen and scholars. It is even more a result of the rapid rise in economic interaction, spurred by the continuing surge of Japan's economy throughout the sixties. In any case, the increase in the number of public and private Americans and Japanese in contact with one another has created informal networks of concerned individuals with compatible perspectives on security and trade issues. These have formed the basis for the building of transnational alliances

19. See Asahi Shimbun Staff, *Pacific Rivals*, pp. 217–18; and George Packard III, *Protest in Tokyo* (Princeton University Press, 1966), p. 288.

20. Edwin O. Reischauer, "The Broken Dialogue with Japan," *Foreign Affairs*, vol. 39 (October 1960), p. 23.

on issues where the domestic interests of actors in the two countries led them to favor the same general sort of resolution.

Such alliances were in evidence on Okinawa and textiles. In the first case the alliance (a successor to that of the fifties) included a small group of State and Defense officials, and an equally small group of Gaimushō officials and scholars with close ties to the Sato government who were sensitized by the events of 1960 to the potential impact of the opposition on the issue and the security relationship that it threatened. In the second case the primary alliance (which helped produce both the Kendall plan and the unilateral Japanese industry program negotiated by Mills) was between free-trade-oriented politicians and businessmen in the United States and compromise-prone Japanese in the government bureaucracy and the textile industry. The Okinawa alliance usefully broadened and supplemented official channels; the nongovernmental actors basically supported the official positions that were evolving and exerted constructive marginal influence on them. The textile alliance, by contrast, worked against the fundamental Nixon administration negotiating position. In both cases, however, alliance reflected not just a convergence of interests on the particular issue but a commitment to the larger institutional structure of the bilateral relationship. Those who pushed Okinawa reversion saw it as essential to prevent a recurrence of the violent opposition to the 1960 treaty and to build a new basis for the security relationship that could carry it into the seventies and perhaps beyond. The textile alliance reflected not just convergence of specific economic interests, but a commitment to the GATT structure of free trade which quota proposals threatened. This liberal trade order was believed essential if the U.S.-Japan economic relationship were to continue evolving toward increasingly open national economies and mutually beneficial interdependence.

Because parties to such alliances value strong U.S.-Japanese ties, and favor resolving issues on terms that preserve or strengthen these ties, such transnational alliances are generally a positive force giving breadth and strength to the relationship. But this does not mean that their specific impact on the course of a particular issue will always be constructive or useful. The very fact that allied actors are oriented toward the relationship may make them insufficiently sensitive to the strength and aims of other domestic political actors with different orientations. Moreover, actors on one side—visibly exploiting the opportunities that the alliance presents—may not fully recognize or carefully calculate how the interests of their allies in the other government differ from their interests, and how this may affect critical choices. Each partner in an alliance may also accept too readily the other's reading of the domestic political situation in the other's country—a reading inevitably colored by specific interests.

In some cases, alliances can facilitate those signals and arguments by actors in one country that strengthen proponents of a desired settlement in the other. As the informal dialogue between Okinawa reversion advocates in the two governments proceeded, for example, Japanese actors were explicitly signaled that they should emphasize the politics of the issue on Okinawa and in Japan proper. They would better promote the right decisions in the American government, they were told, if they emphasized not direct strategic arguments for reversion, but rather the political case: that unless reversion came soon, unrest would intensify and make it impossible to maintain either U.S. administrative control of the island or the broader bilateral security relationship. And in formulating their argument in this way, Japanese leaders thereby reinforced the case that was being painstakingly built and argued by U.S. officials who favored reversion. But sometimes the political advice offered by allies can be wrong—as when Japanese sympathetic to their textile industry's unilateral restraint plan were apparently told by Mills and those working with him that President Nixon would acquiesce in it if not pressed to make an explicit endorsement.

A detailed look at that episode of early 1971 illustrates several potential pitfalls such alliances face. After two years of inconclusive and difficult textile negotiations, there was broad agreement in both countries that some resolution was essential, involving some form of new Japanese export restraint. Mills and the leaders of Japan's textile industry shared this view. They also needed one another. The congressman needed the export control plan that the industry leaders could adopt and implement; he could then argue that the issue was at least tentatively resolved, and thereby divert a new congressional move to enact the textile import quotas he opposed and feared. For Japan's textile leaders, any export restraints were undesirable, but some form of quotas seemed inevitable, and the broad general restrictions in the industry program were far more palatable than the stringent, item-by-item quotas the Nixon administration was pushing. But they needed Mills's active opposition to statutory quotas (he had gone along with quotas in 1970, and they had passed the House) so that he—in his pivotal position as Ways and Means Committee chairman—could protect them against this threat. And by blocking statutory quotas, Mills would also be undercutting the Nixon administration's ability to use the threat of congressional action as leverage with the Japanese government in pressing for negotiated restrictions in the form the administration wanted. All of these things Mills could give them—plus the outside pressure needed to bring industry unity. All would enhance their leverage within Japan—in selling their proposal to those in the textile industry who opposed any form of restraint; in dealing with Japanese politicians and officials who felt that much more stringent limitations were the only way to solve the crisis.

But neither Mills nor the Japanese industry leaders wanted the plan to trigger a crisis in relations between the Nixon and Sato governments. Still less did other actors who accepted and increasingly supported the plan—Japanese bureaucrats and politicians; the American free trade community and its business and political allies. Yet whether it would trigger such a crisis depended on how the Nixon administration would react, above all on the President's personal response. And because no one believed that Nixon could openly endorse a solution far less restrictive than that he had been insisting on, the best the plan's proponents could hope for was his tacit acceptance, presumably because he too had tired of the issue and would be willing to accept half a loaf as long as it could be blamed on others. Nixon's reaction was difficult to be sure of in advance. But in predicting it, Japanese actors relied on the assurances of their American allies—Mills and the lobbyist-intermediary, Michael P. Daniels—that Nixon would in fact go along. These assurances proved inaccurate, so when the plan was announced it exacerbated the crisis it was intended to resolve.

This outcome reflected mistakes by many actors. The Nixon White House, for example, failed to exploit several opportunities to signal its opposition while the situation was still fluid. But the crisis also resulted, in part, from the divergent interests of the actors involved in the transnational alliance. Both Mills and the Japanese industry could gain something from the plan even if the White House denounced it: it would continue in force and weaken the case for statutory quotas or a more stringent negotiated solution. But for the Sato government and the Gaimushō, the Nixon rejection was a disaster. It was particularly so because Nixon clearly felt betrayed by the plan and by the Japanese government's endorsement thereof, and his bitterness would affect his handling of other issues involving Japan in that fateful year. Yet the

Washington embassy and the Gaimushō—which perceived the potential danger of a negative Nixon reaction—allowed themselves to be reassured by the assessments of others—Mills and Daniels—whose stakes were different, who did not want a Nixon rejection and might indeed have delayed action if they had expected one, but who could nonetheless live with it.[21]

This illuminates, therefore, two broader weaknesses of transnational alliances: the dependence of actors in one country on the assessments of their allies in the other of that country's political scene, and the tendency to underrate the divergence of interests within the alliance, the possibility that political outcomes tolerable to one party can be disastrous to another. Engrossed in a complex, fast-moving, indirect negotiating effort such as the Mills plan became, participants tend to forget how much each actor's assessment of his own political system is affected by his stakes in the issue, and how these stakes are predominantly in terms of his position and relationships within his own nation.

Similar problems can arise when negotiated solutions are sought more conventionally—through official negotiating channels.

The Choice of Channels

The standard way governments bargain on issues is through designated official channels. Ideally, unified national positions are worked out internally, and each government then negotiates through a designated official, team, or agency. Thus each can "speak with one voice" in conveying its official stance, notwithstanding the inevitable flow of information and signals through other channels as well.

The value of having a clear-cut, single negotiating channel is illustrated by what can happen in its absence. At one point in the textile negotiations, each of three Americans was conveying to Japanese leaders a distinct formula for an agreement—each with some claim to President Nixon's endorsement, each apparently inconsistent with the other two. At the same time, during the spring of 1970, Americans faced problems in judging whether to take more seriously the strong Japanese resistance expressed through official channels up to the cabinet level, or the much more responsive attitude conveyed recurrently by Premier Sato. For each government the result was confusion joined with bitterness toward

21. This story is told at much greater length in I. M. Destler, Hideo Sato, and Haruhiro Fukui, "The Textile Wrangle: Conflict in Japanese-American Relations 1969–71" (1976; processed), chap. 12.

officials across the Pacific, since the other government seemed to be offering proposals with one hand and taking them away with the other. Such chaos might well have been avoided had a regular, single channel been used throughout the negotiations.

If the general case for some dominant channel is strong, however, there is less agreement on what it should be, or how—on controversial issues—it can be maintained. In postwar U.S.-Japanese relations four types of channels have been used. One, of course, is *diplomatic channels*— negotiation of issues through the foreign offices and their embassies. A second is *functional channels*, direct dealing on issues between those government officials and agencies with particular competence and responsibility in the substantive problem area involved. A third route for bilateral negotiations is *summit channels*, defined most generally as dealings between heads of government or their senior political aides. Finally, there is the not infrequent resort to *back channels*, operating around or above those who have formal negotiating responsibility.

DIPLOMATIC CHANNELS. Embassy–foreign office channels have been heavily employed in postwar U.S.-Japanese relations, not just on routine matters but on major issues as well. Once the decisions to proceed were made by the respective political leaders, security treaty revision was negotiated by Foreign Minister Aiichiro Fujiyama and Ambassador Douglas MacArthur II, though LDP factional strife over the terms intervened at several points. Okinawa reversion was similarly handled primarily through diplomatic channels until the shape of the agreement had emerged. The frequent ability of these foreign offices to retain operational responsibility reflects the national patterns of foreign policymaking. In Tokyo, Gaimushō influence has reflected the traditional leverage of career ministries in their spheres of recognized competence, the lack of a strong military competitor, and the general convergence of foreign policy views between senior Foreign Ministry bureaucrats and LDP leaders. In the United States, the State Department's leverage on Japan issues was founded upon both the lack of day-to-day presidential involvement in these issues from the late fifties to the late sixties, and the general State–White House agreement on policy during this same period.

Employment of diplomatic channels has had major and obvious benefits in resolving U.S.-Japan issues. Foreign office officials are—on the average—the persons most likely in each government to be sensitive to the political and bureaucratic scene in the other. They are thus most likely to be able to calculate what can be negotiated and how to go about negotiating it. In the textile case, U.S. State Department officials were most aware of the volatility of the issue in Japan; on Okinawa, both foreign offices were able to work for a reversion agreement guided by some sense of the domestic constraints on each other's decisionmakers. This sensitivity inclines foreign office officials to favor stances that will bridge the substantive gap between the two sides. This is true in any bilateral negotiations, but particularly so in U.S.-Japanese relations. In the Gaimushō, the dominant postwar policy orientation has been the maintenance of close, constructive relations with the United States. And State Department people involved in U.S.-Japan issues have generally seen the U.S. interest as building a constructive, mutually beneficial partnership and thus solidifying the alliance.

Yet these advantages—understanding of the other country, willingness to compromise—are not always sufficient to resolve bilateral issues. Giving the textile issue to the foreign offices might have avoided the confusion of multiple channels. But it is unlikely that it would have resolved the dispute because of the limited responsiveness of officials in both agencies to the politics of the issue at home. Indeed, critics of diplomatic channels sometimes argue that the other country's politics and interests are all that their foreign office is interested in. In other parts of the American bureaucracy, State is frequently regarded as the spokesman for foreign interests. In Tokyo, the Gaimushō has been dubbed the "Japan branch of the State Department," or "the State Department's annex at Kasumigaseki."[22]

The fact that diplomats are thus not trusted domestically is partly inevitable—special interests can hardly expect an agency that is pressed with many claims to give regular priority to theirs. But partly it reflects how foreign offices view themselves—not primarily as domestic political arbitrators and consensus builders but as protectors of international from domestic politics. They tend to seek not so much to master and manage domestic political forces to their advantage, as to limit the intrusion of such forces into the domain of international diplomacy. Former Gaimushō Vice Minister Shinsaku Hogen has stated "the consensus of professional Japanese diplomats"[23] that "no good can come of a diplomacy that panders to domestic public opinion."[24]

22. Asahi Shimbun Staff, Pacific Rivals, pp. 315–16.
23. Ibid., p. 316.
24. Ibid.; this quotation paraphrases Hogen. George F. Kennan expressed a parallel view in his response to a reporter's argument that he and State had not

One obvious effect of such an attitude in both governments is to limit the utility of foreign office channels for resolving issues where other strong bureaucratic or domestic interests are involved. Another, ironically, is to lessen a major foreign office strength—insight into the politics of the other country. For to the degree that Gaimushō officials, for example, draw their assessments of American domestic politics from conversations with State Department counterparts, they are likely to reflect the same biases, the same relative insensitivity to the particular domestic interests and to domestic opinion generally. Thus, the Japanese foreign office underestimated the strength of the Nixon administration's commitment to a textile agreement in early 1969, despite a number of strong signals. Diplomats sometimes believe too readily that the other foreign office really speaks for its government. Gaimushō officials believed in early 1971 that the two countries' China policies were being coordinated because they were holding regular consultations with State Department counterparts. The Nixon announcement of July 15 showed how wrong such an assumption could be.

And because they are so close to the current officials of the foreign government and their current problems, diplomats have a tendency to exaggerate the long-term cost of being politically and personally unaccommodating to that government's current leaders, or the cost of those leaders departing from power. A rather extreme example of this bias was the U.S. embassy's apparent definition of U.S. interests in Japan in 1960 as not only the continuation of LDP rule, but the preservation of the embattled Kishi cabinet. Despite overwhelming signs that Kishi could not long remain in power, Ambassador MacArthur opposed any U.S. initiative to postpone Eisenhower's visit as likely to "be a mortal blow for Kishi."[25] In fact, the eleventh-hour cancellation of Eisenhower's

---

adequately made the case for the Marshall Plan to Congress: "I pointed out that personally I had entered a profession which I thought had to do with the representation of United States interests vis-à-vis foreign governments; that this was what I had been trained for and what I was prepared to do to the best of my ability; and that I had never understood that part of my profession was to represent the U.S. government vis-à-vis Congress; that my specialty was the defense of U.S. interests against others, not against our own representatives; that I resented the State Department being put in the position of lobbyists before Congress in favor of the U.S. people." *Memoirs*, vol. 1 (Little, Brown, 1967), p. 405n.

25. Cable no. 3824, U.S. Embassy, Tokyo, to Secretary of State, May 25, 1960. In a later cable, MacArthur denied press reports that Eisenhower had decided to go ahead with his visit "to give shot in arm to waning Kishi Administration." They were "not repeat not true." But the reason he urged a strong White House denial of this

invitation and the ensuing resignation of Kishi probably strengthened U.S.-Japanese relations, for they defused Japan's domestic situation and led to another conservative government with stronger domestic support. Kishi's hanging onto power had exacerbated the crisis; his letting go led to its resolution.

To these limits in the capacity of diplomatic channels to take full account of domestic politics must be added a related problem—limits on substantive expertise. Particularly in the economic area, where trade and monetary issues demand special knowledge of domestic and international conditions, the expertise for handling problems is usually concentrated outside of the foreign offices. These issues where such expertise is particularly important become candidates for direct negotiations through functional channels.

FUNCTIONAL CHANNELS. Competing ministries in Japan seem to agree that

diplomacy left entirely to the Foreign Ministry rarely works well. The Finance Ministry shares some of MITI's irritation with the Foreign Ministry. Haruo Nishima, a Finance official who served as minister of the Washington embassy for more than three years, sums up the attitude by noting: "Common nationality is not enough to insure communication. Experts on specific problems, even if they are of different nationality, invariably understand each other better than an expert and a nonexpert of the same nationality." A colleague of his, also with long experience in Washington, agrees: "In negotiating economic matters, discussions between the Japanese Foreign Ministry and the State Department are likely to founder. Since the former is probably being pressured by MITI, anyway, and the latter by the Commerce Department, direct negotiations generally prove far more effective than the roundabout route via the Foreign Ministry and the State Department."[26]

On many U.S.-Japanese issues substantive expertise is clearly greater outside the foreign offices—textiles is one example; monetary relations, agricultural trade, and military technology are others. Economic and military agencies may not be willing to share their expertise with generalists, since it is for the specialists a major source of leverage, a basis for seeking for themselves a central role in influencing and negotiating policy. Moreover, such expertise is usually linked to particular interests

---

report was that it was "damaging both to the President and Kishi." (Cable no. 4028, U.S. Embassy, Tokyo, to Secretary of State, June 6, 1960.) See also Asahi Shimbun Staff, *Pacific Rivals*, p. 217; and A. Merriman Smith, *A President's Odyssey* (Harper, 1961), chap. 17.

26. Asahi Shimbun Staff, *Pacific Rivals*, p. 326.

—whether in or out of government—and its holders do not generally trust the foreign offices to give priority to these interests.

Such expertise is frequently joined with leverage over implementation. In Japan, much of MITI's power over textiles was tied to its indispensable role in developing and monitoring a system of export restraints that would be imposed by the industry itself. Similarly, it is the U.S. military that has day-to-day custody over nuclear weapons, as the controversy of late 1974 once again highlighted. In each case, it would be difficult—close to impossible—for the foreign office to insist on negotiating terms that the implementing party could not live with.

Yet functional channels have sometimes proved too close to domestic interests to permit bilateral agreement. Certainly, MITI and the Commerce Department could more realistically reflect and represent the positions of the textile industries of each country. Moreover, they were better versed in the technicalities of the issue, and would have been unlikely to reach an agreement that could not be implemented. Indeed, the logical extreme of functional negotiations on textiles occurred in the prewar period, when American and Japanese industry representatives met directly and worked out an arrangement in 1937 that placed quantitative limits on Japanese sales in the American market. Unfortunately, by 1969 the positions of the two industries had become virtually irreconcilable. In a series of negotiations that reflected the responsiveness of their agencies to industry positions, Secretary of Commerce Stans and MITI Ministers Ohira and Miyazawa failed to reach agreement. Interestingly, the channel through which a textile agreement was finally negotiated combined a certain functional responsibility for the issue with high-level political interests. A new MITI minister, Kakuei Tanaka, wanted to settle the issue for political reasons and was able to control his domestic situation. His negotiating counterpart, David Kennedy, was committed to winning what the U.S. industry wanted, and as ambassador-at-large was able to mount a closed operation insulated from day-to-day intervention either from hawks in the Commerce Department or doves in the State Department.

A relatively effective use of functional channels was the negotiation on the financial terms of Okinawa reversion, handled mainly by Treasury and Finance in 1969–71. On this issue—and on international monetary and financial matters more generally—the two agencies could exploit their common expertise (and a common interest in dealing directly).

But usually they were free from the directly conflicting constituent pressures that bedevil dealings between MITI and Commerce.

A frequently employed compromise between functional and diplomatic channels is the interagency team—standard practice on trade negotiations. Members of such teams are expected both to contribute their expertise and to uphold their agencies' respective policy concerns. Interagency negotiating groups were employed by both sides in the textile negotiations—but usually for formal, relatively visible conferences rather than serious bargaining sessions. On Okinawa, interagency teams were effectively employed in negotiating the detailed administrative arrangements after the agreement in principle at the 1969 summit.

SUMMIT CHANNELS. Direct contact between the heads of governments and their entourages has been a recurrent feature of Japanese-American relations since the occupation, and a number of important agreements have been negotiated or at least ratified in summit meetings. They played major roles in all three cases highlighted in this study. An Eisenhower-Kishi meeting inaugurated the consultations that led to the security treaty revision negotiations. Sato's meetings with Johnson and Nixon were the major focal points on Okinawa reversion. And Sato's summit talks with Nixon on textiles had very bad consequences for the issue and the relationship.

As the first two cases demonstrate, summit dealings do not always undercut regular diplomatic channels, but can provide diplomats with substantive guidance and support. Negotiations on revising the treaty and returning the Ryūkyūs inevitably rose to the level of heads of government—because they involved important treaties in the sensitive area of territorial jurisdiction and national security; and because they involved powerful bureaucratic and domestic interests, or (in Japan) major domestic political controversy. Resolution of such issues required the engagement of national political leaders; hence summit conferences have proved important—perhaps even indispensable—in achieving breakthroughs on them. Since this is known in the two governments, summits have the effect—once scheduled—of providing action-forcing deadlines for officials who themselves seek progress on such issues (or are pressed by their leaders to achieve it). Thus the drafting of summit communiqués proves an important focal point for bilateral diplomatic negotiations— with Okinawa once again the prime example. And summits play the further role of bringing Japan-related issues to the attention of the American president, who normally gives them little day-to-day attention. And what the president gives his attention to affects what his key subordinates stress as well. Thus, U.S.-Japan summit meetings are likely to raise the perceived importance of U.S.-Japan issues in the American government more generally.

Summit channels also encourage considering particular bilateral issues within the broader context of the overall U.S.-Japan relationship. Bureaucracies would prefer, if possible, to handle each issue on its own terms. But national leaders frequently see their country's relationship with another as an important general concern—particularly if they develop personal ties with a foreign counterpart. Thus escalating the level of attention and responsibility forces consideration of priorities among various policy objectives and raises the possibility that several issues can be brought together in some sort of negotiating package.

Such gains from summit channels in energizing and broadening governmental policymaking have been considerable in U.S.-Japanese relations. There are also public political advantages. Trips by chiefs of government are major press events—in Japan for all American summits, in the United States if it is the American president who does the traveling. Thus, they provide information and publicity about the other country, the relationship, and issues between them. And they may enhance general political support for a friendly bilateral relationship, since they dramatize and personalize it.[27] Yet the textile case illustrates that summitry can create major problems—particularly if national leaders view it as an alternative to other channels rather than as a complement and stimulus to them.

One problem in that case was inadequate substantive preparation. As Fred Iklé has noted, summit decisions generally are risky because they may be taken "with the advice of people who had to master the detailed issues in as hurried a fashion as the President himself."[28] Particularly on the American side, summit conferences tend to bring into the decision process presidential aides and advisers who are more responsive to the president's own domestic needs than they are knowledgeable in the substantive questions at stake. This was clearly the case in the Sato-Nixon textile discussions of November 1969 and October 1970. In 1969, presummit preparations on the issue seem to have been handled mainly

27. The other side of the coin, of course, is that summits provide a target for critics of the relationship—1960 is the obvious case.

28. Fred Charles Iklé, *How Nations Negotiate* (Harper and Row, 1964), pp. 127–28.

by two persons—Henry Kissinger and a Sato emissary—whose expertise on the substance and politics of the issue was grossly inadequate. The result was a basis for agreement that proved politically unviable. In 1970, presummit communications were again carried on through limited, White House–Kantei channels, leading to Sato's endorsement of a formula that once again was not checked out at home for its soundness or its acceptability.

Yet the leaders clearly expected more positive results. And this seems to reflect a more general problem—that because summit meetings can often be a vehicle for promoting major negotiating breakthroughs, leaders are tempted to see them as sufficient for fully achieving such breakthroughs. Summits become not useful vehicles for moving issues forward, but the definitive forum for their resolution whether or not the way is prepared. But this assumes a power that neither chief of government possesses, especially the Japanese premier. Nixon seems to have felt that because he was agreeing to Okinawa reversion, Sato could yield on a politically very different issue—textiles—and that Sato's personal assent would be decisive in bringing about the outcome—restraint of Japanese textile exports—that Nixon desired. This, of course, turned out to be very mistaken.[29] For such trade-offs look much easier from the summit standpoint than they prove to be in real life. Issues with strong domestic political implications just are not that manipulable; textiles-for-Okinawa-type exchanges are appealing to leaders—and to partisans who win their objectives thereby—but they do not resolve the problem of winning domestic consensus on the issue where one's nation does the bulk of the conceding.[30] And this is related to a larger criticism frequently made of Nixon-Kissinger diplomacy—that it exaggerated the maneuvering room, the flexibility, the actual power of choice that national leaders possess in the economically complex, politically alert advanced democratic industrial societies.

Finally, the textile case suggests several problems that can arise from the reliance on a personal political relationship between leaders. The most obvious is that failures are taken personally too—Nixon found Sato

29. It is interesting to note that the major summit successes in U.S.-Japanese relations involved issues where the primary decision required came from the president; the main fiasco, textiles, was where comparable decisiveness was expected from a premier.

30. Nor was this problem reciprocal in this case; a U.S. consensus on Okinawa had largely been achieved before the 1969 summit; on textiles, the achievement of Japanese consensus was left to afterwards.

wanting as a politician for failing to help him after he had given the premier what he needed. Thus an economic dispute of secondary importance was converted into a crisis of personal confidence.[31] In construing his relationship with Sato as one requiring reciprocal political support, moreover, Nixon took no apparent account of the fact that while postwar American leaders had consistently sought to help keep Sato's party in power, the Japanese had no reciprocal preference for Nixon's Republicans.[32] And the significance of textiles to Nixon was almost purely electoral.

And reliance on a personal relationship between a Japanese and an American politician brings the problems inherent in communicating through an interpreter to the fore. Each leader, speaking and listening in his own language, does what his political career has rewarded him for doing—he thinks and acts in terms of the political matrix of his own culture. The danger of misunderstandings based on personal styles and nuances is multiplied, therefore, unless the leaders are supported by the checks against such misunderstanding that established institutions can supply, such as cross-cultural expertise, prior analysis and clarification of the issues at stake, and careful preparation of proposed agreements.

BACK CHANNELS. High officials sometimes resort to secret communications routes hidden from many of the people and offices formally responsible for an issue in their respective governments. Essentially a back-channel negotiation is one that occurs parallel to, but separate from, the regular, formal negotiation on an issue. It is carried on between officials —or semiofficials—who operate with direct authority from the president or premier. Often an intermediary is used in these negotiations.[33] Back

---

31. Again relevant here is Neustadt's characterization of how personal relationships between national leaders can deteriorate, with "muddled perceptions" and "stifled communications" leading to "disappointed expectations" and "paranoid reactions." (See p. 90, above.)

32. When a leading Japanese official in the textile negotiations was asked whether a political obligation to Nixon could have been stressed, in Japanese domestic discussions, as an argument for further Japanese concessions, he replied that the response would have been incredulous laughter—"We want to keep *that* man in office?!"

33. For an extensive discussion of the use of back channels in recent U.S.-Soviet relations, see John Newhouse, *Cold Dawn: The Story of SALT* (Holt, Rinehart and Winston, 1973). For a more general discussion of types of intergovernmental contacts and the roles and functions of unofficial "contact-makers," see Masashi Nishihara, "Kokkakan kōshō ni okeru 'hi-seishiki sesshokusha' no kinō: Nihon to Amerika no taigai-kōshō o chūshin ni" [The function of 'unofficial contacts' in international negotiations: Special focus on external negotiations of Japan and the United States], *Kokusai seiji*, vol. 50 (1973), pp. 66–87.

channels are thus employed, by definition, when at least one of the other types of channel is already in operation. Their use is a special case in the broader area of secret diplomacy, involving keeping information not just from the public but also from large portions of the governments involved. Back channels were employed at critical points in the Okinawa and textile negotiations. Their use has also been reported in the prewar and peace treaty negotiations.

Back channels are used for two overlapping purposes—to convey and obtain information, and to work out the actual terms of bilateral agreements on particular issues. An example of the first occurred midway in the textile negotiations, at a time when they were deadlocked. The parties with assigned responsibility in each government were Minister of International Trade and Industry Kiichi Miyazawa and Secretary of Commerce Maurice Stans. Neither knew the other personally. Each felt the need to get a better feel for the other's position and for whether there might be a basis for agreement between them. Hence, they found it useful to communicate through an intermediary, an American who had gotten to know Miyazawa during the postwar occupation and Stans during the Eisenhower administration. Similarly, Premier Sato in 1967, wishing to make substantive progress on Okinawa reversion, sent an emissary to the Johnson White House to communicate how important the issue was to him, and to learn what Johnson's price might be.

Yet another back-channel effort of a sort was the Ikeda mission of May 1950. Premier Yoshida wished to sound out Washington on a particular formula for future U.S.-Japanese relations—trading U.S. base rights on the Japanese mainland for American military protection and economic concessions. But as Langdon describes it, "the trip would have been disallowed by General Douglas MacArthur's staff for its real purpose." So "it was represented as an inspection tour for the Finance Minister to familiarize himself with the latest techniques abroad."[34] With this as his cover, Ikeda was able to take his trip and help lay the substantive foundations for the peace and security treaties negotiated by John Foster Dulles in the succeeding fifteen months.

In these cases, back channels offered a way for a responsible actor on

34. Frank C. Langdon, *Japan's Foreign Policy* (Vancouver: University of British Columbia Press, 1973), pp. 8–9; Langdon's source is Kiichi Miyazawa, *Tokyo-Washinton no mitsudan* [Tokyo-Washington secret talks] (Tokyo: Jitsugyo no Nihon Shu, 1956), pp. 47–52. On this episode, see also Frank Gibney, *Japan: The Fragile Superpower* (Norton, 1975), pp. 47–49.

one side to get through more or less directly to a key actor on the other side and learn what his interests and stands were on an issue, and what he thought his government would ultimately require. Communicating through regular channels usually means that an official has many audiences inside his own government. This is likely to discourage frankness about what he might really be willing and able to concede. By limiting his audience to a counterpart with comparable responsibility, he may be able to communicate with greater frankness. And if he uses an intermediary, the communications can be more tentative and exploratory than direct encounters with his counterpart might allow.

Communicating in this way is not, however, simple and trouble-free. Particularly if a new intermediary is being introduced, his technical expertise in dealing with the subject may prove shaky, or his personal relations with one of the parties may not be sufficiently close and dependable for him to speak reliably for that party. If these problems can be overcome, however, significant benefits can result. Sato seems to have been quite successful in communicating with Johnson through an agent in 1967, even though the immediate result fell short of the premier's maximum goal. A much more qualified success was the Ikawa-Iwakuro mission of early 1941; it conveyed Premier Konoye's interest in peace negotiations sufficiently to help get such negotiations inaugurated, but the talks themselves proved frustrating and unproductive.[35]

The use of back channels becomes more complicated when the aim becomes actual negotiation of specific terms for resolving an issue. Here the potential political benefits of employing such channels can also be substantial. They give the officials thus dealing directly and secretly a temporary freedom from political and bureaucratic struggles, and from cumbersome interagency clearance procedures that are often a part of

35. Two Catholic priests visiting Japan in November 1940, Bishop James E. Walsh and Father Drought, first proposed the idea of opening U.S.-Japanese talks for avoiding a war to Tadao Ikawa, who was a director of the Central Agricultural and Forestry Bank. Ikawa conveyed this idea to Premier Fumimaro Konoye, and the latter basically favored it. Instead of formally bringing it up at a cabinet meeting or at a liaison conference with the military, Konoye privately instructed Ikawa and Colonel Hideo Iwakuro to follow through on the idea in January 1941. This eventually led to the opening of negotiations between Secretary of State Cordell Hull and Ambassador Kichisaburō Nomura in Washington in April. For details, see R. J. C. Butow, *The John Doe Associates: Backdoor Diplomacy for Peace, 1941* (Stanford University Press, 1974); and Gaimushō Hyakunenshi Hensan Iinkai [Japanese Foreign Ministry], *Gaimushō no hyakunen* [A one-hundred year history of the Japanese Foreign Ministry], vol. 2 (Hara Shobo, 1969), pp. 541 ff.

such struggles. And if back-channel negotiations do lead to a basis for agreement, the existence of such an accord becomes something that can be used to mobilize the domestic support in the two countries that is required to make the agreement effective. This is a special case of the political argument for secret diplomacy: "Once the agreement is signed, it tends to act as a *fait accompli*, weakening dissent and mobilizing interest groups in support of it. Thus the requisite domestic consent may be obtained in the end, whereas the individual concessions would have been opposed."[36]

In the textile case, the advantages of using secret channels must have seemed obvious to officials employing them. With both governments pressed by strong textile industry spokesmen with close governmental ties, alert to the significance of every technical detail, and with these industries taking sharply divergent—in fact, irreconcilable—substantive positions, an escape from the need for each government to clear its position with domestic interests virtually day by day seemed a prerequisite for a solution. Yet to placate these domestic interests while the dispute continued, visible initiatives (or rebuffs of initiatives) were called for— hence the need to have a formal negotiation also. But the fact that a back channel seemed necessary did not make this approach sufficient. For on textiles, back channels did not eliminate the problems of achieving support domestically; they just changed the character of these problems, and not always in a beneficial way.

First of all, officials excluded from the action did not develop any commitment to agreement formulas negotiated in back channels, such as might have followed from their involvement. Moreover, they resented the exclusion, giving them a double motivation for resisting the secretly developed accord. After Premier Sato acceded to Nixon's textile wishes at the November 1969 summit, he returned home to encounter noncooperation from his MITI minister, who was unwilling to take much heat for sponsoring concessions made without his knowledge. Sato also met strong resistance from Japan's textile industry leaders, fueled by their conclusion that the premier was deceiving them, going around them, acting without the consultation and consideration of their interests that were the norm in consensus-style decisionmaking.

Such opposition was especially potent because the textile industry, and the allied MITI bureaucracy, had to play a key role in implementing

36. Iklé, *How Nations Negotiate*, pp. 134–35.

the export controls. There was no precedent for handling such export limitations without industry acquiescence and constructive cooperation. Efforts to win concessions by working with MITI and the industry had not been effective, and this was why the back channel was resorted to. As Henry Kissinger wrote (prophetically) in 1968 about American decisionmaking, an "unpopular" negotiating stance would have been— and repeatedly was—"fought by brutal means, such as leaks to the press." Hence back-channel negotiations: "the only way secrecy can be kept is to exclude from the making of the decision those who are theoretically charged with carrying it out."[37] But if those "theoretically charged with carrying it out" in fact have close to a hammerlock on the instruments of implementation, then the strategy is likely to backfire— and it did on textiles.

Yet another problem in that case was the emergence of the back channel itself as a major source of controversy in domestic politics. Premier Sato never exploited the potential leverage of an already-existing accord because he was unwilling to risk admitting that he had concluded one. He was reluctant to invite denunciation of a "textiles-for-Okinawa deal" (a "secret deal" has a particularly "dirty" connotation in Japan), fearing that this might force him to resign under fire and threaten those close Japanese-American ties that he felt were essential to Japan's welfare. Thus, an effort was made to transform the Sato-Nixon accord into a final formal agreement while concealing the existence of the accord from most participants in these formal negotiations. Predictably, it proved impossible to get the Japanese government, under heavy pressure from the industry, to arrive at the substantive position demanded by a Nixon administration determined to satisfy the American domestic industry, just as it had before the summit. For to Japanese officials, nothing fundamental had changed.

All of these problems in the use of back channels are, of course, part of a larger limitation applying also to summitry. If the power of the official at the other end of the back channel is limited, or if his role in the general decisionmaking system is constrained, then getting agreement with him is of limited value, for he will not be able to deliver. This proved true not just of the Nixon-Sato channel, but also of the Stans-

37. "Bureaucracy and Policy Making: The Effect of Insiders and Outsiders on the Policy Process," in Henry A. Kissinger and Bernard Brodie, eds., *Bureaucracy, Politics and Strategy*, Security Studies Paper 17 (University of California at Los Angeles, 1968), p. 5.

Miyazawa channel when the commerce secretary sought to pin down a basis for agreement through it.

This would be true even if both key actors were of the same mind as to what they had agreed to, and what the status of their agreement was. But it is anything but clear that they will be under such circumstances, and it remained uncertain in the textile case. One problem is expertise—limiting the direct action to generalist senior officials multiplies the possibilities for technical errors, or for agreements whose substantive and political implications are badly assessed by at least one of the negotiating parties. Both were recurrent problems in back-channel textile dealings. Kissinger did not understand the substance and thus seems to have taken, at times, positions inconsistent with his purposes. Sato, the evidence suggests, did not realize how restrictive was the agreement to which he had acceded.

Nor is it clear whether what was agreed to was conceived of in the same way on both sides. Both leaders did apparently see Sato's 1969 promise as a definite commitment to negotiate a textile restraint agreement, as Nixon desired. But did Sato, like Nixon, feel committed to the substantive details, to the particularly restrictive formula developed in the back channel? Or did Sato see it a bit differently, feeling that it left him some substantive room for maneuver? The latter seems more likely. For there may be significant differences between the ways that American and Japanese officials view the role of intermediaries, or go-betweens. And contrary to the assumptions of some American officials who seem to believe that intermediaries are the best way to negotiate with Japanese, it may be that such channels are generally considered more definitive, more final, by Americans than by Japanese.

Back-channel agents or intermediaries are frequently employed in Japan, probably more so than in the United States. In a society where individuals go to great lengths to avoid direct confrontations, go-betweens provide a vehicle for sounding out the real intentions of another party, encouraging franker communication than would be likely face to face.[38] But because of the strong bureaucratic tradition and the consensus decisionmaking style, official or "front" channels are generally the authoritative ones in Tokyo. Tacit understandings reached through behind-the-scenes bargaining are not considered final until they have

38. On this point, see Edwin O. Reischauer, "Introduction: An Overview," in Priscilla Clapp and Morton H. Halperin, eds., *United States-Japanese Relations: The 1970's* (Harvard University Press, 1974), p. 11.

been approved by the official decisionmaking body, such as the cabinet. Behind-the-scenes bargaining, then, becomes a step or an instrument toward creation of consensus among the parties concerned. Toland in describing a prewar episode comments that the use of go-betweens "was common in critical times, since telephones might be tapped; moreover, ideas could be expressed through a middle-man which would have been difficult to bring up face-to-face; and *if things didn't go well, the go-between could simply be repudiated.*"[39]

For Richard Nixon and Henry Kissinger, by contrast, back channels were unambiguously the place where the serious business of foreign policy negotiation normally took place. Similarly, Stans—in contact with Miyazawa via their intermediary in May and June of 1970—would likely have discounted the information appearing daily in the Japanese press portraying stances and proposals Miyazawa was putting forward that were inconsistent with Stans's minimum requirements. For he would have given more credit to the private signals he was getting, the basis for agreement he felt was emerging through the back channel. But after three days of Washington talks between the two men that ended in

39. John Toland, *The Rising Sun: The Decline and Fall of the Japanese Empire, 1936–1945* (Bantam, 1971), p. 130. Emphasis added. Nishihara also emphasizes the frequent resort to intermediaries by Japanese. He argues that employment of back channels is a product of a "diffuse" system of decisionmaking responsibility, which he compares with the "specific" system in the United States, where decision responsibility is more clearly focused. ("Kokkakan kōshō ni okeru 'hi-seishiki sessho-kusha' no kinō," pp. 82–83.) This is certainly true in the sense that consensus policymaking leads, in practice, to shared responsibility, though such diffusion would seem to make it harder—not easier—for intermediaries to operate effectively. But Nishihara's argument does not take account of the particular importance in Japan of responsibilities and procedures based on formal organizational roles and processes. On textiles, for example, the MITI minister was almost always the central policy figure in Tokyo, whereas President Nixon could and did shift responsibility for the negotiations among several officials with varying responsibilities. It may sometimes be more difficult in the Japanese system to attribute a particular decision to a particular individual, but Japanese nonetheless are more likely than Americans to follow established institutional patterns, at least in a formal sense. Back-channel agreements become authoritative only when accepted within the formal system. When working at its best, the system thus combines respect for formal prerogatives with flexible communication through intermediaries with personal ties to leaders.

In *The John Doe Associates*, Butow concludes that despite their apparent success in initiating negotiations in 1941, the overall impact of intermediaries Drought, Ikawa, and Iwakaro was "pernicious," misleading each government (especially Tokyo) as to the other's position, making the Hull-Nomura conversations "more muddled and ineffective than they would otherwise have been," and generally undercutting—despite noble intentions—whatever prospects for peace remained (pp. 315 ff.).

impasse, it became clear that the position Miyazawa was taking vis à vis other Japanese actors in his broader domestic policy process was a more reliable indicator of his ultimate stand.

Finally, there may have been mistakes or misinterpretations made by one or more of these intermediaries. Such a person may be so motivated to press a basis for agreement that he exaggerates the commitment of one principal or the other; he may misinterpret what is said; he may have ambitions or interests or values of his own that color his judgment or his action. Indeed, to play such a role in an error-free way, a person must have a formidable list of talents—political savvy, inside connections, intercultural sensitivity, substantive grasp, and personal self-effacement. Principals are, of course, not entirely at the mercy of a go-between—they can develop ways of checking or testing the information he conveys. But as long as they are conducting a concealed operation, their means of double-checking are necessarily constrained.

All of these considerations suggest that, in recent U.S.-Japanese relations, the advantages of back channels for serious negotiations have usually been more than outweighed by the risks. This does not mean they are not occasionally useful as a tool. It does mean that officials in both countries, frustrated by the constraints of domestic politics on bilateral issues needing resolution, need to guard against the temptation to overuse them. As a route to political intelligence, back channels have clearly proved helpful. As a device for resolving politically volatile issues, they need to be sparingly employed. At the very least, there needs to be clear reason to believe that dealing in secret will lead to resolution, not exacerbation, of the domestic political controversy that made the back-channel approach tempting in the first place.

Conclusions

The Okinawa reversion negotiations attest to the fruitfulness of reliance on regular diplomatic channels. But the three other types of channels were effectively employed in these negotiations as well. Progress was made through the summit of 1967, and agreement was reached and announced by Nixon and Sato in November 1969. Back channels played a key role in political intelligence. And while the weakness of the Japanese military ruled out the use of functional channels on issues related to the military bases, they were successfully employed in negotiating the financial arrangements of reversion after the 1969 agreement to proceed in principle.

Okinawa was also the most successful achievement of the transnational alliance between Americans and Japanese in and out of government who were concerned with protecting and strengthening the political foundations of the security relationship. Actors in both countries moved with increasing coordination and sophistication in pushing both governments to the solution they felt soundest on policy grounds—and salable on political grounds. The precursor of this alliance was important also in paving the way for security treaty revision in 1960, particularly in bringing American demands for Japanese military activity down to domestically realistic levels. Its failure was that it was too narrow, insufficiently sensitive to the power of the opposition to challenge the new treaty and the government that negotiated it. The Okinawa coalition was also limited, by and large, to members of the establishment in Japan, but it included nongovernment academics who were aware of broader intellectual opinion. And all of its main actors had the 1960 experience before them as a lesson in what to avoid.

On textiles, by contrast, the major transnational alliance was unsuccessful—partly because of misreading of decisionmaking in both countries, but even more because it was in competition with the established negotiating channel, and in direct opposition to the interest group the U.S. president was determined to satisfy. In textiles, every type of channel was also used, but often in conflict one with another, and with notably counterproductive results. Negotiators at the bureaucratic and even the ministerial level operated—especially in Japan—in ignorance of the summit-level understanding. Diplomatic channels were intermittently employed, but never firmly based domestically. Back channels and intermediaries were given burdens greater than the politics of the problem would bear. By contrast, the use of other channels in Okinawa was, in general, both substantively and operationally consistent with what the diplomats were seeking, and subject to their influence if not always their control.

For these and other reasons, Okinawa was also handled on both sides with unusual sensitivity to the impact of their actions on the politics of the problem in both countries. One important factor in Japan was Sato's political style—the very caution and indecision that so muddied the waters on textiles. The premier became committed to the Okinawa issue quite early, but he successfully avoided making his demands so urgent, so immediate, that he needed U.S. action faster than the American government could be expected to move. Sato's "indecisive" style also allowed enough internal debate in Japan to clarify what terms would be viable in Tokyo—in contrast to the 1960 crisis where the domestic political parameters became clear only after the treaty's conclusion.

In the United States the political problem was different—premature exposure of State (and Defense civilian) support for reversion ran the risk of triggering strong and immovable military and congressional opposition. Time was needed to negotiate with the military inside bureaucratic walls. The need for secrecy was met partly by the "attention gap" —Japanese calls for reversion did not turn up on the front pages of American newspapers, even when voiced by a premier, whereas U.S. demands for new textile quotas were inevitably prominent in Tokyo. But the Americans' ability to keep the issue a closed one also owed much to the restraint with which Japanese politicians and officials handled the issue. On textiles, American public statements of objectives were not restrained—especially after the mandate passed to Maurice Stans. Thus the Okinawa issue could rise to importance in the U.S. government through the reports of officials especially sympathetic to and oriented toward Japan; textiles reached Japanese political leaders through daily press reports and through complaints from industrialists and nationalists angered by these reports.

In its initiation, the subsequent interaction, and ultimate resolution, then, Okinawa once again demonstrated that a volatile U.S.-Japan issue can be effectively resolved. And textiles once again offers an example of what to avoid.

CHAPTER SIX

Managing Future U.S.-Japanese Relations

"UNTIL THE reversion of Okinawa is accomplished," said Prime Minister Eisaku Sato in 1965, "the 'postwar period' will not end so far as our country is concerned." From our vantage point ten years later, Sato's comment seems prophetic in more ways than he could have known or intended. For as final negotiations were being conducted for the return of Okinawa, the postwar period indeed came to a dramatic end. But the events that punctuated this finale included much more than reversion. From 1969 to 1971 there was the bitter dispute over textile quotas. In July and August 1971 Japan was confronted with the "Nixon shocks": the sharp turn in U.S. policy toward China, and the harsh announcement of unilateral measures to improve the U.S. balance of payments. By the time Okinawa returned formally to Japan in May 1972, Tokyo had responded to the second of the Nixon shocks by revaluing the yen and was lifting the most onerous of its remaining import barriers. The following September a new Japanese premier, capitalizing on the momentum of the sudden American move toward China, moved Japan one step ahead of the United States by normalizing diplomatic relations between Tokyo and Peking. By the close of 1972, therefore, the last major elements of American infringement on Japanese sovereignty had—by one means or another—been removed. Japan had emerged from America's cold war shadow on China policy; it had abandoned, under American pressure, most of that sheltered international economic position that Washington had initially encouraged and long accepted; and it had retrieved full sovereignty over the last of its territory taken over by the United States in 1945. The postwar period had indeed ended.

Our study has dealt mainly with this postwar period, concentrating on bilateral issues that were raised and resolved then. But it has been animated by concern for the future, and its conclusions and recommendations must be relevant to things not only as they were, but also as they are and will be. Thus before moving to conclusions drawn from past experience, we must address two broader questions. (1) Granted that the alliance relationship was very important to both countries in the period of cold war confrontation and Japanese economic and political reemergence, does it remain so in an era of American détente policies and a wider ranging Japanese diplomacy? (2) Assuming its continuing importance, can an analysis of past bilateral crises yield conclusions relevant to present and future problems?

The Importance of U.S.-Japanese Relations

Throughout this study, the importance of harmonious U.S.-Japanese relations has been assumed rather than demonstrated. We asserted the need in chapter 1; thereafter, it became the objective and the premise upon which this study was built. This was consistent with our purpose—to concentrate on the politics and the processes that have affected the attainment of this goal. And the conclusions reached in this chapter will also relate primarily to means. But they depend ultimately on the reader's acceptance of the ends to which they are addressed. Therefore, it seems appropriate at this point to offer a concise statement of why we believe a strong and cooperative Japanese-American relationship, lasting through the seventies and beyond, is so vital to both countries.

The primary reason why U.S.-Japanese relations are important is that the countries are important. In terms of gross national product, they are the world's first- and third-ranking nations, with Japanese output now above that of any Western European nation. For this reason alone, their cooperation has a major constructive impact on the international order, and a serious conflict between them could spell disaster.

The American commitment to Japan's defense responds to no immediate military threat. But it does serve to stabilize a relatively benign pattern of great-power relations in East Asia. Within the current security framework Japan is able to remain a lightly armed, nonnuclear power oriented toward the West but increasingly confident in developing its relations with communist countries. Conversely, the undermining or abandonment of the U.S. defense commitment could have very serious consequences. One need not accept the probability of any particular scenario—a militarily resurgent Japan with advanced nuclear armament arousing deep anxieties throughout East Asia and beyond; a weak and vulnerable Japan buffeted by international threats and domestic turbulence—to conclude that many of the alternatives to the existing arrangement could pose significant new threats to regional and world peace.

We do not mean to suggest that Japanese-American security relations should not continue to evolve to meet changing circumstances, or that they must always be based on the existing mutual security treaty. Other bases for bilateral security cooperation are certainly conceivable. And it is quite possible that one or both governments may one day seek to change the current security arrangement, perhaps in response to domestic pressures or leadership changes (such as the emergence of a coalition government in Tokyo). But were such a renegotiation to take place, a relationship of reciprocal political understanding and mutual credibility would be all the more important—to minimize the danger of a sharp break at a time likely to be punctuated by domestic controversy; to maintain a basis for continued constructive cooperation on security as well as other issues.

The importance of Japanese-American economic relations rests on two simple propositions: that each nation has a large stake in an open, liberal world economic order and that their cooperation is necessary in multilateral efforts to sustain such an order.[1] The fact that the two nations' approaches may diverge on issues such as energy does not refute this basic interest held in common. The Japanese economy, though not so foreign-trade-dominated as sometimes believed, does depend on access both to markets for its products and to commodities for import, particularly raw materials and agricultural products. The United States, while relatively more self-sufficient, nonetheless gains much, both economically and politically, from an open international trading and financial order. It gains particularly from commerce with Japan, its largest overseas trading partner; the recent lifting of Japanese restrictions on product and capital imports increases these gains. Here again the costs of a sharp break would be severe. Current economic interdependence is sufficiently great, particularly for Japan, that a major economic rupture would almost inevitably throw into question U.S.-Japanese relations across the board.

1. For a development of this argument with particular reference to the evolving Japanese economy, see Edward R. Fried and Philip H. Trezise, "Japan's Future Position in the World Economy" (Brookings Institution, 1974; processed).

For all of these reasons, it would be senseless and contrary to the interest of both countries to allow their relationship to unravel through mismanagement, or lack of political support, on either side of the Pacific.

The Relevance of Past Cases to Future Problems

But granted the continuing importance of strong U.S.-Japan ties, what relevance does the practical experience with bilateral crises of the postwar period have to the current, somewhat different situation? Are not emerging problems both different in substance and more multilateral than bilateral—like the energy question? And hasn't the unusual asymmetry of the postwar period been sharply reduced, with Japan both relatively stronger today and less dependent upon the United States?

Certainly the nature of the problems affecting U.S.-Japanese relations has changed in all of these directions, although it is difficult to say exactly how far these changes have gone or how long they will continue. But they do not, we believe, undercut the relevance of our analysis in any fundamental way. Different substantive problems will engage different groupings of actors in each capital, but this is hardly new. And barring major institutional changes these actors will be working within governmental systems very similar to those we have described. The major business of U.S.-Japanese relations has shifted notably in the past several years from bilateral to multilateral issues. But the two nations' cooperation is required to resolve most of these issues, and the development of common or compatible positions within multilateral negotiations will require the same sort of care in U.S.-Japanese dealings, the same effort to make mutual perceptions as accurate as possible. Indeed, it may require greater care. As for asymmetry, it has undeniably diminished at least in the economic area. It may one day disappear. But neither government is yet behaving as though that day is imminent; indeed, the psychological and behavioral tendencies associated with the postwar relationship of dependence remain strong.

Thus, if the episodes we have described will inevitably grow more dated, the larger political patterns and problems emphasized here should remain relevant. In the future as in the past, the issues most likely to endanger U.S.-Japanese relations will be those involving strong and conflicting domestic political values and stakes. And the ultimate course of U.S.-Japanese relations will continue to be shaped not simply by the

broad policy conceptions and objectives of national leaders, but importantly by the day-to-day management and mismanagement of specific
issues. Thus, although for simplicity of presentation we will frame our
conclusions in terms of bilateral negotiations or issues in which agreement between these two governments is the ultimate objective, the conclusions will apply also, we think, to U.S.-Japanese cooperation on issues
requiring multilateral resolution.

Explaining Success and Failure

Our concern throughout this study has been the resolution of U.S.-
Japanese issues. And our general criterion for judging effectiveness in
resolution has been political: the feasibility or sustainability of a bilaterally negotiated outcome (or series of outcomes) in the domestic
politics of both countries.

There are, of course, other criteria for measuring the success or failure
of bilateral interaction. Instead of concluding that the decision of Okinawa reversion was successful because it met the basic demands of both
American and Japanese politics and interests, one could measure it
against U.S. base policy worldwide and ask whether the maintenance
of a large base like the Okinawa complex is still desirable in the current
strategic situation. Instead of criticizing the mutual indisposition to
compromise on textiles, one could ask what general pattern of international trade regulation was desirable and evaluate the two countries'
positions in terms of their proximity to this pattern. We would not deny
the importance of such substantive policy questions; indeed, each of us
has particular views on them. But we believe also in the importance of
strongly based U.S.-Japanese relations. The cause of bilateral harmony
cannot always take precedence over other policy concerns, nor should it.
But it is a worthy objective and merits careful analysis of how it can
be attained.

This being our purpose, the existence of many other policy objectives
and interests in both countries has entered our study not on the assumption that they should or could be eliminated, but as the endemic, enduring characteristic of the politics of U.S.-Japanese dealings which
people committed to the relationship ignore at their own peril. We have
found that U.S. officials recurrently take actions or make statements that
damage or complicate U.S.-Japanese relations because their minds and

interests are elsewhere. This applies also, to a somewhat lesser degree, to Japanese politicians and bureaucrats. But these other interests are real and legitimate. They cannot be overcome by exhortations about the overriding importance of U.S.-Japanese relations because to most actors this will *not* be the primary value or interest. Thus for both governments the need is to protect and enhance the relationship by accommodating, modifying, or otherwise coping with these other values and interests in order to move toward common ground on particular issues, ground defensible in both Tokyo and Washington. This requires effective dialogue and mutual understanding between representatives of the two countries, but it requires also effective political management and consensus-building by these representatives at home. And the dialogues both within and between the two countries must proceed more or less simultaneously in the move toward accommodation.

Applying these criteria, and drawing on the analysis of previous chapters, we can arrive at a general explanation of the contrasting experience with Okinawa and textiles that has been highlighted throughout this book.

The underlying reason for success on Okinawa was the unusual degree of reciprocal political sensitivity. Washington policymakers saw the problem, above all, as one of Japanese domestic politics; if reversion were not expeditiously accomplished, opposition groups in Japan could use the issue to mount a strong attack on the overall alliance relationship when the ten-year treaty term expired in 1970. Their Tokyo counterparts were sensitive to U.S. politics because they had to be—they required a substantial, timely U.S. policy change which they lacked the power to force. Thus they needed to relate the form and timing of their initiatives to the needs of those Americans working for reversion within the U.S. government.

But on neither side did sensitivity to the politics of the other country mean a failure to respond to the politics at home. In Washington, military interest in protecting the Okinawa base complex was recognized; civilians and military leaders worked together to assure that reversion could be accomplished on terms consistent with this interest. And in Japan, of course, Prime Minister Sato worked consistently and effectively to avoid the sort of crisis in U.S.-Japanese security relations that confronted his brother and predecessor, Kishi. Once Sato made his decision about the minimum terms his domestic situation required, he went to great lengths to be sure Nixon would grant them. (This included, ironically, the textile promise that caused him so much trouble both with Nixon and within Japan.)

Because of this basic sensitivity on both sides to the politics of both countries, the more specific political requirements for resolving the issue could be met. In both countries the political groundwork could be carefully laid for a consensus on reversion, with key officials in each determined that the two national policy stances would emerge compatible with one another. In both, a relatively small circle of experts could control the issue because they made steady progress in satisfying the needs of major actors in both countries; the incentive for others to fight them or to open up competing channels was minimized. Thus the issue could be negotiated through a mutually reinforcing combination of diplomatic and summit channels; thus moderates in each country were able to strengthen one another. Many of these same strengths were present in the security treaty negotiations in the late fifties, which led effectively to agreement between the governments. But the Japanese opposition and the widespread public anxiety about the treaty had not been brought into the political equation. In 1969, by contrast, the agreement on nuclear-free, home-level reversion was directed explicitly toward meeting broad Japanese domestic concerns. The fact that several of the Japanese and Americans involved on Okinawa had dealt with one another on security treaty revision reinforced their determination to avoid a replay of the 1960 crisis, and their already established personal relationships limited the range of potential misperception as the Okinawa talks proceeded.

In the textile negotiations, such reciprocal political sensitivity was usually absent among those responsible for the issue in both countries. Instead, they took hard-line positions shaped almost entirely by how they construed domestic necessities. Consequently they were frustrated in their efforts to resolve the issue. Other channels then proliferated, and when these too yielded no solution, universal confusion and frustration were the inevitable result. Because moderates who sought compromise were on the defensive in each government, they were not able— as they had done on Okinawa—to deliver specific actions from one capital that would strengthen moderates in the other. On Okinawa, the few important actors outside the two governments who became involved worked with officials who controlled the action within these governments, to common purposes. On textiles, insiders and outsiders were frequently at cross-purposes, and the most remarkable outside initiative

—the alliance of Congressman Mills with the Japanese textile industry—involved designedly limited communication with top Nixon administration leaders and ended up in bitter confrontation with them. Thus Japanese-American interaction on textiles took the form of recurrent polarization, confusion, frustration, and enduring mutual resentment.

It is tempting, then, to attribute success on Okinawa almost entirely to the political sensitivity and skill of those who negotiated it, and to find the roots of the textile crisis in the lack of such sensitivity and skill on the part of those responsible there. But there were other reasons also that Okinawa proved the easier of the two to resolve, factors beyond the control of officials handling one or the other.

On Okinawa, for example, it was Japan that was doing the asking. If international negotiations were simple power contests where the stronger country is likely to prevail, then textiles should have been rather easily settled, whereas Okinawa should have festered unresolved. And between 1955 and 1965 that was what happened; Japanese repeatedly agreed to limit textile exports, while Americans treated Okinawa reversion as out of the question as long as international tensions persisted. But, as the experience of 1965–71 suggests, things can work the other way. Once the wall of U.S. resistance began cracking, the fact that Japan was the initiating country made Okinawa reversion easier for at least two important reasons. One was that the chief executive of the country from which concessions were sought, the American president, had considerable authority and leeway on the issue, much more than his Japanese counterpart had on textiles. A second was that the "attention gap," the relative neglect of Japan issues by the U.S. media, made it possible to avoid a premature Okinawa debate in the United States, which might have hardened military and congressional opposition before inside consensus-building could do its work. The U.S. textile initiative, by contrast, was front-page news in Tokyo, and it triggered a particularly volatile combination of strong Japanese textile industry resistance and broader nationalist resentment both reflected and fueled by the press.

There were also differences in the structure of interests on the two issues that made textiles particularly difficult. In the Japanese government, a strong role was unavoidably played in those negotiations by industry-responsive MITI officials, whereas Tokyo decisionmaking on Okinawa was controlled by politicians and foreign office officials with broader international perspectives. In Washington, the key special interest on reversion—the U.S. military—depended on tolerable U.S.-Japanese relations, and on reasonable tranquillity in Okinawa, in order to maintain viable base operations and thus its overall pattern of force deployment in the Pacific. Moreover, U.S. military leaders operate within a constitutional tradition that predisposes them to accept an unambiguous presidential decision unless it goes very deeply against their values and interests. The U.S. textile industry had no evident stakes in U.S.-Japanese relations that might have encouraged it to moderate its demands. And it was under no comparable presidential authority and discipline, though its leaders might have accepted a more moderate textile agreement without breaking with Nixon if he had confronted them with one and said it was all he could get.

Finally, Okinawa reversion was to most Americans a legitimate goal for the Japanese leadership to be pursuing, whether or not the same Americans felt that they could accommodate it. New textile quotas were, to many Japanese, an illegitimate, unreasonable demand for the U.S. leadership to make. Part of this critical difference involved yet another aspect of the asymmetrical relationship. There was a long tradition of American efforts to accommodate and bolster the conservative Liberal Democratic party leadership, whereas there was no comparable Japanese policy or interest in helping maintain a particular U.S. political party in power. The perceived illegitimacy of textiles stemmed also from the fact that it originated in "low politics"—a deal with a particular industry aimed at votes and money—whereas Okinawa involved the territorial identity of a nation.

Thus in considering why Okinawa was resolved effectively, and textiles was not, we have found part of our answer in how officials perceived the issues and their politics and how they managed national decision-making and bilateral negotiations. But we have also found part of our answer in differences between the issues, differences beyond these officials' control. There will surely be much in future U.S.-Japan issues also that officials will have to accept as given—in how particular domestic actors construe and press their interests, for example, and in the leverage they may be able to exert over the stands their government takes. Thus recommendations for improving the management of such issues should not be represented as a cure-all for future bilateral ills.

Still, Okinawa could easily have become a very serious political crisis without skillful and mutually sensitive diplomacy and political management. Textiles would have been difficult even with such skill, but damage to broader U.S.-Japanese relations could have been much better contained. And the crisis leading to cancellation of Eisenhower's visit in 1960 stands as a pertinent reminder that astute diplomacy within government channels may not be enough, if the broader domestic politics of an issue, in either country, is not effectively addressed.

Skillful and sensitive handling of the politics of U.S.-Japanese relations will remain a necessary, if not sufficient condition for maintaining strong bilateral ties. The remainder of this book considers how this goal can most effectively be advanced. The next two sections address how Americans should deal with Japan.[2] Assuming that influential U.S. actors give high priority to maintaining a strong relationship, how should they handle the difficult political issues that are certain to arise? The final section then deals with the problem of enhancing sensitivity to Japan in Washington. In a government where many others will not have such day-to-day concern, how can the voices of those sensitive to U.S.-Japanese relations be made more influential, or at least more clearly heard?

Japan as a Typical Large Ally

In fundamental respects, Japan is typical of the major countries with whom the United States has developed alliance relationships since World War II. Japan is a large democratic state with a strong bureaucracy and an advanced economy. Like their counterparts in the United States, politicians in Tokyo take varying stands on particular issues with an eye to their present standing and future prospects; officials operate from particular bureaucratic vantage points, with specific interests to defend and roles to play. On important foreign policy issues, influential actors are typically divided not only on ends and objectives to be pursued, but also about the means of pursuing them, and about who should have which responsibility for such means. In all of these respects, foreign policymaking in Japan is comparable to that in European countries with which the United States has close relations—Germany, for example, and the United Kingdom.

Similarly, the postwar Japanese-American alliance has been comparable in its origins and evolution to U.S. alliances with Western European

2. From this point on, we will address our recommendations primarily to the U.S. side, because we write principally for an American audience. In many cases, however, they are applicable to Japanese officials as well.

countries. It was formed under conditions that required dependence on the United States for economic survival, recovery from the war, and military security. It passed through a period during which Japan—like America's European partners—accepted and encouraged a dominant role for the United States, and formulated its own policies in deference to the patron nation. The hard necessities of this dependence limited, for a time, the influence of competing domestic interests and values on policies of the dependent nation's government and leadership, reducing the likelihood of major policy crises. This led many American policy-makers to assume a commonality of interest, a unified approach to international problems that would prevail over any wayward internal tendencies in its client. Moreover, the cold war made the United States subordinate its particular economic interests in the immediate postwar years to the need for alliance solidarity.

But as Japan recovered from abject dependence, strong competing forces inevitably reemerged to influence her policies, and Americans' tendency to underrate such forces contributed to the major, unanticipated bilateral crises that followed—in 1960 over the new security treaty, in 1969–71 on textiles. And the fact that these crises occurred between allies compounded the hurt and the frustration, because political leaders in one allied country expect their interests to be understood and accommodated by their counterparts in another. When this does not happen, their natural reaction is to feel let down personally, even betrayed. Again none of this is unique to U.S. dealings with Japan. Neustadt depicts a similar pattern in the Suez and Skybolt crises, even in an alliance between two nations with the strongest common cultural heritage.[3] And comparable problems resulted from the interplay of American and German politics in the negotiations of the mid-sixties over German balance-of-payments "offsets" for U.S. troop expenses.[4]

Yet despite these basic similarities to U.S. experience with Western European nations, Americans have tended to view Japan through very different lenses. Japanese differ in race, and speak a language very few Americans understand. Their culture appears as exotic and fundamen-

3. Richard Neustadt, *Alliance Politics* (Columbia University Press, 1970).

4. See "Offsets and American Force Levels in Germany: 1966, 1967, 1969," based on a case by Gregory F. Treverton, in Graham T. Allison and others, *Adequacy of Current Organization: Defense and Arms Control,* app. K to the Report of the Commission on the Organization of the Government for the Conduct of Foreign Policy (GPO, 1976), pp. 240–51.

tally alien, their modes of communication somehow purposive but hard to fathom. Successful in adopting the technology of the West, in emulating its pattern of industrialization, Japanese have somehow retained their cultural identity. Given this anomalous pattern of achievement, Japan's alternating role in U.S. history as friend and foe, the relative newness of extensive Japanese-American contact and communication, and the tendency of many Americans to fall back on racial stereotypes, it is not surprising that Americans' images of Japan have been fluctuating and simplistic. Thus, economically, Japan has been seen (by some as late as 1969) as an imitative, low-wage country producing shoddy goods for world markets at low prices, or (more recently) as a finely tuned modern industrial machine—Japan, Inc.—marching relentlessly to new economic conquests and threatening ultimately to subdue the world.

These views of Japan have colored concepts of the bilateral relationship and affected how Americans have handled that relationship. Just as the slow-dying "occupation mentality" among Japanese has perpetuated an attitude of dependence, an expectation of being "taken care of" well beyond the period when actual Japanese weakness justified such an attitude, Americans have found the role of patron and tutor all too congenial and hard to shake. As long as Japan behaved cooperatively— and postwar weakness often left her leaders little choice—Americans were friendly and even appreciative, impressed by her devotion to national economic and political reconstruction. American officials argued Japan's interests in international forums; and not merely because these interests were largely compatible with America's own. But the relationship was a somewhat patronizing one, and when Japan became visibly strong once again—this time economically—Americans reacted with concern, even alarm. For those whose cultural arrogance and racism made it inexplicable to them that an Asian country should seem to be beating the West at its own economic game, conspiracy theories became an easy explanation. Among officials, responses were usually more sophisticated, but the feeling was widespread that it was somehow wrong and unappreciative of past favors for Japan not to yield to U.S. needs on textiles once they were forcefully stated. When Japanese did not yield, they were "arrogant." Such expectations would not have been present in a negotiation with Great Britain or Germany. Indeed these countries were major textile exporters to the U.S. market in 1969, but the United States did not even press the issue seriously with them, much less employ the type of insensitive, sometimes brutal, negotiating tactics it employed toward Japan. Not surprisingly, much of the Japanese resentment in that case stemmed from the conviction that this was one more example of Western discrimination against Eastern products and countries. The fact that the U.S. initiative lumped Japan with Korea, Taiwan, and Hong Kong as a "low-wage" textile producer could only reinforce this conviction, and the broader ambivalence toward the United States within Japan.

This tendency to treat Japan as different from other major allies is both outmoded and damaging to U.S.-Japanese relations. Japan is far more like modernized Western countries than the enduring stereotypes suggest, though important political and cultural differences remain. And dealing with Japan as American officials deal with other major allies is likely to be far more productive, to produce considerably fewer misunderstandings and resentments, than treating Japan as a mystery that can be unlocked only with an entirely different sort of key. For whether they make Japan to be a docile partner or a relentless ultimate adversary, simplistic images of a unified, calculating Japan blind Americans to what they need above all to recognize—that Japan is a plural, many-sided country, home to a welter of competing viewpoints and interests, whose government and policies reflect the semiresolved conflicts among these views and interests. America's major postwar problems with Japan have arisen not from her unity but from her disunity—ideological conflict over the revised security treaty, governmental inability to win textile industry agreement to quota concessions, slowness in reaching consensus on measures to correct the trade imbalance.

Thus, the first lesson for American officials dealing with Japan is that she should be thought of like any large allied country. *In analyzing a particular U.S.-Japan political problem and deciding how to handle it, Americans should ask the same sorts of questions, and employ the same sorts of negotiating tactics, as they would when dealing with Britain, Germany, Canada, Italy, or France.* Japan—like these countries—is not a unified entity whose every act is part of a coherent bargaining strategy, but rather a complex political system where issues are being argued out internally even as they are being negotiated externally. In choosing which issues to press and how hard to press them, in selecting which signals to send and how to send them, *American officials need to make explicit, careful calculations about the internal politics of such issues in Tokyo*—about what outcomes seem feasible within this politics, and about which American steps are likely to strengthen the chances for the Japanese decisions and actions the Americans seek. At the same time, they need to be moderate in their expectations (as Neustadt emphasizes in U.S. relations with Britain). The U.S.-Japanese alliance has spawned a large area of overlapping interests, and a considerable range of transnational alliances and channels, both formal and informal, for handling issues; these suffice for resolving the majority of bilateral issues, or at least averting crises on them. But where domestic interests and stakes in particular issues are high, resolution becomes far more difficult. On such politically sensitive issues, U.S. officials must recognize how strong domestic forces inimical to agreement can prove, how hard it often is to calculate the other country's politics correctly and how difficult to control their own government's action, even if they calculate correctly about the "other side." This is true of difficult issues with Britain; it is no less true with Japan.

It follows that, as a general rule, *major issues should be initiated and emphasized only if analysis of the Japanese political scene indicates reasonable prospects for a favorable outcome.* Often, such analysis is undertaken too late—an issue is pressed, and Japanese political receptivity is considered only when resistance arises. Sometimes, as in the textile case, American officials seek an international agreement in the hope that Japanese cooperativeness will solve their political problems in Washington. Thus Nixon sought to control textile imports through international negotiations not because of positive findings abroad but because of negative findings at home. Like Kennedy before him, he did not want to go to Congress for the statutory authority to impose textile quotas unilaterally, fearing Congress would force on him broader trade restrictions that he did not want.

What one would like is the opposite—a presumption against choosing as a major priority objective something for which there is little apparent support and strong potential opposition in Japan. And if such an objective is chosen anyway, as in the textile case, it should be pressed with restraint—taking care not to provide a target for critics in Japan; recognizing that the maximum substantive goal may prove unattainable. Japanese initiatives on security treaty revision and Okinawa reversion were better received than the American textile proposal because important American actors saw revision and reversion as important means of protecting and strengthening the security alliance, something the *Americans* valued. Similarly, American pressure for relaxation of Japanese import barriers benefited from a growing body of official and business opinion in Tokyo that saw such liberalization as both inevitable and desirable. There was no such support in Japan for textile quotas in 1969.

It is easier, however, to argue the need for such timely political assessments than to prescribe a fool-proof procedure for making them. One important if oft-cited rule is to *keep open a range of information sources* about the politics of an issue in Tokyo, as one should do in any major capital. Foreign office officials are frequently limited in their domestic political sensitivity; actors generally interpret their domestic scene in terms of their particular interests; even the Tokyo allies of American officials will have different stakes that color their perceptions. To avoid overdependence on one information channel, U.S. officials need not only to keep a number of lines open, but also to understand the vantage points, biases, and limitations of them all. Another means of assessing political prospects is *to take advance, "unofficial" soundings* through diplomatic or other bilateral channels, raising an issue tentatively in order to "test the water." Sometimes this can be done by a public statement, though this risks activating opposition once the statement appears in the Japanese press. (If an issue needs to be aired publicly, in fact, it is often better for Japanese actors to launch the trial balloons, since this avoids the connotation of American pressure or an attempt by the "senior partner" to dictate a solution.)

To suggest such general rules is not to imply that U.S. officials with day-to-day responsibility for Japan are typically insensitive to such matters. On Okinawa they were very sensitive, and the actions of particular officials on other specific issues have frequently been animated by a rather sophisticated awareness of the politics of such issues in Tokyo. On occasions where biases and misreadings have plagued U.S. policymaking, the fault has rested not so much with officials specializing in Japan as with political leaders and functional officials who were rejecting their advice. In the 1960 crisis, however, the embassy's readings were wide of the mark, and State Department officials in 1969–70 did underestimate the depth of Japanese textile resistance, though they were sensitive enough to its presence. Even if they do consult many sources and take advance soundings in sophisticated ways, of course, U.S. officials cannot fully judge whether an initiative might win acquiescence in Tokyo if they fail to consider one major influence on Japanese decision-making—how much energy and bargaining leverage U.S. leaders are willing to apply to the issue. But on a case like textiles, a careful advance analysis would have concluded that a very large American effort would be required, and that even such an effort might not prove successful. Such a finding would not, by all evidence, have deterred President Nixon from pressing the issue, given his prior political commitment. But assuming that Nixon had a will to listen to such analysis and take it seriously, he and his advisers might conceivably have selected their means more carefully and been more flexible on terms at critical negotiating junctures.

Once an issue is initiated, the next rule in politically difficult negotiations with allies becomes: *don't expect too much too soon*. Major initiatives are almost always calls for major adjustments of interests within the target country. These almost always take time. It was wrong to hope for quick Japanese adherence to comprehensive textile restraints in 1969 —the Japanese industry saw too great a stake in exploiting rapidly growing markets for manmade fibers; it felt too deep a resentment against the enforcement of existing cotton textile quotas; it was able to mobilize quickly and seize the banner of nationalist resistance to "unreasonable" American demands; there was no strong counterpressure in Tokyo. Since the textile industry not only had strong support on the issue in governmental and political circles, but also controlled the means of implementing an agreement, its acquiescence to any agreement was essential, and it would not be quickly attained. (Nor, conversely, could Sato have won return of Okinawa in 1965 or 1966, no matter how hard he had pressed for it; the adjustment of U.S. military interests could not be accomplished in a day.)

In working toward an objective, *it is often useful to seek limited concrete steps* to create momentum toward a goal. On both security treaty revision and Okinawa reversion, agreement on intermediate goals proved useful—the joint committee to study the security relationship established at the 1957 Eisenhower-Kishi summit; the Johnson-Sato agreement of 1967 on negotiating reversion within "a few" years. And in both cases these steps established a presumption favoring further action that advocates of such action could exploit within their own governments. On textiles, however, the United States (under industry pressure) repeatedly rebuffed proposals for partial restraints to take effect soon, holding out for a "comprehensive" accord covering all textile trade. Americans in charge of the negotiations do not seem to have given much thought to how such a partial accord might have been designed so as to lead to broader coverage later. Of course, one problem was that Japanese negotiators wanted to assure that any partial accord would not lead to broader restrictions, but stand as an alternative to them.

While an issue is being negotiated, *U.S. officials should regularly seek to provide signals that strengthen moderates in Tokyo who are working to bring about agreement.* The aim should be to enhance the latter's ability to serve as brokers between domestic and U.S. interests. This must be done, however, with a good deal of care and finesse. In some cases it may be well to respond positively to proposals by Japanese moderates even if they fall short of what is desired—to encourage further efforts on their part; to make them appear to their colleagues as officials taken seriously in Washington. Unless taken with subtlety, however, such action on the part of American officials may well embarrass the Japanese moderates and discredit them in the eyes of their more nationalistic opponents in the government, mass media, and the general public. In any case, it will almost always be prudent to avoid the opposite—the sweeping denunciations of Japanese "arrogance" and "inflexibility" that Americans sometimes indulged in during the textile negotiations. Not only do these undercut Tokyo moderates by making the Americans with whom they do business appear insensitive and even "anti-Japanese"; they are bound to be picked up in the Tokyo press and to fuel nationalist resistance to concessions. A much more positive and promising line would be to develop arguments in support of U.S. proposals that Japanese actors can pick up and use domestically, arguments that are relevant to the main issues as seen in Tokyo. Still another way to strengthen the hand of Japanese moderates is by granting concessions in the course of particular negotiations that are designed to give them what they need politically at home—like the provision in the 1967 communiqué for gradual adjustment of Okinawan economic and administrative structures to prepare for reunification with Japan. Once again, through these and other actions, U.S. officials should conceive of policymaking in Japan as a typical political process and think about how best to help those who are fighting within that process for actions leading toward bilateral agreement on controversial issues.

Finally, some conclusions common to the handling of all relationships can be drawn about U.S.-Japan summit diplomacy. Like most leaders in parliamentary systems, the Japanese prime minister is limited in his power, so his acquiescence is not equivalent to delivering the Japanese government on an issue. Another postwar lesson, however, is how closely the resolution of major issues has been tied to the current political situation of the reigning premier. The crisis of 1960 reached such a peak because an unpopular treaty was identified with an unpopular premier, Nobusuke Kishi. His brother, Eisaku Sato, failed to move more aggressively on textiles ten years later because of his particular vulnerability to charges he had "tainted" Okinawa reversion by making a textile promise to Nixon.

The basic conclusion that emerges is that *Americans should avoid placing too great a domestic burden on a prime minister in the pursuit of an objective*. If an alliance relationship is to endure, it is important to show reasonable sensitivity to the political constraints within which a counterpart leader must operate. Moreover, *U.S. leaders should normally avoid linking negotiations on politically controversial issues that are essentially separate in substance and involve separate Japanese domestic constituencies*. However attractive—even inevitable—a textiles-for-Okinawa trade may have seemed to Nixon, the two issues were in different political arenas in Tokyo. What Sato gained on Okinawa was not of direct benefit to the industry-related interests most resistant to a textile accord. To them, such a trade-off was all loss and no gain; hence they fought it.[5]

Japan as a Special Case

In all of the ways just cited, Americans can best deal with Japan by behaving very much as they would—or should—toward a major European ally. But dealing with any country requires sensitivity also to its unique features. Japan particularly requires such sensitivity, because the language and cultural gap remains deep, because misunderstandings and misperceptions have been uncommonly frequent.

The ways Japanese policymaking is "different" bear little resemblance to the extreme stereotypes recapitulated earlier in this chapter. The

---

5. There was also a particularly Japanese reason why this "secret deal" issue proved so volatile in Tokyo. To most Japanese, reversion was an issue of national integrity and honor, an overdue vindication of basic Japanese rights. It was therefore, in a certain sense, illegitimate for the Japanese government to bargain for it, and for the Americans to demand a price for it. For Nixon, holding back on Okinawa to extract textile concessions must have seemed like natural bargaining behavior. But for Japanese the sacred historical event of reversion would be severely tarnished if their government had to make "unreasonable" concessions on an unrelated trade issue in order to bring it about.

Japanese government is not monolithic. Its institutions are neither unusually disciplined nor overridingly purposive. Postwar economic growth policies have been impressive, and relations between officials and industrialists have had a more cooperative, less "adversary" character than in the United States. But there is no "Japan, Inc.," no relentless government-business combine. To the degree that the "special" character of U.S.-Japanese relations has been a product of Americans holding to such erroneous perceptions—and some of it has—their correction can contribute to reducing the degree Americans wrongly treat Japanese as "different," to both nations' benefit. But Japanese policymaking *is* different in that it exhibits, in particularly acute form, the dispersal of influence and decision power found in all modernized democratic societies.

In all modern democratic societies, major policy steps require reasonable political consensus. But in Japan this extends to a belief that all major views and interests relevant to a decision ought somehow to be taken into account, that all those with important stakes in the outcome have a right to a hearing and some influence. Achieving consensus by this broad criterion can take considerable time on controversial issues, if it is attainable at all.

In parliamentary systems generally, the chief of government is a less commanding figure than an American president. But in Japan the constraints on the premier are particularly great—because of consensus values and expectations; because of fragmentation within the ruling party; because of the strength of the permanent bureaucracy; because of the ability of the opposition to exert effective public pressure notwithstanding its permanent minority status.

In every country, the politics of national defense and security has particular features, but in Tokyo the legacy of World War II combines with more general features of Japanese politics to impose constraints unlike those in any other major country.

In many bilateral relationships, there are differences in negotiating styles, but those between the United States and Japan can cause particular trouble unless officials are sensitive to them.

The lessons arising from these differences do not conflict in any fundamental way with our primary injunction—do unto Japanese as you would do unto other important allies. But they do add an important dimension to the relationship, and thus to our conclusions about how it should be handled day by day.

Japan's unusually weak and constrained political leadership reflects the never-ending competition among the Liberal Democratic party's senior members for the premiership. The prime minister's dependence on factional balance within the party limits his authority and shapes the composition of his cabinet. However adept he may be politically, the Japanese prime minister lacks the authority and autonomy of a strong American president in deciding how an issue will be resolved. Moreover, attempts to assert such authority are likely to be resisted as arbitrary or undemocratic. For in Tokyo the premier is expected to move slowly and carefully, articulating the existing consensus on an issue or nurturing gradual changes in it rather than issuing clarion calls for fundamental new policies.

The premier and his cabinet are further constrained by the strong bureaucracy. The major ministries are dominated by elite senior officers who seldom shift between ministries, and are almost never challenged by the kind of in-and-out officials identified with particular U.S. presidents or administrations. Nor is there any layer of politically appointed officials between the cabinet and the bureaucracy. All of this strengthens the ministries as self-confident, elite institutions, and increases the ministers' dependence on them. And it is reflected in conceptions of what is proper for political leaders to do. In Washington it is accepted practice for the president to circumvent the bureaucracy. But in Tokyo the permanent government remains, in many respects, the ultimate, legitimate locus of responsibility.

For Americans dealing with Japan the strength of the bureaucracy can sometimes be helpful; it offers a clear target for communications, a clear locus of responsibility. But when the desired decisions or concessions are not forthcoming, as in the textile case, it produces frustration. Not surprisingly, U.S. leaders then seek to negotiate above or around Japan's bureaucracy. Just as predictably, these efforts usually fail, for there seldom exists an authoritative political counterpart with whom a binding deal can be struck. Acting as further barriers to resolving issues through summit conferences and back channels are the Japanese aversion to "secret deals" and the prevalence of leaks to the Tokyo press.

In general, therefore, *American leaders dealing with Japan should employ summit channels not to substitute for diplomatic or functional channels, but to reinforce them, in careful coordination with them. Americans should confine the use of back channels in U.S.-Japanese relations to the gathering of political intelligence about what agreements may be possible, rather than employing them to negotiate such agreements.* Behind these operational recommendations, however, is a broader conclusion. The concessions sought by Americans will often be politically unattainable, especially if what is asked for is quick Japanese action on contentious issues. *Rather than employing weakly based back channels, or pressing for personal concessions from a prime minister unlikely to be able to deliver his government, Americans dealing with Japan need to lower their expectations about what can be quickly accomplished. The general rule for all alliance relationships—don't expect too much too soon—applies with particular force to Japan.*

Further constraining Japanese political leaders is the ideological split between conservatives and opposition. Though Americans tend to discount the opposition parties because of their extreme ("irresponsible") policy positions, their anti-American stance, and their lack of visible power, the opposition does exercise important inhibiting influence on Japanese foreign policy. In seeking to deny the opposition openings to exploit, conservative governments are moved to caution. Such caution is likely to increase if the conservative Diet majorities diminish further— or disappear. In order to assess accurately the impact of opposition parties on Japanese policymaking, *U.S. officials need to extend their contacts beyond the conservative establishment, probably to a greater extent than they have to date.* The problem of broadening such communications unfortunately is not one resolvable simply by Americans, for part of the difficulty is that opposition figures are often reluctant to be "tainted" by too much contact with U.S. officials. And the fact that American diplomats are accredited to the current government—and must negotiate day-to-day issues with that government—imposes inevitable constraints, of course, on how much they can build relationships with outside groups. A notably encouraging recent development was the successful September 1975 visit to the United States by a delegation of prominent Japan Socialist party members; the fact that the last previous such visit was eighteen years before suggests the gap in communications that remains.

Pressure from the opposition is particularly pervasive on defense and security issues, fueled by ideological opposition to the Self-Defense Forces and the alliance with the United States. Nor is this pressure countered by the kind of institutional strength inside the government that the Pentagon provides. The Japanese military is essentially uninvolved in foreign policy, shies away from strategic discussion, and takes its direction from political leaders and civilians in the Japan Defense Agency. This, plus the enduring popular antimilitary and antinuclear sentiment which is a legacy of World War II, makes Japanese military and security policies far more inhibited than those of any other important nation. Despite American urgings to do more, postwar Japanese governments have consistently avoided major rearmament and military commitments outside Japan's borders. Because of this unique combination of political pressures and because the resulting Japanese security policies are, we believe, generally consistent with U.S. interests, American officials should exercise restraint in pressing Tokyo on defense questions.

The Japanese pattern of decentralized policymaking and the inhibitions on defense issues cause Japanese officials to exercise considerably greater caution in bilateral negotiations than their U.S. counterparts. This Japanese tentativeness, their preference for talking generally about and around a problem, attending first to forms and general principles and leaving the details to a later stage, often comes across to Americans as delaying tactics, and delay may well be its outcome whether intended or not. To Japanese, by contrast, the U.S. push for specifics often seems overhasty, perhaps even rude, and certainly insensitive to the need for time to develop mutual confidence and a general framework for understanding. The Japanese relative lack of verbal assertiveness in communications—particularly in dealing with Americans in English—reinforces this difference in style. And even in the use of go-betweens, a practice particularly attractive to Japanese as a means of facilitating indirect communication, it is the Americans who tend to expect quick and definitive results, while the Japanese consider employment of intermediaries as exploratory and tentative.

Such divergence in negotiating styles is not easy to bridge; nor will greater sensitivity to Japanese negotiating preferences always bring Americans the results they seek. Tentative, informal communication about an issue is certainly useful in its early stages, as officials begin to focus on its substantive and political ramifications. And in initial negotiating sessions, it may well be useful for Americans to follow Japanese preferences and talk about the issues at hand in an exploratory, general, tentative manner. But if they keep doing so, they may contribute to delay rather than resolution; conversely, a clear-cut U.S. stance on specifics is often necessary to move the Japanese government to reach its own specific position. *But while maintaining their preference to push specific issues where possible, American negotiators can pay greater heed to questions of timing—seeking to judge whether a move to specifics is premature or whether the issue has been sufficiently vetted in Japan to make possible a concrete response to a specific initiative.* Americans can also give heed to Japanese concern for form by seeking to put their specifics within a framework acceptable to Japanese involved in the issue (as was done on Okinawa), and by understanding that ambiguous Japanese responses do not necessarily have negative connotations. And in cases where Japanese officials seem personally reticent about pressing policy views that conflict with the Americans', U.S. officials can sometimes move things along if they spend less effort pushing their own positions and more time encouraging the Japanese to articulate theirs. Of course, when the U.S. substantive stance on an issue triggers broad opposition in Japanese domestic politics, delay and more delay is likely to be the ultimate—if not, for all actors, the intended—Japanese response. But where a substantive basis for compromise seems politically attainable, Japanese ambiguity may well reflect a serious feeling out of the domestic and bilateral politics of the issue, and may then be followed by a more specific and constructive substantive reaction.

Yet these recommendations for handling negotiations with Japan differ only slightly from the kind of negotiating practice that would be appropriate toward other countries. And it is particularly important that U.S. officials not allow their awareness of the particular features of Japanese policymaking to move them to treat Japan issues, and Japanese negotiators, in a fundamentally different and perhaps invidious manner. Too often Americans have done that, with unfortunate consequences. For Japanese officials—long sensitive to and resentful of discrimination in the international community—are likely to perceive themselves as being treated differently by Americans, even on the basis of limited evidence. The result can be a clouding of interpersonal dealings that can hinder particular negotiations even though the Americans involved may not be fully aware of what the problem is. Thus, *American officials need to show, in their dealings with Japanese counterparts, the same personal respect, the same avoidance of condescension and cultural arrogance, that they should evidence in dealings with Europeans.* And on substantive issues like trade policy, where Japan is still emerging from a long experience of discrimination against her products, *Americans should avoid both the fact and the appearance of seeking arrangements vis à vis Japan that are inequitable by comparison with parallel arrange-*

ments with European countries. In contrast to the security sphere—where arrangements differing from those in NATO have strong political and substantive justification—Japanese-American economic relations need to be based, to the greatest extent possible, on full reciprocity in benefits and obligations within a larger world economic order founded on the same principles.

Thus, even attention to Japan as a special case yields recommendations similar to what one would urge in U.S. dealings with other allies. American officials should be sensitive to the particular features of Japanese politics, but all countries have unique political configurations which need to be understood and dealt with. The cultural style and language differences are particularly important in this bilateral relationship. But once we focus on how Americans should seek to bridge these differences, we end up saying, in various specific ways, that they should deal with Japanese as they deal (or ought to deal) with representatives of other large countries. The cultural gap does require some extra effort, greater attentiveness so that reciprocal political understanding and communication can be adequate and effective. But it is the same sort of effort that Americans should devote to Anglo-American or German-American relations. Japan remains, of course, special in significant ways, and these need to be recognized. But *Americans dealing with Japan will do so far more effectively, with far fewer mistakes, if they approach Japan and Japanese as a country and people whose government and politics are not all that different, fundamentally, from those of large, modern societies elsewhere in the world.*

Increasing U.S. Government Sensitivity to Japan

All of our recommendations to this point have been based on the assumption that there are U.S. officials who give high priority to U.S.-Japanese relations in their daily work. And clearly there are. Yet only a small minority of American politicians and bureaucrats will be interested in any continuing way in such recommendations. For the rest, concern about Japan is at best rather general and intermittent; their interests, their jobs, their expertise, their institutional and personal stakes involve mainly other things.

How then does one get the U.S. government to act with sensitivity toward Japan and the politics of the relationship? If U.S. government policies toward Japan were clearly separable from other important American objectives and interests, the answer would be obvious—that government decisions with major impact on U.S.-Japanese relations should be made and influenced, insofar as is possible, by those in the U.S. government and society who are expert in the substance and politics of the relationship, and by the overlapping group of those whose jobs make them feel especially responsible for keeping U.S.-Japanese relations on a reasonably even keel.

This is in fact the way things worked on Okinawa. The political case for steps toward reversion was voiced by the dean of America's "Japan experts," Edwin Reischauer, from the beginning of his ambassadorial tenure in 1961. In 1966, after Sato had identified himself personally with the islands' return, the State Department's country director for Japan seized hold of the issue. Working with the new U.S. ambassador U. Alexis Johnson and with civilian and military officials in the Pentagon, he quietly but adroitly built a working-level bureaucratic consensus within which reversion came to be seen as both inevitable and acceptable to U.S. interests.

But the experts' ability to move this issue within the U.S. government did not result from their sensitivity to Japan. From such sensitivity they drew the objective and their determination to press it. But their success arose from their ability to understand the stakes of other key American policy actors on the issue—mainly the military and their potential congressional allies—and to engage them in a dialogue from which a resolution satisfactory to both emerged. Indispensable also was the positive orientation of two presidents—Johnson and Nixon—and the ability of the officials involved to understand and operate within their priorities and constraints. Had there been important presidential political objectives inconsistent with what these officials were doing, or had these officials been perceived as unresponsive to the program interests of the military, they could not have controlled the issue as long as they did. On textiles, where the priorities of key State Department officials were in conflict with the President's (and with those of the commerce secretary and his department), policy determination and management were kept out of their hands.

In the late fifties and early sixties, of course, U.S.-Japan issues did not typically engage competing American political and functional actors in a major way. Bilateral security and economic dealings had little immediate impact on broader U.S. strategic policies or the international economy; Japan was not a focal point for domestic political contention. So in the United States, Japan issues could be left more or less consistently to the country experts at the State Department and its Tokyo embassy. The presence of strong officials in both locations worked also to this end, and the general sympathy and support of senior Kennedy and Johnson administration officials for the alliance was of course essential for the experts to be able to play this role. But this period appears to have ended as the postwar era ended, with Japan's emergence as a front-rank economic power with significant impact on world economic patterns and institutions and growing impact on U.S. domestic markets. And while American political concern about the "Japanese threat" has fallen off since it reached its peak in 1971 and 1972, the pattern of "leaving things to the Japan experts" is unlikely to reemerge. At the very least, these experts on Japan must now share responsibility with other government experts—in monetary and trade matters, for example—whose claims to involvement are no less legitimate than their own. This has become particularly important now that so much bilateral U.S.-Japan interaction is taking place on multilateral issues, and often in multilateral forums.

Thus, if they are to operate effectively within this broader substantive and political arena, *there is a need to strengthen the sensitivity of those expert in and specifically responsible for the U.S.-Japan relationship to other major values, interests, and objectives that affect U.S. national policymaking, thus improving their ability to coordinate the politics of the process and to build internal consensus in support of their policy initiatives.* For good U.S.-Japanese relations cannot be effectively advanced by officials insensitive to other legitimate U.S. policy objectives. Rather, such officials must be knowledgeable and credible mediators between the needs of the relationship and the concerns of other U.S. policy-influencing actors. The U.S.-Japan relationship will be well served if those with responsibility for it are doing the coordinating, but only if they are successful in satisfying, placating, or combating other relevant interests inside their government, as State officials were on Okinawa. And they must also be sensitive enough to the broader political feasibility of a settlement to avoid provoking a crisis domestically with the terms they negotiate, as occurred in Tokyo in 1960.

Yet on many issues the country specialists cannot play a central management role whatever their responsiveness to other interests. They may lack functional expertise or authority. It was Treasury Under Secretary Paul Volcker, not an official of State's Bureau of East Asian Affairs, who coordinated the second dollar devaluation in February 1973 and flew secretly to Tokyo to consult just prior to its implementation. Or the president may view an issue as belonging primarily in a sphere where the Japan specialists' expertise and credibility are limited—electoral politics (textiles), or relations with another country (the July 1971 China shock), or domestic economic policy (the "soybean shock" of U.S. export controls in June 1973). Looking at U.S. foreign policymaking more generally, a State Department skeptic concluded in 1970 that the country director was typically "too far removed from the source of political power to evaluate, reconcile, and arbitrate the U.S. interests involved in any important issue."[6] And if Okinawa is an example to the contrary, it is hard to find very many others.

If those whose principal concerns lie elsewhere are bound to control many issues of major importance to U.S.-Japanese relations, then *those officials not specifically responsible for U.S.-Japanese relations need to be made more sensitive to the politics of the relationship and to how the issues that they help decide will affect Japan and the relationship.* At minimum, the aim would be limitation of damage—officials close to President Nixon and politically credible to him might have argued for a somewhat less demanding stance on textiles, on the ground that it would in fact resolve the issue and could be effectively sold to U.S. industry leaders even if it did not give them everything they wanted. This might have terminated the dispute in December 1970 if not before. More ambitiously, the aim would be to build the needs of U.S.-Japanese relations into broader policy initiatives that a government was pursuing, and into the concepts of international reality that national leaders hold. Again, the examples are negative. The 1971 Nixon shocks reflected no positive concern with Japan ties and Japanese political impact. And the Nixon administration's "five-power world" concept of power centers flexibly adjusting their policies to balance one another does not seem very realistic when set against the politics of a bilateral relationship where (especially in Tokyo) governmental decisionmaking is slow and issues must

6. Dissent of Arthur Allen, in U.S. Department of State, *Diplomacy for the Seventies* (1970), p. 357. For a comprehensive assessment of the role of country directors in U.S. foreign policymaking since the position was established in 1966, see William I. Bacchus, *Foreign Policy and the Bureaucratic Process: The State Department's Country Director System* (Princeton University Press, 1974).

be carefully bargained internally before moves can be made externally. Political leaders seldom have the leverage and authority they would need to make such a system work.

A prerequisite for reciprocal sensitivity between Japan experts and other U.S. officials is, of course, continuing intragovernmental communication. Particularly important is a steady, two-way dialogue between the Japan specialists and each administration's political leadership. That communication seems to have been most effective between 1961 and 1969, but under circumstances where the White House gave little day-to-day attention to Japan and tended not to press the priority of other policy values on key issues affecting Japan—a situation not too likely to recur. The nadir of such communication came in 1971, when the Nixon White House—frustrated by the textile case, tending to view Japan experts as Japan apologists—took major actions affecting Tokyo without the experts even being informed, much less involved. There were, of course, particular advantages to the Nixon administration in springing its new China and economic policies on an unexpecting world. But there is no evidence that the costs to U.S.-Japanese relations were seriously addressed, much less the possibility of the United States taking other actions toward Japan to ease or compensate for the shocks.

High American policymaking is peculiarly a product of presidential style, which limits the potential of institutional remedies for this sort of internal noncommunication. *One possibility, however, would be for each president to assign, to one of his senior foreign policy advisers, a "watching brief" for U.S.-Japanese relations, establishing as one of his explicit responsibilities the task of following major U.S.-Japan issues and defending the needs of the relationship both on these issues and on other issues with substantial impact on Tokyo.* This adviser would serve as a natural contact point for Japan desk or embassy officials who needed to raise problems at the presidential level, and also for impressing on these officials the strength of presidential priorities not related to Japan. To be effective in this role, the official assigned this brief would require, at minimum, near-cabinet rank and intermittent access to the oval office.[7]

The future of U.S.-Japanese relations remains anything but assured.

7. We do not mean to suggest that a president apply this prescription uniquely to Japan. A senior official might ideally have several such briefs covering major areas of continuing American policy concern. It might prove desirable, for example, for an official to have such responsibility for a number of major American alliance relationships.

In the era of détente, there is no credible, immediate great-power threat from which the alliance seems to offer shelter; thus the task of its maintenance lacks day-to-day urgency on both sides of the Pacific. This opens the relationship to neglect, even abuse, in the pursuit of other interests domestic and foreign, as the textile dispute and the 1971 Nixon shocks testify. The fact that broader international economic and political relationships were changing in the early seventies fed fears, in Japan, that the United States might be moving to abandon the alliance entirely or at least to reduce it to a formal shell without substance. Time and effort on both sides of the Pacific have repaired much of the damage of 1971, and the alliance has been given renewed priority in Washington. Yet should the future bring crises comparable to those of the early seventies, characterized by misperception, malcommunication, and growing mutual bitterness, a Japanese political leader, incumbent or aspiring, might choose to give voice to such bitterness rather than seek (as did Sato and Tanaka) to dampen it. Or events initiated by other countries could create sharp new difficulties for the U.S.-Japan relationship—war or threat of war in Korea, or a new and perhaps more stringent Arab oil embargo. Either would pose acute domestic and international dilemmas for both countries, taxing their capacity for reciprocal political sensitivity and cooperation.

Whatever the major U.S.-Japan problems of the next decade may be, an approach to avoiding or ameliorating future crises can be found in the roots of past ones. Successful resolution of controversial issues requires effective mediation, in each capital, between the requirements for U.S.-Japanese relations and the claims of actors representing other policy priorities and interests. Those in each country seeking such constructive resolution must be sensitive to the position of their counterparts in the other, and try to shape their official actions so as to strengthen these counterparts. The task is anything but easy. Some degree of misperception and recurrent tension is inevitable between two such large pluralist states. But a constructive long-term relationship requires continuing efforts to contain such tension, and to resolve—gradually sometimes—the issues that produce it.

For Americans dealing with Japan, this means approaching Japan as they would any modern democracy, alert to its particular political features but expecting the sorts of political and bureaucratic divisions, the patterns of recurrent misperceptions and misunderstandings, that they would expect in dealing with other major U.S. allies. And it means following rules of caution and prudence that they would follow toward these allies: assessing the political scene with care; shaping initiatives to be effective in Tokyo but still sustainable in Washington; treating counterparts with sensitivity and respect. The postwar U.S.-Japanese relationship has managed to survive many departures from these rules, but it needed also to survive the two severe crises that resulted. In the future we might not be so lucky.

Bibliography

TWO MAJOR sources for this study were case studies by the authors based on extensive interviews with participants in both national capitals: "Decisionmaking in U.S.-Japanese Relations: Okinawa Reversion," by Priscilla Clapp and Haruhiro Fukui; and "The Textile Wrangle: Conflict in Japanese-American Relations 1969–71," by I. M. Destler, Hideo Sato, and Haruhiro Fukui.

Foreign Policymaking and Organization: General and U.S.

Allison, Graham. *Essence of Decision: Explaining the Cuban Missile Crisis.* Boston: Little, Brown, 1971.

Allison, Graham T., and Morton H. Halperin. "Bureaucratic Politics: A Paradigm and Some Policy Implications," in Richard H. Ullman and Raymond Tanter, eds., *Theory and Policy in International Relations.* Princeton: Princeton University Press, 1972. Brookings Reprint no. 246.

Bacchus, William I. *Foreign Policy and the Bureaucratic Process: The State Department's Country Director System.* Princeton: Princeton University Press, 1974.

de Rivera, Joseph M. *The Psychological Dimension of Foreign Policy.* Columbus, Ohio: Merrill Publishing, 1968.

Destler, I. M. *Presidents, Bureaucrats, and Foreign Policy.* Princeton: Princeton University Press, 1972 and 1974.

Halperin, Morton H., with the assistance of Priscilla Clapp and Arnold Kanter. *Bureaucratic Politics and Foreign Policy.* Washington: Brookings Institution, 1974.

Hilsman, Roger. *The Politics of Policy-Making in Defense and Foreign Affairs.* New York: Harper and Row, 1971.

Hoffmann, Stanley. "The American Style: Our Past and Our Principles," *Foreign Affairs,* vol. 46 (January 1968).

Iklé, Fred Charles. *How Nations Negotiate.* Written under the auspices of the Center for International Affairs, Harvard University. New York: Harper and Row, 1964.

Jervis, Robert. "Hypotheses on Misperception," *World Politics*, vol. 3 (April 1968). Reprinted in Morton H. Halperin and Arnold Kanter, eds., *Readings in American Foreign Policy: A Bureaucratic Perspective*. Boston: Little, Brown, 1973.

Keohane, Robert O., and Joseph S. Nye, Jr., eds. *Transnational Relations and World Politics*. Cambridge: Harvard University Press, 1972.

Neustadt, Richard E. *Alliance Politics*. New York: Columbia University Press, 1970.

Newhouse, John. *Cold Dawn: The Story of SALT*. New York: Holt, Rinehart and Winston, 1973.

Steinbruner, John D. *The Cybernetic Theory of Decision: New Dimensions of Political Analysis*. Princeton: Princeton University Press, 1974.

Japanese-American Relations

Armacost, Michael H. "U.S.-Japanese Relations: Problems and Modalities of Communications," *Department of State Bulletin*, vol. 68 (January 15, 1973).

Asahi Shimbun Staff. *The Pacific Rivals: A Japanese View of Japanese-American Relations*. New York: Weatherhill, 1972; Tokyo: Asahi, 1972.

Clapp, Priscilla A., and Morton H. Halperin. "U.S. Elite Images of Japan: The Postwar Period," in Akira Iriye, ed., *Mutual Images: Essays in American-Japanese Relations*. Cambridge: Harvard University Press, 1975.

————, eds. *United States–Japanese Relations: The 1970's*. Cambridge: Harvard University Press, 1974.

Clough, Ralph N. *East Asia and U.S. Security*. Washington: Brookings Institution, 1975.

Cohen, Jerome B., ed. *Pacific Partnership: United States–Japan Trade*. Lexington, Mass.: Lexington Books, for the Japan Society, 1972.

Destler, I. M. "Country Expertise and U.S. Foreign Policymaking: The Case of Japan," in Morton A. Kaplan and Kinhide Mushakōji, eds., *Japan, America, and the Future World Order*. New York: Free Press, 1976.

Fried, Edward R., and Philip H. Trezise. "Japan's Future Position in the World Economy." Processed. Washington: Brookings Institution, 1974.

Hunsberger, Warren S. *Japan and the United States in World Trade*. New York: Harper and Row, for the Council on Foreign Relations, 1964.

Kitamura, Hiroshi. *Psychological Dimensions of U.S.-Japanese Relations*. Occasional Papers in International Affairs, no. 28. Cambridge: Center for International Affairs, Harvard University, 1971.

Meyer, Armin H. *Assignment: Tokyo*. New York: Bobbs-Merrill, 1974.

Nagai, Yōnosuke. "Dōmei gaikō no kansei" [Trap of alliance diplomacy], *Chūō kōron*, January 1972.

Nishihara, Masashi. "Kokkakan kōshō ni okeru 'hi-seishiki sesshokusha' no kinō: Nihon to Amerika no taigai-kōshō o chūshin ni" [The function of 'unofficial contacts' in international negotiations: Special focus on external negotiations of Japan and the United States], *Kokusai seiji*, vol. 50 (1973).

Reischauer, Edwin O. "The Broken Dialogue with Japan," *Foreign Affairs*, vol. 39 (October 1960).

Rosovsky, Henry, ed. *Discord in the Pacific: Challenges to the Japanese-American Alliance*. Washington: Columbia Books, for the American Assembly, 1972.

Sato, Hideo. "United States–Japanese Relations," *Current History*, vol. 68 (April 1975).

Taylor, Allen, ed. *Perspectives on U.S.-Japanese Economic Relations*. Cambridge, Mass.: Ballinger Publishing, for the U.S.-Japan Trade Council, 1973.

Japanese Decisionmaking and Organization

Campbell, John Creighton. *Contemporary Japanese Budget Politics*. Berkeley and Los Angeles: University of California Press, forthcoming.

Fukui, Haruhiro. "Bureaucratic Power in Japan," in Peter Drysdale and Hironobu Kitaōji, eds., *Japan and Australia: Two Societies and Their Interactions*. Oxford: Oxford University Press, forthcoming.

―――. "Foreign Policy-Making in Japan: Case Studies for Empirical Theory." Processed. Paper prepared for delivery at the 1974 annual meeting of the Association for Asian Studies.

―――. "Policy-Making in Japan's Foreign Ministry." Processed. Paper prepared for delivery at the Conference on Japan's Foreign Policy, Jan. 14–17, 1974, Kauai, Hawaii.

Hellmann, Donald C. *Japanese Domestic Politics and Foreign Policy: The Peace Agreement with the Soviet Union*. Berkeley: University of California Press, 1969.

Hosoya, Chihiro. "Characteristics of the Foreign Policy Decision-Making System in Japan," *World Politics*, vol. 26 (April 1974).

Johnson, Richard Tanner, and William G. Ōuchi. "Made in America (Under Japanese Management)," *Harvard Business Review*, vol. 52 (September–October 1974).

Kusayanagi, Daizō. "Tsūsanshō: Tamesareru sutā kanchō" [MITI: Star agency on trial], *Bungei shunjū*, August 1974, p. 114.

Matsuyama, Yukio. "Japanese Press and Japan's Foreign Policy," *Journal of International Affairs*, vol. 26, no. 2 (1972).

Misawa, Shigeo. "An Outline of the Policy-Making Process in Japan," in Hiroshi Itoh, ed. and trans., *Japanese Politics, An Inside View: Readings from Japan*. Ithaca: Cornell University Press, 1973.

Oberdorfer, Don. "The Lockjaw of Tokyo Dailies," *Washington Post*, Jan. 4, 1975.

Trezise, Philip H., with the collaboration of Yukio Suzuki. "Politics, Government, and Economic Growth in Japan," in Hugh Patrick and Henry

Rosovsky, eds., *Asia's New Giant: How the Japanese Economy Works.* Washington: Brookings Institution, 1976.

Vogel, Ezra F., ed. *Modern Japanese Organization and Decision-Making.* Berkeley and Los Angeles: University of California Press, 1975.

Japanese Politics, Culture, and Foreign Policy

Brzezinski, Zbigniew. *The Fragile Blossom: Crisis and Change in Japan.* New York: Harper and Row, 1972.

Doi, Takeo. *The Anatomy of Dependence.* Translated by John Bester. Tokyo and New York: Kodansha International, 1973.

Emmerson, John K. *Arms, Yen and Power: The Japanese Dilemma.* Rutland, Vermont: Charles E. Tuttle, 1972.

Fukui, Haruhiro. "Factionalism in a Dominant Party System: The Case of Japan." Processed. Paper prepared for delivery at the 1974 annual meeting of the American Political Science Association.

————. *Party in Power.* Berkeley and Los Angeles: University of California Press, 1970.

Gibney, Frank. *Japan: The Fragile Superpower.* New York: W. W. Norton, 1975.

Kaplan, Eugene J. *Japan: The Government-Business Relationship.* U.S. Department of Commerce. Washington: Government Printing Office, 1972.

Langdon, Frank C. *Japan's Foreign Policy.* Vancouver: University of British Columbia Press, 1973.

Morley, James W., ed. *Forecast for Japan: Security in the 1970's.* Princeton: Princeton University Press, 1972.

Mushakōji, Kinhide. *Kokusai seiji to Nihon* [International politics and Japan]. Tokyo: Tokyo University Press, 1967.

Nakamura, Hajime. *Ways of Thinking of Eastern Peoples: India-China-Tibet-Japan.* Honolulu: University Press of Hawaii, 1964.

Nakane, Chie. *Japanese Society.* Berkeley and Los Angeles: University of California Press, 1970.

Packard, George III. *Protest in Tokyo.* Princeton: Princeton University Press, 1966.

Pempel, T. J. "Japan's Nuclear Allergy," *Current History,* vol. 680 (April 1975).

Reischauer, Edwin O. *Japan: The Story of a Nation.* New York: Alfred A. Knopf, 1970.

Scalapino, Robert A., and Junnosuke Masumi. *Parties and Politics in Contemporary Japan.* Berkeley: University of California Press, 1962.

Thayer, Nathaniel B. *How the Conservatives Rule Japan.* Princeton: Princeton University Press, 1969.

Watanabe, Akio. *The Okinawa Problem.* Melbourne: Melbourne University Press, 1970.

Watanuki, Jōji. "Japanese Politics: Changes, Continuities, and Unknowns."

Processed. Institute of International Relations for Advanced Studies on Peace and Development in Asia. Tokyo: Sophia University, 1973.

Weinstein, Martin E. *Japan's Postwar Defense Policy, 1947–1968*. New York: Columbia University Press, 1971.

Yanaga, Chitoshi. *Big Business in Japanese Politics*. New Haven: Yale University Press, 1968.

Yukawa, Hideki. "Modern Trend of Western Civilization and Cultural Peculiarities in Japan," in Charles A. Moore, ed., *The Japanese Mind: Essentials of Japanese Philosophy and Culture*. Honolulu: University Press of Hawaii, 1967.

Memoirs and Histories: Pre-1960

Acheson, Dean. *Present at the Creation*. New York: W. W. Norton, 1969.

Allison, John M. *Ambassador from the Prairie: or Allison Wonderland*. Boston: Houghton Mifflin, 1973.

Borg, Dorothy, and Shumpei Okamoto, eds. *Pearl Harbor as History: Japanese-American Relations, 1931–1941*. New York: Columbia University Press, 1973.

Burns, James McGregor. *Roosevelt: The Soldier of Freedom*. New York: Harcourt Brace Jovanovich, 1970.

Butow, Robert J. *Japan's Decision to Surrender*. Stanford: Stanford University Press, 1954.

Coughlin, William J. "The Great *Mokusatsu* Mistake," *Harper's*, March 1953.

Craig, William. *The Fall of Japan*. New York: Dial Press, 1967.

Dunn, Frederick S. *Peace-Making and the Settlement with Japan*. Princeton: Princeton University Press, 1963.

Feis, Herbert. *The Atomic Bomb and the End of World War II*. Princeton: Princeton University Press, 1966.

———. *The Road to Pearl Harbor*. Princeton: Princeton University Press, 1950.

Hoopes, Townsend. *The Devil and John Foster Dulles*. Boston: Little, Brown, 1973.

Iriye, Akira. "The Failure of Military Expansionism," in James William Morley, ed., *Dilemmas of Growth in Prewar Japan*. Princeton: Princeton University Press, 1971.

Kido, Kōichi. *Kido Kōichi nikki* [Kōichi Kido dairy]. Vol. 2. Tokyo: Tokyo University Press, 1966.

Kurzman, Dan. *Kishi and Japan: The Search for the Sun*. New York: Ivan Obolensky, 1960.

Smith, A. Merriman. *A President's Odyssey*. New York: Harper and Brothers, 1961.

Toland, John. *The Rising Sun: The Decline and Fall of the Japanese Empire, 1936–1945*. New York: Bantam Books, 1971.

Yabe, Teiji. *Konoye Fumimaro* [Fumimaro Konoye]. Tokyo: Jiji Press, 1958.

Index

Academic community, effect on government policy, 56–57
Acheson, Dean, 92
Agency for International Development, 83
Agriculture, U.S. Department of, 83
Aichi, Kiichi, 32, 63, 95n
Allen, Arthur, 193n
Allison, Graham T., 3n, 91n, 96n, 136, 177n
Allison, John M., 14n, 15n
All Japan Prefectural and Municipal Workers' Union. *See* Jichirō
Amae, 108–11, 116
Amaya, Naohiro, 81n
Armacost, Michael H., 94n
Army, U.S. Department of, 25, 28
Asahi Shimbun Staff, 15n, 127n, 138n, 144n, 150n, 152n

Bacchus, William I., 193n
Back negotiating channels, 149, 157; advantages of, 158–59; decisionmaking and, 161; problems involving, 159–64; purpose of, 158; recommendations for use of, 186–87
Baerwald, Hans, 163n
Balance of trade, U.S.-Japan, 1–2, 38, 42, 45
Bator, Francis, 105n
Bilateral issues: back channels to resolve, 149, 157–64; balance of interest during negotiations over, 135–38; broadening political arena of, 138–39; criteria for evaluating resolution of, 171–72; declining importance of, 170–71; diplomatic channels to resolve, 149–52; functional channels to resolve, 149, 152–54; indirect communications over, 129, 130; informal direct communications over, 129; Japanese caution in negotiating, 188; management of, 74–76; political reasons for initiating, 126–29; problems in solving, 125–26; recommendations for initiating, 179–81; recommendations for negotiating, 186–90, 192–94; summit channels to resolve, 149, 154–57; transnational alliances on, 143–48. *See also* Interaction, between political systems; Signals; United States-Japanese relations
Bonin Islands, 24, 30, 31
Borg, Dorothy, 50n
Brodie, Bernard, 161n
Bureaucracy: careerists in, 72–73; comparison of Gaimushō and State Department, 69, 73–76; consensus procedures in, 103–04; for foreign policymaking, 50, 70–71, 73; for national security policymaking, 84–86; policy-influencing role of, 71–72; political leaders and, 68, 69, 71, 76–77; size of, 70–71. *See also* Decisionmaking; Interagency relations
Burke, Arleigh, 137, 138
Burns, James MacGregor, 93n, 113n
Business community, 50–51, 53, 54, 59
Butow, Robert J. C., 120n, 159n
Byrnes, James F., 133n

Cabinet Research Office, Japan, 85
Cabinet Secretariat, Japan, 66–67
Campbell, John Creighton, 75n, 78n
Caraway, Paul W., 26
Central Intelligence Agency, 71
China, Nationalist, 11–12, 64
China, People's Republic of, 1, 2, 44, 114